Charles Edwardes

Rides and Studies in the Canary Islands

Charles Edwardes

Rides and Studies in the Canary Islands

ISBN/EAN: 9783743323193

Manufactured in Europe, USA, Canada, Australia, Japa

Cover: Foto ©ninafisch / pixelio.de

Manufactured and distributed by brebook publishing software (www.brebook.com)

Charles Edwardes

Rides and Studies in the Canary Islands

RIDES AND STUDIES

IN THE

CANARY ISLANDS

BY

CHARLES EDWARDES

AUTHOR OF "LETTERS FROM CRETE," &C.

ILLUSTRATED.

London

T. FISHER UNWIN

26, PATERNOSTER SQUARE

1888

Inscribed to
DON BENJAMIN RENSHAW,
OF
LAGUNA, TENERIFE.

INTRODUCTION.

This book is written for the entertainment both of those who visit the Canary Islands and those who do not.

The fortunate few who propose to sojourn under the palms and sunshine of Tenerife may be glad to learn from it something about the early Canarians, whose bones alone remain to us. The Guanches, for example, were a race deserving of a fair niche in the mausoleum of defunct human types.

These fortunate few may also welcome the book, because it assumes to give a description (inadequate enough) of what they hope to see.

On the other hand, the "Rides and Studies" appeals no less to those discreeter travellers who do their journeying by the fireside. There is worse pastime than climbing a mountain with one's feet on the fender. And though it is a pleasure to ride, agape with expectation, among strangers in a strange land, it is even pleasanter to sit at ease in one's arm-chair, under our dull homely skies, and amid familiar faces. This the sage majority who travel only among the octavos know by heaven-born instinct.

INTRODUCTION.

In the building of this little book, I have had help which I must gratefully acknowledge.

To my comrade-in-affliction in the island of Palma, (the Rev. C. V. Goddard), I am indebted for most of the sketches. Like other human creations, they are imperfect; but, for that, "circumstances" are to blame, rather than their author.

The drawing on page 41 is by Miss Yeatman.

For the photographs here reproduced, I render thanks to Mr. A. Samler-Brown and Señor Baeza.

I have read and digested, with more or less effort, a quantity of literature about the Canary Islands: histories, epics, rhymes, chronicles, and fables. The usage that I have made of this literature seems to empower me to set the somewhat responsible term "Studies" a-pillion to the "Rides" of my title. But there is in truth nothing very scholastic about the book. And if aught in it appear to savour of erudition or antiquarian exploits, let praise for this be offered at a venture to the memory of the Abbé Viera who, a hundred years ago, unravelled the tangle of Canarian history.

Fragments of the "Rides and Studies" have already appeared in print in sundry magazines. The proprietors and editors of the *Cornhill Magazine*, *Temple Bar*, *The Graphic*, the *St. James's Gazette*, and other periodicals are hereby thanked afresh for their courteous permission to incorporate these fragments in the structure of the book.

WOLVERHAMPTON,
Nov. 10, 1888.

CONTENTS.

CHAPTER I.

The S.S. *Niger*—West Coast merchants—Santa Cruz from the sea—The Anaga Hills—The Mole—Nelson and July 25, 1797—The Churches of Santa Cruz—The workhouse — Street architecture and the *Postigos* — The *Alameda*—Emigration—Santa Cruz a Spanish foundation—Statuary in the *Plaza*—The defects of a cosmopolitan seaport .   1

CHAPTER II.

The Grand Hotel and Sanatorium of Orotava—Commercial decay of the islands—An early ride—Roads and roadside scenes—The ungallant driver—Laguna — The north side of Tenerife—Matanza—Bencomo, the King of Taoro—Victoria—The Valley of Orotava and Humboldt's praise of it—The Peak   .   . 16

CHAPTER III.

Sweet idling in Puerto—Trivial excitements of a health resort—Puerto as it is and as it was—The old wine trade- Irish monuments in the Church- Puerto's harbour—La Paz—A Guanche sepulchre—Guanche skulls—A southern villa—The cochineal insect—Sugar, tobacco, and wine—The ruin of 1826 . . 28

CHAPTER IV.

Various conjectural origins of the name, people, and land of the Canary Islands—The island of San Borondon—The legendary first inhabitants—The Canaries and the Elysian Fields identical 55

CHAPTER V.

Tacoronte—Its museum and miraculous crucifix—The Guanches—Their mummies and method of embalming—Their polity—Coronations—Ceremony of ennobling—Religion—The vestal virgins of Grand Canary—Education—Morals—Trial by smoke—Punishment of crime—Dress—General character—Food—The Palma mode of dying—Dwellings and furniture—Inscription of Belmaco—Strength and agility—Reflections . . 67

CHAPTER VI.

The Gardens of Acclimatization—Eccentric trees and shrubs—The dragon tree—Orotava Villa—The private gardens of the Villa—The Castillo monument—The Villa Church de la Concepcion—The Dominican nuns and the Jesuit fathers—Periodical eruptions of Teide—Philosophy of life in the Villa . . . 86

CHAPTER VII.

A tour round Tenerife—The boys and the bell-tower—The configuration of Tenerife—*Barrancos*—Zones of tem-

CONTENTS. xiii

perature—Realejo, Upper and Lower—Bencomo and Realejo—The Church of Rambla—Icod—The dragon tree—The sad citizen—Garachico—The story of 1706—The drunken prisoner—Sunset on the Peak—Playing the pedagogue .   .   . 104

CHAPTER VIII.

A trait of Icod character—A fair morning—Pumice plains and lava beds—Gomera—On the Cañadas—A *volcancta*—The Peak at its toilette—Palm Sunday service—Garachico from above—A valley bivouac—Santiago—A severe mountain—Chia -Guia—Excitement in Guia—Hospitality of Guia—For and against country life   129

CHAPTER IX.

The hot south side of Tenerife—The Euphorbia—José's bragging—Adeje—Its Casa fuerte—Its population—Ascent to Chasna—Chasna of the clouds—The doctor and his daughter—A morning outlook—Flower customs—The Eve of St. John—Granadilla—Its oranges—A sturdy gentleman—Granadilla's church, club, and tobacco factories—Rio—*Barrancos* and cave dwellings—Flies—Arico—The ex-dockman—Fast life in Arico . 146

CHAPTER X.

A dilemma—Spanish generosity—The *Barranco* de Herque—Fasnea—The genial householder—A downpour—Escobonal and the *Carretara*—View of Guimar—The procession of Holy Thursday—Fanaticism—Candelaria—Rude burial—The camel—Santa Cruz—Strategy—Laguna—Orotava   167

CONTENTS.

CHAPTER XI.

Easter morning—A Guanche festival—Bencomo—The city of Laguna—Its history—The romance of Dacil and Castillo—The pestilence of Laguna—Ecclesiastical appropriations—Public festivities and mourning—The miraculous sweat—Some governors of the Canaries—Bishops, and Murga's injunctions—The expulsion of the Jesuits—Laguna as it is 184

CHAPTER XII.

The Laguna Churches—Social difficulties—Scheme for the emancipation of women—A working men's club—Ecclesiastical treasures—The library—The Professor and his pamphlet—Superstitions—The burning of Judas Iscariot—A diocese without a head . . . 200

CHAPTER XIII.

The Anaga Hills—The woods of Mercedes—A dainty greensward—The Anaga edges and abysses—The " Cruz del Carmen "—The " Cruz de Afur "—Taganana woods and village—The " Cura "—A rustic beauty—A Guanche idyl—" El Roque de las Animas "—The monk and the nuns—Bencomo and Zebensin—Tenerifañ economics—Return up the " Vuelta " . . . 210

CHAPTER XIV.

Traditions about the Peak—First account of an ascent—Preparations for the climb—Our start—Glorious day—In the clouds—Above the clouds—El Pico de Teide—Stages of the ascent—The Retama Plain—Obsolete hardships—At the foot of the pyramid—The Estancia—Bed-making and eating—Sunset—A restless night—On by moonlight—An unexpected meeting—The Rambleta—Sunrise—On the summit—In the crater—Hot and cold—Sulphur men—The ice cave—The descent . . . 224

CHAPTER XV.

Palma from Tenerife—The weekly *correo*—The misery of it—A fair night at sea—Topography of Palma—Origin of its name—Guayanfanta—Conquest of Palma—The brave king of the Caldera—Alonso de Lugo's mean shift—Later history of Palma—Tenerife named by the people of Palma—The Bishop and the convent cake—Independence of Palma—The Vandewalle family, past and present . . . 261

CHAPTER XVI.

Santa Cruz of Palma—A warm town—The mole—Steep streets—Palma women—Don Pedro and his wife—Palma fashions—Morning routine—The craterette of Santa Cruz—Architecture and industries of Santa Cruz—The Church of San Salvador—Altar machinery—Our Lady of the Snows—The cockpit—A series of fights—Palma's dependence on England—Local wines and tobacco—Weevils—Locusts—Legend of the Peak of Tenerife and the Caldera of Palma . . . 270

CHAPTER XVII.

Preparations for a tour round Palma—*Barranco* de Galga—A red land—San Andrés—Los Sauces—Its merry mill—*Barrancos* de Herradura—Gallegos and Peleos—Awful roads—A beautiful country—We lose our way—The timid shepherd boys—A fairy fog—The kindly

proprietress and her hospitality—Tricias—Its elevation
—Primitive quarters—A mill by cow-power—More
barrancos—Bad water—Candelaria—Its ancient church
—A gracious noonday rest—On the Caldera edge—Indescribable panorama—The Caldera—Its colours and
immensity—The Pico de Bejanao—Volcanoes and lava
flows 290

CHAPTER XVIII.

Los Llanos'— Its *fonda* — Curious visitors and fellow
guests — Argual — Paso and the *Alcalde* — Paso's
school—The Caldera by the *Barranco*—Under the
Pico de los Muchachos—The Caldera bed—The Cumbrecita Pass—Steep crags—Clouds brewing in the
Caldera—The old and the new road over the *Cordillera*
—The volcano of Tocade—We desert Don Pedro—A
cruel voyage from Palma . . . 310

CHAPTER XIX.

Historical summary—Béthencourt and his successors—Disputes about the Canaries between Spain and Portugal
—Generous native princes—Rejon and the conquest of
Grand Canary—Los Palmas—Ascension Day in the
cathedral—Bones and copes—Paintings—The hospital
—The English sailor among the Spaniards—Theatre
and markets—Spanish justice—The harbour—Cloudy
weather—The evening promenade—A funeral and
burial 325

CHAPTER XX.

Characteristics of Grand Canary—The noisy sleeper—A
sudden idea—Pancho and the Andalusian—The Cal-

dera de Vandama—Tafira—Atalaya—Probable pedigree of the dwellers in Atalaya—Santa Brigida—San Mateo—Pancho's relations—The priest and his assistants—Across country—Guimar—A pretty prospect —Telde—Troglodytes and aristocrats—A brisk ride in the dark—S.S. *Opobo*—The last of the Peak . . 349

APPENDIX 363

LIST OF ILLUSTRATIONS.

	PAGE
OLD CONVENT AND CHURCH TOWER IN SANTA CRUZ OF PALMA ...	*Frontispiece*
MAP OF TENERIFE ...	7
A WATER CARRIER ...	19
THE PEAK: FROM A ROOF IN PUERTO	30
A PICTURE IN PUERTO ...	34
A BUSY DAY IN PUERTO ...	38
VIEW FROM A GARDEN NEAR HUMBOLDT'S VILLA	41
A GUANCHE SEPULCHRE ...	45
AN ENGLISH RESIDENCE BY PUERTO ...	48
A VILLA OF TENERIFE ...	52
THE ISLAND OF SAN BORONDON ...	64
FACSIMILES OF THE INSCRIPTIONS OVER THE CAVE OF BELMACO, IN THE ISLAND OF PALMA ...	82
SCENE ON THE ROAD TO THE VILLA ...	87
A DRAGON TREE	92
THE VILLA ...	101
LOOKING WEST FROM PUERTO ...	108

LIST OF ILLUSTRATIONS.

	PAGE
BALCONY IN SAN JUAN DE LA RAMBLA ...	116
ICOD AND THE PEAK ...	126
THE PEAK IN MARCH: FROM ABOVE ICOD ...	136
A CLUMP OF EUPHORBIA	148
A TENERIFAN IN HIS MANTA	152
A LAGUNA PORTAL ...	198
A GOATHERD OF TENERIFE	229
A BEGGAR OF TENERIFE	234
THE PEAK FROM PUERTO: SHOWING THE TIGAYGA RIDGE...	237
OUTLINE OF CHAHORA, AS SEEN FROM THE SUMMIT OF THE PEAK	260
MAP OF PALMA ...	271
MAP OF GRAND CANARY	333

RIDES AND STUDIES IN THE CANARY ISLANDS.

CHAPTER I.

The S.S. *Niger*—West Coast merchants—Santa Cruz from the sea—The Anaga Hills—The Mole—Nelson and July 25, 1797—The churches of Santa Cruz—The workhouse—Street architecture and the " Postigos "—The " Alameda "—Emigration—Santa Cruz a Spanish foundation—Statuary in the Plaza—The defects of a cosmopolitan seaport.

Our ship, the *Niger*, of the African Steamship Company, dropped anchor off Santa Cruz on the morning of Sunday, the 20th March. So many of our country folk had come on board at the last moment, in a scamper from the east winds and sleet of " dear old England," that throughout the voyage the vessel had carried a freight of human flesh much beyond her capacity. Some of us had in consequence been put aft like stowaways. The Bay of Biscay had drenched us by bucketfuls in our nightly stumble and slide down the wet decks to these sad quarters, and the pitching was as if we had been in a swing at the mercy of lusty arms. At Madeira certain pale invalids and knickerbockered tourists enlarged our circle, so that for the final two days of the eight from Liverpool to Tenerife people slept on the dining tables and under them, like the dregs of a debauch. For the Steamship Company this was admirable, but for us who were not interested in its dividends it was not so pleasant. Besides, the provisions had begun to fall off : there was not enough marmalade for the tenth day. Taking these various circumstances into account, it was joy to know that the voyage was at an end. The twentieth of March is a day on which, in the Catholic calendar, souls are released from the pains of Purgatory. It is also the first day of Spring, according to Spanish reckoning. Thus our landing on Spanish and Catholic soil was doubly auspicious.

We parted with the half-dozen passengers whom we left on the *Niger* to proceed to Sierra Leone and the West Coast, much as one might part with an explorer bound for the North Pole. Over brandies and sodas these heroes of commerce had told us of the heat, ennui, and flavour of doom that marked their life at the lonely trading stations in the mangrove swamps of the wide river mouths. King Chance rules in Benin during the wet season as grimly as when he held court in Paris, with Robespierre for his prime puppet.

These merchants were married. Their wives lived in England, and made them welcome for a couple of months every alternate year. One gentleman, bolder or more pitiless than the rest, was, this trip, accompanied by his wife: it was an experiment.

SANTA CRUZ.

Six weeks after I left the *Niger* her death was in the papers.

Is it not ghastly? Black men and women, gold dust, elephants' teeth, leopard skins, blue skies, palm-trees, and freedom from the restraints of convention, cannot give charm to these cruel shores, which force white men to solace themselves with the old hectic and deluding cordial, "Let us eat, drink, and be merry; for to-morrow we die!"

From the water Santa Cruz has the gay air of a Levantine city. Its bulk of white houses with flat roofs, the two dark campaniles of its principal churches, the pale pink or ochre bodies and yet brighter turrets of mercantile and municipal buildings, the flutter of flags, and the heavy curl of surf on its sandy beach, give it a lively look. But the town is nothing to its surroundings. Imagine a mass of pointed and serrated mountains hedging it close on one side, and the long backbone of Tenerife, springing behind the town from these chaotic hills, and rising gradually in the opposite direction until, thirty miles away, it culminates in the Peak itself, 12,180 feet above the sea: you may then have an idea of the mere land frame of Santa Cruz.

The Anaga hills, near our anchorage, drop into the sea by stern red precipices. Their summits, winningly fantastic, two and three thousand feet high, are crested with laurels and heaths, the leafage of which is wonderfully clear against the blue background of sky. For the rest, there are many palm trees among the houses of the city, and beyond it, where the land swells to the watershed, are fields of barley, and patches of the cochineal cactus. These last, decked in their white rags, are curiously suggestive of extensive laundry grounds.

One word, however, about the Peak. In Santa Cruz it is little more than a tradition. The buttresses of the Cañadas, or old crater, eight or nine thousand feet from the level, and upon which the Peak proper is built as a precise pyramid, stand like a distant wall between the capital and the mountain top. Thanks to this foreshortening, only enlightened eyes can identify a tiny purple pimple, peering over the great wall, as the Teide long believed to be the highest elevation in the world.

After eight days at sea, some of us were hasty in our efforts to land on Tenerife. But the health officer had first to certify that we were bringing no infectious disease to this little island which has suffered so many scourges of various kinds since it came into civilised history. " Patience ! " therefore, was the word. Indeed, this was a plea to which we soon got habituated. If the dinner came not for an hour or two after it was ordered, " Patience, señor," murmured the landlord. If the horse I had engaged for a week's riding tour appeared as an animated sheaf of bones, the livery man remarked that with " patience " the " beast would improve in looks." If, in a clumsy attempt to eat a prickly pear, I ran four or five spines into my thumb, and groaned while trying to extract them, a swarthy native was sure to be near to assure me that with " patience " the wound would fester comfortably and allow the venomous points to expel themselves. And when the southern husband, in a rare moment of petulance, complains of the screaming of his babe, ten to one the mother will whisper "Patience," and remind the father that by and by the squaller will become a man.

About three hundred years ago, when the populalation of Santa Cruz was under a thousand, the inhabitants began to build a mole for the protection of their harbour. This mole is still unfinished. A long line of gigantic cubes of concrete are waiting to be hurled pell-mell into the sea for the due continuance of the work; but it is impossible to say how many years they have thus been waiting, or when the mole will be completed. "Patience!" however.

This thick fragment of a pier, with the lighthouse upon it, has strong interest for an Englishman. It was while he was standing on it during the night of the 24th July, 1797, that a brilliant shot from a field-piece under the *alameda*, about two hundred yards distant, carried off Nelson's right arm, killed Bowen, the captain of the *Terpsichore*, wounded the captain of the *Seahorse* and two seconds in command. and killed a score of others. We had already captured the mole, but had been forced to abandon it. It was doubtful if Trowbridge and his thousand men had succeeded in their endeavour to row upon the shore, march into the town, and bring the Governor-General to a surrender. In this strait Nelson himself came into the strife, just in time for the cannon shot which, in the words of the Spanish rhymer—

> "Maté á Bowen atrevido,
> Á Nelson le quité un brazo,
> Á veinte y dos de un balazo
> Muertos, al inglés vencido."

The citizens of Santa Cruz are proud of the memory of this battle, and with good reason. Nelson was not accustomed to be beaten. His tone in demanding the Philippine treasure-ship, *Principe de Asturias*, which was the ostensible cause of his coming to Tenerife, was, therefore, high-handed, not to say insolent. Trowbridge, when he had safely got through the surf in the teeth of the shore guns, and brought his small body of men into the heart of the city, was even more peremptory than Nelson. His force had got divided, so that he found himself in the Plaza, face to face with the castle and its guns, with only about 340 men around him. Nelson's co-operation had failed. The rest of his troops were isolated elsewhere in the city. Nevertheless, says the Spanish historian, "in spite of this false position, Trowbridge had the hardihood to send a sergeant to the castle, demanding its surrender, and threatening else to burn the town." Later, when the reunited British force had taken shelter in the convent of San Domingo, and Nelson's second attempt to relieve him had been defeated, Trowbridge altered his tone. He sent to the Spanish general to say that he did not wish to injure the town, but that he was determined to have the bullion of the Manila ship. Such persistence, in such a situation, was heroic. But when the Governor, in reply, threatened at once to besiege the convent, and to give no quarter, our sturdy Trowbridge returned to his right senses. A flag of truce ended the engagement. The 675 survivors of the original 1,000 assailants marched with all honours of war through the Plaza, between the French and Spanish soldiery of the defence, and embarked for their ships. It is worth mention that the victors, as courteous after as they were brave and intelligent during the battle, gave our men a breakfast before allowing them to re-embark.[1]

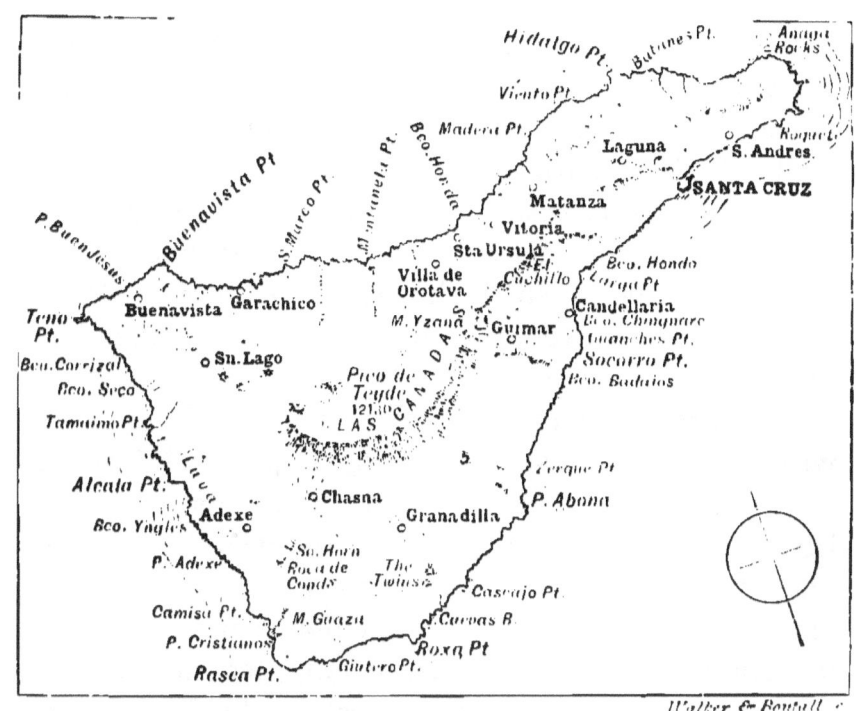

TENERIFE: Extreme dimensions, 60 miles by 30.

[1] Nelson's letter to the Governor shows how he appreciated this civility:

"THESEUS, *July* 26, 1797.

"SIR,— I cannot quit this island without thanking your Excellency most sincerely for your extreme kindness to me, for your humanity in regard to our dead and wounded in your power and under your care, and for your generosity towards all

The total number of men engaged in the defence of Santa Cruz was only 1,669. Trowbridge estimated them at 8,000, and English historians have held to his estimate. But he did not know that, by a trick of war, the same troops were being marched backwards and forwards, like pantomime dummies, to make an effective show.

It is the fashion with visitors to decry Santa Cruz. They use it as a stepping-stone to the other side of the island, and lament when they are obliged to return to it. This is hard on the town, which is at least worth a leisurely inspection. Its two large churches are full of the heavy gilded carving and spiral wooden pillars of which the Spaniards are so fond. Their canvasses, too, are characteristic. Either the figures portrayed are grotesquely out of drawing, or the colours have vanished. The subject of Purgatory, with the elect presided over by Popes and Jesuits, is treated as coarsely in Santa Cruz as in every little village church throughout the islands. When one has looked on Nelson's flags, in a chapel of the cathedral, and admired the ingenious carved work of a certain Spaniard who died in 1743, leaving this as his monument, the real interest of the building is exhausted. The flags are in elongated cases, under lock and key, and hung on the wall high out of reach. This was deemed essential after the rude

who are disembarked. I will not fail to inform my sovereign of this, and I look forward to an opportunity when I may personally assure your Excellency how much I am your Excellency's most obedient and humble servant,

"HORATIO NELSON."

theft of them, once upon a time, by a British midshipman, who thought his and his country's honour depended on their recovery.

The workhouse of Santa Cruz seemed to me almost an ideal place for the long death of old age. It was far from depressing. The good sister who led me through its airy, clean, whitewashed corridors and wards laughed cheerfully all the while. I found fifty well-knit boys busy with slates and pencils and problems of long division. They rose to their feet with pleased alacrity when we appeared, and enjoyed the diversion. From the boys we went to the girls. They were of ages from eight or nine to fifteen, and some of them gave promise of great beauty. Dark eyes that go to the heart are common in Spain; but here, among these well-bred orphaned girls, were also complexions worthy of England, as well as eyes lucid with sweet expression. The girls were variously employed; some embroidering, some cutting paper patterns for the decoration of church statuary, or devising bouquets of paper roses and geraniums, for use in this land teeming with natural flowers. In this democratic establishment there was work for all who could work. Even the crones, poor ugly old creatures, found pastime in picking corn from a mammoth heap in the midst of their apartment, and they chattered vociferously over their labour. For the men there was bootmaking, carpentering, tailoring, &c. None were degraded to the task, fit only for Bridewells, of meddling with oakum. We discovered seven little urchins making their midday meal, in truly national style, round one big bowl of *gofio*. They paused with uplifted spoons at the sight of us, but soon resumed their repast. Thus, down the scale, we arrived at the nursery, where a couple of young mothers began to tidy their babes, but a few weeks old, for our entertainment. " That one is blacker than it ought to be," remarked the sister, with a shake of the head, to one of the mothers. But we did not tarry to listen to the voluble explanations which the girl offered on behalf of the child and its parentage. Lastly, we went into the *patio* or inner courtyard of the building—a garden full of flowers, with palms, bananas, and orange trees interlaced between the sky and the earth. Here the veterans of the workhouse strolled and sunned themselves, free from anxiety. I daresay the southern sun has something to do with it; but the contrast between this workhouse in a colony of Spain, and the prison-houses to which in England our unfortunate paupers are consigned, was startling.

The streets of Santa Cruz, though not elegant, are by their narrowness adapted for the shade one sighs for under a tropical sun. They are uneven and cobbled, and to drive through them is torture. The houses are lofty, with carven balconies, doors, and window shutters, painted green, with no small degree of individuality. Some of the older buildings on the Marina are palatial in their woodwork—especially the consular houses. From the *patio* of palms and orange and lemon trees, with a fountain in their midst, one looks up broad heavy staircases with twisted banisters at dainty supports with elaborate capitals and embossed roofs that would have done credit to Nuremberg in its best days. Piazzi Smyth reproaches the Canarians because their "liliputian panelling" is of American deal, instead of the tougher olive or walnut wood. Of course the labour of carving olive timber as they have carved the deal would have been greater; but the work ought surely to be judged only according to its pretensions. It assumes to be ornamental, and it is ornamental. It does not assume to be high art, and therefore it merits no blame because it is not high art.

These wooden window shutters play an important part in the domestic life of the Canarians. They keep the house cool by the exclusion of light and heat: but they also bring the ladies of the house into immediate though delicate association with their friends and acquaintance outside. The shutters are invariably pierced at the base by a small movable trap which goes outwards on hinges; and with this *postigo* pressed open more or less wide by their heads, the women pass hours of the day looking forth into the street, their powdered cheeks level with the cheeks of the pedestrian. At first it is a little embarrassing to walk down one of these long, close, empty streets between a file of faces, the black eyes of which are merciless and unswerving in their concentrated scrutiny. But, after a time, one perceives that it is a gracious custom whereby a stranger may at small cost see the pretty faces of the town in very agreeable contiguity, and contrast the one with the other as easily as if they were photographs in a shop window.

The *alameda* (from *alamo*, a poplar — the tree favoured in the Peninsular for these public places) of Santa Cruz is a remarkable little tract of forestry in the middle of the town. Here the botanist may try his erudition with almost certain discomfiture. Among date palms and royal palms he will find laurels as tall as a house, and many a plant indigenous to the tropics, but quite at home in this dry, warm air, which knows hardly anything of a temperature below 50° Fahrenheit. On the hottest of days one may breathe at ease under this thick foliage, or even indulge in a paddle in the fountains of the *alameda*, like a certain maid whom I caught knee-deep in the water, whiffing a cigarette.

The familiarity gained by the Canarians with such tropical vegetation as they see in the *alamedas* must in some measure make the expatriation that is so common here less irksome and harsh. We landed on the mole at a time when several score of agriculturists and their families were embarking on an emigrant ship bound for Venezuela. The mother country acts wisely in giving her colonists every facility for dispersion over her own colonies. The advantages of Porto Rico, Venezuela, and Cuba, with assisted passages and so forth, are broadly placarded in Tenerife; and yearly the deportation from the Canaries is large. People marry so young here, and the women are so prolific, that, considering the limited area of the archipelago (about 3,300 square miles), there is no resource but emigration. Prior to the invasion of Spain, the old inhabitants were posed with the same difficulty. In Lanzarote, for example, a law was passed, sentencing to death all children of a family except the first-born. But this uncommon regulation was soon afterwards rendered unnecessary by a pestilence which almost depopulated the island. It may not be generally known that the first civilizers of Florida were Canarians, and the city of St. Augustine in that state, which claims to be the oldest European settlement of the United States, was founded in the sixteenth century by a contingent of seventy families from Santa Cruz.

But it is early to begin sketching the past history of the Canaries. This subject is so gigantic in proportion to the smallness of the islands and their distance from the great centres of civilization in past ages, that it demands very careful and precise "boiling down" to the degree at which it may interest and adequately instruct without being tedious or pedantic.

Enough if for the present I remind my readers that Santa Cruz is a Spanish foundation in the midst of the other towns and villages which mostly existed when the Guanches held Tenerife. Orotava, Guimar, Teide, Icod, Taganana are all immediate derivations from the dead Guanche tongue. Santa Cruz, on the other hand, merely marks the place where Alonso de Lugo, the conqueror of the island, first set foot in Tenerife, holding a great cross of wood in his arms. Like other disseminators of European customs among peoples who are so far barbarians that they have not yet succeeded in discovering gunpowder and the art of printing, De Lugo was, above all things, bent on Christianizing the Guanches. And so the cross was set in the ground, the chaplains said mass in the open air, surrounded by the thousand grim warriors in armour, who had come from slaying the Moors in Granada to a new kind of blood-shedding, and the place was christened Santa Cruz, and annexed to the domains of their Majesties of Spain.

In the Plaza of Santa Cruz is a stately marble obelisk which in its own way is pathetic. In the centre of it is a representation of the Virgin of Candelaria, a village on the southern coast of Tenerife; and this figure is flanked by four marble survivals of the Guanche kings, clad in skins, and bearing their royal sceptre—the thigh-bone of Tinerfe, that Homeric and legendary first monarch of the whole island. I hope I may be able to show that the Guanches, who have been exterminated, were a people of many virtues and much nobility. As for the Virgin of Candelaria, that potent legend, with all its influence over the minds of many generations of island Catholics, may tell its own tale in due course.

But it is now time to leave Santa Cruz. It is a city of meagre entertainment after all, and of very mixed blood. Ships of many nations call here week by week, and the sight of tipsy tars and brawling travellers does not work in the cause of virtue upon the youth of cosmopolitan seaports like this. In back streets I was confronted with staring signboards inviting the stranger, in bad English, to enter, drink rum, and have a good time. There are two hotels, at least, where English is nearly as much the mother tongue as Spanish; and each advertises its rivalry to the other by conjuring me to believe that it is the better, and that nowhere else in the town is English spoken. The Anglo-mania has touched Santa Cruz. Pale ale in the familiar bottles is an article of common use here. And oh, *horribile dictu!* I cannot go into my hotel without passing two or three Spanish young men in large check coats and trousers, an attitude of supreme impertinence, their hats cocked on one side, and the crook of their walking canes resting on their molars. These young gentlemen think it "chic" to behave as they imagine the English behave; and so they idle away the hours in this way, and ogle everything female that comes under their gaze.

CHAPTER II.

The Grand Hotel and Sanatorium of Orotava—Commercial decay of the islands—An early ride—Roads and roadside scenes—The ungallant driver—Laguna—The north side of Tenerife—Matanza—Bencomo, the King of Taoro—Victoria—The Valley of Orotava, and Humboldt's praise of it—The Peak.

SINCE the opening of the English Sanatorium on the northern side of the island, English faces are common objects along the road which joins Orotava and Santa Cruz. Indeed, the islanders think their fortunes are to be made by the exodus hither year after year of an increasing number of strangers with their pockets full of money. A few years ago the mere name of "invalid" made a Spaniard of Tenerife shiver and turn away. He imagined that lung disease, for instance, was contagious; so that, however poor he might be, he would not dream of letting an empty house to a person affected with phthisis. The same reason makes it customary to hide the fact when a native is in a decline.

I do not know how the change has been wrought, but wrought it has been. For a long time European physicians have praised the air of the Canaries as curative, *ne plus ultra*, for certain maladies. Its dryness is extraordinary. The average annual rainfall is under fifteen inches. The average winter temperature on the coast is 63·8°. It was whispered that if only some millionaire could get from the Spanish Government a concession of the island of Tenerife, he might, by judicious outlay, turn it into a health ground for Europe and the West Coast of Africa, such as the world would be grateful for. But the very extravagance of such a reputation seems to have been fatal to its acceptance. Besides, of what use was this admirable climate to the ordinary health-seeker if there were no hotels to offer him the comforts on which, equally with the climate, his health depended? In a common wayside *venta* he might get a truckle-bed, an oily diet of little variety, and the companionship of innumerable fleas; but, not unwisely, he preferred to leave Tenerife to itself rather than accept these certain evils as a part of his cure.

A year or two ago, however, a company of Spanish nobility and others put their heads together. Bad times had come upon Tenerife, no less than upon England. Cochineal, of which, in 1860, more than a million pounds weight had gone from the islands to Europe, at a price of about a dollar a pound, had fallen before the modern invention of aniline dyes. The demand had become trifling, and the price had diminished to a quarter of a dollar. It was a severe blow to cultivators, many of whom at once gave up all hopes of the affluence they had expected. Later, the wines, which of old, before the ravage of the oidium disease, had produced the most excellent Malvasia, were studied with renewed interest. Tobacco also was planted largely where the cochineal cactus had formerly held the ground. By these means, prosperity might be coaxed back to the islands, which no longer merited the name of "Fortunate." Yet another opening for capitalists was suggested. Why should not Tenerife bid for a few of the thousands who annually go from the north to the south, in terror of the winter? Why, indeed, with such claims as hers?

It has eventuated in the Orotava Grand Hotel—Sanatorium and health resort—a speculation in the interest of humanity, for the profit of the various marquises and counts who have subscribed the capital for its institution. Thanks to the Sanatorium, the people in the north-east of Tenerife are already familiarized with the sight of Englishmen. They see them by carriage-loads, or galloping themselves into health, pursued by swarms of flies. Their energy is a marvel to them. Their evident wealth is an endless subject of conversation and envy to them. But the wisest and best-cultured of them are beginning to fear that in course of time they may have to pray for deliverance from them, even as they seek deliverance from the locusts when a south-east wind brings a ravening scourge of them upon the land.

I took the early mail coach from Santa Cruz to Orotava, and sat by its coarse but hearty driver. The tender colour of the Oriental neighbourhood of the capital soon after dawn, the placid ocean, with the outline of Grand Canary, forty-five miles distant, and the warm fresh air, were alike exhilarating. But the Anaga hills are the supreme beauty of Santa Cruz. Their greenery on this spring morning was delicious, and their tortured summits, connected one with another by narrow edges that piqued the fancy, made my feet itch to be upon them.

The distance from Santa Cruz to Orotava is about twenty-five miles. In the first five miles we rise nearly 2,000 feet, to the ancient capital of Tenerife, the city of Laguna. Never was there a more erratic road. We take long sweeping curves to the right, and then corresponding curves to the left. Of course this is for the good of the horses; but here methinks the authorities have exceeded discretion. As engineering work, however, these roads of the first class in the Canaries are beyond praise. The Romans could not have made them better. But at present Tenerife is girdled hardly more than a third by the first class roads. The remaining tracks are infamous; and years will elapse before the tourist can order his carriage to drive round the Peak as if it were the Acropolis of Athens.

The scenes on the road outside Santa Cruz are lively and interesting. We meet files of women of the most robust build, tripping lightly down the incline, with eggs, poultry, vegetables, and fruit on their heads. They move with their arms akimbo, laughing and joking, so that their fine, white teeth are for ever flashing across their dusky skins. There are also mules and mule-carts laden with barrels of wine of country pressing, or sacks of charcoal, cases of bananas for shipment to England, and the like. Here and there we pass a district customs' house. The Canaries are a free port for strangers, but, internally, there is a universal octroi. Thus, for every fowl taken into Santa Cruz, the market woman pays about 2½d., and the goatherd who drives his flock from door to door, milking them according to the demand, pays a little more than a halfpenny a day for every goat thus employed.

As I have said, the coachman was a rough fellow. He and I got to be good friends ere I left the island: but his conduct towards his countrywomen was so unchivalrous on this March morning, that I did not at first think well of him. He flicked at their stout brown calves with his long whip, and made some of them dance their eggs into jeopardy. He did it all in the merriest humour, however, and when his compliments were of the grossest they were met with unvarying smiles or amiable retorts. But soon the horses exacted his attention in our pull up to the level of Laguna. "Go on, little boy!" "On, white horse!" "On post!" Thus he stimulated his ragged steeds to do their best. The bony animals were tied to our old green coach with bits of rope that threatened momentarily to break; but they brought us over our difficulties in praiseworthy style.

Of the mouldering, sombre old city of Laguna, than which there is none more poetical in the islands,

I shall have something to say by and by. It kindles the imagination. It resembles a white-haired old man who has lived safely through a stormy youth and a vigorous and influential prime, but who is now content to glide down to oblivion and decay, soothing his decline with harmless babble about the red days he has seen, and the history he flatters himself he has helped to make. But it is saturated with that "worst symptom a town can have"—silence.

From Laguna to Orotava is about twenty miles, or four hours going in the coach. We are now on the north side of the island. The sunlit blue of the sea is below us, at the base of the broad slopes which fall to the coast from the high road. These slopes are assiduously cultivated, for this is the richest part of the island. Fields of maize, lupins, potatoes, vineyards, brakes of fig-trees, orchards, groves of orange trees, tufts of bananas, cover the land, with the fullest suggestion of opulence and fertility. We pass groups and avenues of superb palm trees, standing among the grain, or leading to the villas which dot this divine stretch of country. Thus the villages of Tacoronte and Sauzal are left behind, and near noon we halt at the inn of Matanza, sensibly browned by the sun, and already conscious that the flies are likely to prove a serious pest in this Garden of the Hesperides.

In all Tenerife there is no better country inn than that, or rather those (for there are a rival pair of them), at Matanza. The hostess of the one I favoured was buxom and comely, and she had learnt to a nicety how to fracture the shell in which the common Englishman thinks fit to ensconce himself. None but the stiffest of necks could stay unbent before her hospitable endeavours, and her sweet if flattering commiserations with the wayfarer on the hard luck that has compelled him to battle with heat, flies, and dust on that particular day. Her smartness, too, was a pattern for all Spain ; though this was no doubt due to the exigencies of the mail, and its assumed punctuality in leaving when the half-hour for luncheon had expired. Ere I was well settled in my chair the ragout of eggs and meat and broth, which stands in Tenerife for a soup *de pays*, was smoking before me ; and beefsteaks, cutlets of kid, chickens, *dulces* (biscuits and other sugary confections), and fruit of bananas, figs, oranges, and apples succeeded each other like the carriages of a train. " Ah! the dear English ! " she muttered, while bustling about with dishes and bottles ; and she carried her affection for us so far as to attack and rout the bevy of barelegged beggar boys and girls and old crones who kept up a tiresome clamour for coppers at the window of the inn.

Matanza is the Spanish for " slaughter." The village and its little church with a lozenge-shaped tower, under the lee of some high pine-clad bluffs facing the Atlantic, marks the site where Alonso de Lugo and his first body of invading Spaniards were brought to a pitiful plight. They supposed that they had but to show themselves to the Guanches and to Bencomo the king of Taoro and prince of the first Guanches, to ensure a victory and an immediate surrender of the island. It was far otherwise. Here at Matanza the Guanches attacked the Spaniards, and put no fewer than nine hundred *hors de combat*. The remaining handful fled with all speed back to the coast and the wooden cross which had been set in the ground, as a place of sanctuary. It was here that the Spaniards first learnt that the Guanches were as powerful individually as the Canarians of Grand Canary, of which island Lugo had recently completed the conquest. Certain armoured crossbowmen of Spain plied their bows from an eminence so as to annoy the Guanches. Their position was unassailable. What could the Guanches do? This: they deliberately undermined the rock itself, so that in a short time it collapsed, crossbowmen and all.

It was a famous victory, and had Bencomo, the king, followed it up by a pursuit of the remnant of the Spaniards, he might have postponed the conquest of Tenerife until the sixteenth century. But this monarch was not only unwilling to harass a beaten foe: he pitied the very prisoners he had taken, and let them go to swell the broken forces at Santa Cruz. Not that he was wholly of a mild and gentle disposition. His indignation was prodigious when, on the eve of the invasion, a native seer dared to prophesy misfortunes for his country. "I swear by the towering Peak of Teide, by the blood of Tinerfe, by the heavens with all their stars, and by the sun now shining on the other world (it was night)—by these I swear that never will I thus be cast down. Thou a prophet, with knowledge of the future! Dost thou, villain, liar, fool, and madman, dare thus to mock at me? . . . Hang him up without loss of a moment!"

When the luckless augur was swaying in his death agonies from the bough of the tree, Bencomo, unconsciously plagiarising from the Scriptures, taunted him with his inability to foretell his own dismal ending. Again, when later the " white wings " of the Spanish ships appeared, and the herald of Spain presented himself before the king with three demands—Peace; the acceptance by the Guanches of Christianity; and the acknowledgment of King Ferdinand of Spain for their sovereign lord—Bencomo treated the two first proposals with bland indifference, but flew into a royal rage about the third demand. " We are not so weak that we are unable to defend ourselves. I was born a king, and a king I mean to die, in defence of my honour, my country, and my subjects."

Matanza was the first battle between invaders and invaded. Here, among the barley and potatoes and vines, relics of the fight of 1495 are still upturned from the reddish earth—bones, fragments of jerkins, helmets, spurs, and weapons.

Leaving this place of slaughter, we now drive through the villages of Victoria (where the Spaniards subsequently atoned for Matanza by a bloody massacre of Guanches) and Santa Ursula, gradually descending from the high ground of Laguna. The palms thicken, and the country gets more and more fertile. We are nearing the vale of Orotava—the most beautiful valley in the world, said Humboldt; and also approaching the base of the Peak.

Soon after traversing Santa Ursula, a deep ravine is crossed by a strong lava bridge, and then we mount the intervening shoulder of mountain, and have Orotava at our feet.

This landscape, like so many others, does not, I think, captivate fully at first. It were better for Orotava had Humboldt never given it such responsible praise. One looks for such transcendent beauty, and the fancy is heated to such a pitch of expectation, that nothing less than Eden could satisfy. Besides, in a valley so laboriously cultivated as Orotava, the colours which help so much to beautify it vary greatly according to the season. In April the barley is ripe, and, amid the green vines, palm, and fig trees, the bronzed hue of autumn shows with brilliant effect. A month later, when the sun has gained in heat, and the fields are already nude and grey, the charm is distinctly lessened. And in midsummer, when the very springs which in winter and March and April send full currents down to the gardens in the valley, are almost dried up, and a coat of dust covers even the leaves of the trees—then a man must take with him a light heart if he is to see aught extraordinary in Orotava, in spite of its blossoms, its surrounding hills, its blue sea breaking in high surf upon the shore, and its supreme guardian, the Peak.

I saw Orotava at its best. The valley is really an amphitheatre, about ten miles long by six from the lip of the bowl to the Atlantic bordering its arena. Where the sea touches the centre of the so-called valley, is the red and white town of Port Orotava, or Puerto, as it is known locally. Two miles higher, and joined with Puerto by a road hung with blossoming trees, and bushes of geraniums, heliotrope, jasmin, and red roses, is the city of Orotava, or the Villa, an imposing coterie of tall buildings, from the midst of which the dome of its large parochial church glints in the sunlight. Beyond Orotava, on all sides, are villages and country houses, thickset in verdure, though the nature of the verdure depends, of course, upon the zone of vegetation which their respective height above the sea-level procures for them. Thus the highest of these villages, while we look upon the valley from our surroundings of flowering geraniums, bananas, and prickly pear, is in a wood of great chestnut trees, the purple hue of which tells us more easily than the naked eye that they have not yet unfurled a single leaf. In one part of the valley all is florid and tropical; in another we are, as it were, in Norway or Sweden; and both are visible at the same time.

But though the various greens of this Garden of the Hesperides are sufficiently pleasing for a connoisseur of Nature's colours, without the Peak, Orotava would have no claim to be called magnificent. The mountains which gird the valley are from six to seven thousand feet high. When I saw them first from Santa Ursula they were in black shadow; indeed their summits were cloaked in the darkest of clouds. But over these clouds, and glowing effulgent against a zenith of intense blue sky, stood the Peak —like a superhuman guardian, suspended above the valley between earth and heaven. It stood as a vast pyramid of snow, with glistening lines upon it where runlets of snow water were melting down to the hot valley at its base. The Peak of Tenerife is 12,180 feet above the sea, according to Humboldt's measurement. As the cloud stratum which, with remarkable obstinacy, forms almost daily at nine or ten o'clock round its great body, hangs at an elevation not exceeding five thousand feet above the level, the mountain is then invisible from Orotava. At such times the whole valley seems to be living in the gloom precedent to a violent thunderstorm. But by climbing the hills sufficiently high, or getting an outside view of the valley, the Peak itself is seen presiding over valley, clouds, and sea alike. This is one of those memorable sights that the mind holds fast to as a pure incomparable pleasure. Recalling it, one is then willing enough to justify Humboldt for his bold commendation of the valley of Orotava.

CHAPTER III.

Sweet idling in Puerto—Trivial excitements of a health resort—Puerto as it is and as it was—The old wine trade—Irish monuments in the Church—Puerto's harbour—La Paz—A Guanche sepulchre—Guanche skulls—A southern villa—The cochineal insect—Sugar, tobacco, and wine—The ruin of 1826.

Two or three days' experience of life in Puerto makes one feel that if change is good in proportion to its completeness, this is a royal health resort.

The eye can look nowhere without being charmed. The sorriest palm tree among the chimney pots of the town seems as happy in its surroundings as if it were one of a grove in a desert oasis. The brilliant green of the young vines and barley a stone's throw from my window is not less beautiful than the olive of the distant country, where it swells upwards to the dark pine forests on the slopes, 5,000 feet above Puerto; nor the deep clear blue of the Atlantic, where it beats into surf against the black scoriated strand of the town, than the pure azure of the heavens above the white crest of Teide.

All is cheerful—from the rhythmical boom of the sea-surge to the singing of the birds in the adjacent

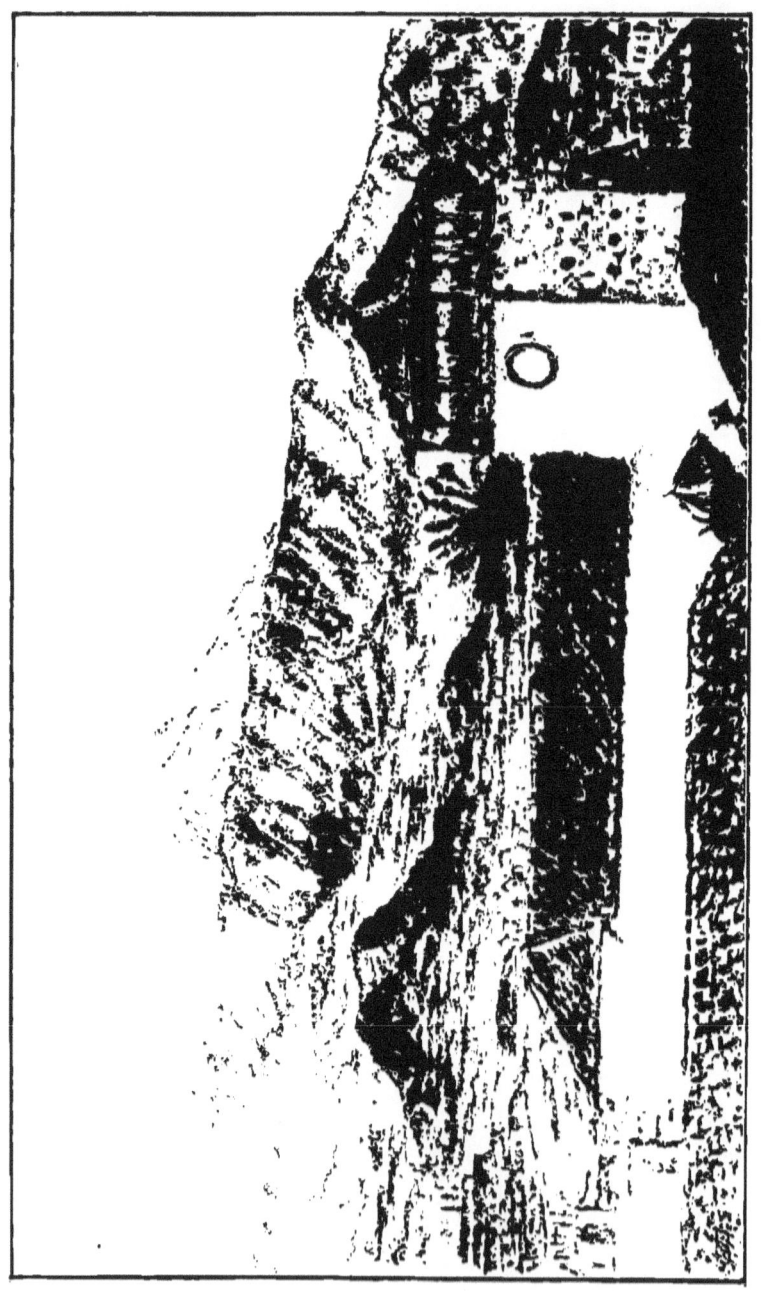

THE PEAK: FROM A ROOF IN PUERTO.

magnolias and orange trees, the singing of men in the streets, and the tinkle of the bells of the goats as they browse towards their upland pasture grounds.

It is warm, but not too warm. During the midday heat, one may lounge the hours away under the shade of the palms, in an atmosphere sweet with heliotrope and orange blossom, and cooled by the splash of the water in the marble fountains among the trees.

By and by the shadows slide fast to the west. The day dies briefly in a wrack of blood-red vapour. The stars hurry forth their light. The little green frogs in the water tanks break into loud amorous babble. The clouds lift from the loins of the Peak, and the great cone of glowing snow shines down on the valley with a lustre that mocks the ray of the baby moon, rising feebly behind it.

But voluptuousness and inertia do not here rule with absolute despotism. There is a measure of what is called "life," even at this young health resort. One day, for instance, with the early cup of coffee, news comes of the death of your neighbour. It is not unexpected, of course. Here nothing is unexpected. But, within the next twenty-four hours, the poor fellow is buried and nearly forgotten. It was a little disturbing to have the men with the black coffin on their shoulders, cigarettes in their mouths, and a bucket of quicklime in their hands come into your room by mistake. Yet even this gives occasion for some dry humour before the week is out. Again, it made one wince for the moment, when, during the funeral service in the small whitewashed cemetery for those "outside the Church," full of big scarlet geranium bushes, and shadowed by tall date palms, a lavender-coloured dog, like a wolf-hound, found his way into the midst of the tearless throng of strangers at the grave of their comrade who has gone into the strangest of all strange places, and sniffed unctuously at the ill-made coffin ere he was kicked off by the burly tourist in a pugaree. These little extraordinary events of the day are not such bad condiment for the evening dinner, with its average hour and a half of tediousness. As for the morrow, it may be devoted to the dance at the Governor-General's in Santa Cruz, his Excellency, with a keen sense of the benefit his province is likely to get from the influx of foreign purses, having sent an invitation for a score or so of the English of Puerto. And on the following day there is a riding party and a picnic for those who think it not unbecoming to take their pleasure on Sunday, and a new preacher for those who attend service.

Add to these mild diversions the excitement that comes in with every steamer bearing its quota of new visitors, letters, newspapers, &c., and the consciousness, individual and collective, that the place is health-restoring in a remarkable degree, and you will see that this Grand Hotel of Orotava, with its tropical gardens, lofty irreproachable rooms, and comforting *cuisine*, is not to be despised.

Puerto is a comatose little town of about 4,000 inhabitants, built on a bed of lava, which in the thirteenth century flowed hither and into the sea from one of the three small volcanic humps that

A SCENE IN PUERTO.

stand up with an air of menace in the midst of the valley of Orotava.

In half an hour one may walk by a narrow and tortuous river-bed, with pent precipitous walls like a miniature cañon, to the base of this pyramid of iridescent ash, whence the foundations of Puerto issued in fiery solution.

With patience and another half-hour one may climb to the top of the *volcancta*. It is already crumbling away, even as the lava it exuded is disintegrating, and become a prey to vines, mulberry, and peach trees. Wild fig and euphorbia bushes have taken root in it, and their twigs are bound together by the stout webs of fat, mottled spiders, who look able and willing to resent the collapse of their careful establishments. From this vantage ground there is a broad view of the villages of Orotava and the sea, even to the island of Palma, fifty miles away.

Puerto, like Laguna, is a moribund town. It has many substantial houses, with fascinating *patios* and balconies, and the urchins who ascend to the belfry of its parish church, and work the clappers of the bells, daily make noise enough for half a dozen active seaports : but the grass in the slippery streets bears witness against Puerto. In the seventeenth and eighteenth centuries the English agents of the London wine merchants who bought Canary wine, mainly resided here. They were the authors of the best of Puerto's houses. They made much money, lived jovially, married the prettiest Spanish girls of Tenerife, and left their progeny to perpetuate the virtues of Englishmen in the island. Indeed, they were so keen commercially, that at one time they all but had the monopoly of the local wines. The growers got pinched under this mercantile pressure, and, after protesting in vain, attacked the English warehouses. Thus it happened that in 1666, at Garachico, a few miles west of Puerto, scores of barrels of wine were burst in the night by bands of masked peasants, and the liquor was sent flowing down the gutters into the sea. In the eighteenth century we had begun to tire of Canary wines: Madeira was superseding them. Nevertheless, as Viera says, though we spoke ill of Canary, we still bought it. We continued, in fact, to buy it, until the oidium disease, early in this century, came disastrously upon the vineyards of Tenerife. The cloud which then fell upon Puerto has not yet lifted.

Both the church and the present inhabitants of Puerto show traces of Anglo-Saxon and Anglo-Celtic blood. One, Don Bernardo Walsh—" vir bonus et justus . . . omnibus innocuus "—who died in 1713, is responsible for a chapel of St. Patrick in the church, and for a red and green altar of stupendous ugliness. He also was the donor of the font. His wife, a dame of the Fitzgerald family, lies buried here by his side. In the Chapel of St. Joseph, opposite to that of St. Patrick, is similar witness to the fellowship between Puerto and Ireland. The handsome heavy wood screen behind the altar is surmounted by a harp, and here, too, lie members of the family of Don Bernardo, who seems to have assumed the euphonious alias of Valois, and the titles of nobility deserved by such a name. A certain medical man named Shee, "Apollo

A BUSY DAY IN PUERTO.

Hesperidum," who died in 1724, and whose earlier associations with Ireland are referred to on his tombstone, shares this mortuary chapel with the Valois or Walshes. I do not know how to explain this exodus hither of Irishmen, apparently about the time of the War of the Spanish Succession. The Canarians supported Philip V. against the Archduke Charles, our candidate for the throne, and therefore we were on terms of enmity with them. Blue eyes, wit, and a pleasant touch of Irish brogue, are, moreover, the characteristics of several residents still in Puerto.

Two hundred years ago Puerto was dignified as "the key of the island." This does but prove how deficient is Tenerife in harbourages. The port is a tiny inlet made by the inclination of its mole towards the gnarled black rocks of lava on one side of it. It will hold a smack of a few score tons; but so terrific is the surf that the open sea is safer than the harbour. Even when there is no wind, the waves thunder into the little bay, and fly a hundred feet high into spray against the roofs of the houses which perch on the shore rocks.

South-west of the bay is a battery as diminutive as the harbour. It was erected to guard this precious position; but I doubt if it ever had cause to fire one of the toy guns with which it was furnished. For, as old Glas, the first English historian of the Canaries, says—" The surf that continually breaks upon the shore is a better defence than a garrison of 10,000 of the best troops." Most of the Canarian seaports at one time or another had to repel privateers, or submit to be sacked by them; but Puerto de la Cruz has no such records in its history. To the east of the port is a limited stretch of black basaltic sand, bordered with tamarisk bushes. A shrine is the only guard-house here; but, indeed, though rocks are wanting, the surf is even more violent than in the harbour.

Above this hot black sand (Humboldt found its refracting power to be 9° Réamur greater than that of the ordinary white quartzose sand) is a precipitous rock, which soon excites the interest of a visitor. It rises about three hundred feet over the sea-level, and its brow is daintily fringed with palms. The villa property which runs to the very edge of this rock is known as La Paz (Peace). Here Humboldt spent a day or two during his hasty view of Tenerife. He is now succeeded by a British officer and his family, who have rented the villa, and made it as like an English country house as a Spanish bungalow can be, with its surroundings of sugar cane, bananas, plumbago bushes, and palms, instead of turf, trim garden plots, high elms, and oaks.

Under the edge of this precipice, I found a trace of old Guanche times that set me reflecting. In scrambling obliquely down the rock sides among the euphorbia, prickly pear, and scrub fig trees, I all but slipped feet first into a pit which suddenly appeared in the sand and scoriæ of the surface. This hole, about twenty feet deep, held an immense medley of human bones—shins, ribs, arms, and crania, all intermixed with the earth that had fallen in from the top of the cave. It was an ancient burial place of

VIEW FROM A GARDEN NEAR HUMBOLDT'S VILLA.

SEPULCHRAL CAVES.

the aborigines of Tenerife, who made it a point of honour to inter their dead in holes almost inaccessible to ordinary human beings. I had ere this seen from below a circular opening in the face of the cliff where it is actually perpendicular, with a cluster of thigh bones lolling in view against the parapet, like men and women in an opera box. This opening seawards sufficed to throw a dim light into the sepulchre.

But, indeed, Tenerife must teem with the bones and mummies of the Guanches. The problem is— to get at them. Given a ravine with sides more or less precipitous, and one may be sure that the natural caves in its scoriated walls have been used as chambers for the dead. Viera, the best historian of the Canaries, had the luck to enter one of these caves, containing more than a thousand mummies, some recumbent, others erect and leaning against the walls. He attributed a fabulous age to these dead. Some, he thought, might date from the time of Juba. But for ages it was the fashion with the apothecaries of Europe to pay good prices for Guanche mummies, which were esteemed as very valuable ingredients in divers mediæval medicines. British sailors and others have therefore transported as many as they could lay hands upon, and these halls of the dead are now denuded of their occupants.

During my stay in Orotava, however, a Swede with a rage for ethnic types, scented out a cave that had not been much disturbed, and carried off to his native land, for the enrichment of the museums, a hamper full of skulls. Another cave was explored with difficulty, aided by ladders and ropes, by some Englishmen, who trod knee-deep in brown dust and skeletons, and contrived to dig from out this dry swamp of dead humanity, fish hooks, needles of bone, and scalps of the ruddy hair that adorned the Guanches, It appeared that the cave had long been the resort of a family of poor agriculturists, who found that its dust was much liked by the beans and potatoes of their garden.

The cave of La Paz is too exposed to have been exempt from rifling. It has yielded some well-developed heads to the collection of an enterprising chemist of Puerto, and innumerable teeth for retail by the Puerto boys at so much a dozen. We got into it one day with a rope, and toiled among the dry bones, to little antiquarian purpose; but we raised a dust that was as pungent and operative as Scotch rappee.

The Guanche skulls are remarkable for their breadth at the cheek bones, and the fine preservation of the teeth. In the museum of Tacoronte are heads of admirable symmetry, and also heads of a base type. Probably the structural difference between a Guanche noble and a common peasant, or a member of the degraded class of butchers or embalmers, was as emphatic as if they were of different human families.

Besides La Paz, there is another villa in the neighbourhood of Puerto which may vie with it for beauty and luxuriant vegetation. This also is at present occupied by an English person, the widow of an English gentleman who came here ill, and lived

A GUANCHE SEPULCHRE.

AN ENGLISH RESIDENCE BY PUERTO.

through several decades in excellent health. The garden contains some gems of the tropics, and very many dissimilar fruits and flowers. There is also a croquet lawn enclosed by palm trees, jasmin, plumbago, and bougainvillea bushes, all in full bloom, young dragon trees, and custard apple trees, with a bower of vines as a shelter at one end, and a mixed perfume of incredible richness. When this English invalid came here, the land was *malpais*, or good for nothing, because of the lava which overwhelmed it. Now, a gay ochre villa, with palm tufts before and behind it, this glorious garden, and careful vineyards, irrigated by as careful canals of flowing water, show what industry and energy can do with even the worst of soil. But it must be admitted that the lava, which had then been out about five centuries, and was friable from decomposition, only needed the hand of a master to turn it to account.

On the skirts of this delightful property I was introduced to the cochineal insect: as usual, in a cloud of white dust, on the eccentric ear of the prickly pear. He is a fat, dark, spherical little creature, looking like a black currant, and with neither head, legs, nor tail, to the casual observer. In fact, he is so inanimate that one may squash him between finger and thumb without any qualm of conscience. He is nothing but a black currant, sure enough, though the bright carmine or lake exusion from his body, which serves him for blood and us for dye, is a better colour than the juice of the currant.

It was the cultivation of these pleasant little individuals which, a score of years ago, put no less than

40 per cent. per annum upon investments into the pockets of the cultivators. Such prosperity was too good to last. The insect was not introduced into Tenerife until 1825 ; and for a time it could not be encouraged to propagate successfully. A priest was the discoverer of the right method of nurture, and to him it is due that from 1845 to 1866 an annual crop of from two to six million pounds of cochineal was produced.

A cochineal plantation has a singular aspect. The larvæ, being very delicate, and rather thick-witted, have to be tied upon the cactus plant, which is to be their nursery and their nourishment at the same time. Thus one sees hundreds of the shoots of the prickly pear—the cactus in question—all bandaged with white linen, as if they had the toothache. In this way the insects are kept warm and dry during the winter, and induced to adhere to the plant itself. When they are full grown, they are ruthlessly swept from their prickly quarters, shaken or baked to death, and dried in the sun. The shrivelled anatomies are then packed in bags, and sold as ripe merchandise at about £5 a hundredweight.

Besides the cochineal, Tenerife grows a little sugar and tobacco. A century and a half ago not fewer than a thousand negroes were employed on a single plantation of the island—that of Adeje. Nowadays, however, the sugar industry has fallen, and the newer industry of tobacco is likely to supplant it.

The local wines are in as low a state as the sugar and cochineal of the island. They have lost ground sadly since the time when Falstaff blurted their

A VILLA OF TENERIFE.

praises. As a matter of form, the hotel list included two or three varieties of Tenerifan wine, though it was notorious that none but case-hardened stomachs could endure them. Even the Malvasia, in spite of its reputation and agreeable savour, plays tricks in an ungenerous manner upon the man who patronises it. Hence the anomalous and humiliating custom of drinking Bordeaux and Burgundy in a country that ought to put France to the blush for its wines. When I ordered a bottle of Malvasia at dinner, the head waiter, a good and considerate man, asked, in a whisper, if I knew what I was doing. It is considered wise to talk with the doctor before making such a bold experiment.

No wonder, therefore, that there are so many empty warehouses at Puerto, or warehouses that once held tuns of Canary, but now are stacked with maize, or with salt fish for Lenten consumption. During my strolls through the silent streets I looked into deserted houses, conventual and other buildings, with overgrown gardens, and monstrous accumulations of foul dirt and cobwebs. "Ah! if only the disease had not come to us!" wailed the son of one of the ruined wine merchants. "It was different before. And the flood of 1826 too—that was bad for Puerto! It rained for hours and hours, and for days in the mountains, so that the water ran down the river beds with the noise of guns. But the river beds could not hold it, there was so much! And thus it swept into the town, and drowned hundreds of men and women and beasts, and carried them and the very houses out on to the Atlantic."

As a matter of fact, this terrific inundation destroyed 225 houses, and drowned 235 people and 804 head of cattle. In the district of Laguna, it was not satisfied with such superficial havoc. Whole estates were washed from the steep hill sides into the valleys; so that the unfortunate proprietors saw nothing but the bare rock-bed of their fields remaining to them.

Forgetting for the moment the balmy luxurious air and charming scenery of these islands, and turning to the category of evils they have suffered from storms like this storm, from piratical ravages, locusts, pestilence, drought and earthquakes, one cannot but realise that the term Fortunate Isles, applied to them of old, has and has had only a comparative meaning after all.

CHAPTER IV.

Various conjectural origins of the name, people, and land of the Canary Islands—The island of San Borondon—The legendary first inhabitants—The Canaries and the Elysian Fields identical.

I HAD hoped to be able in this little book to give a concise yet complete account of the early traditions and history of the Canary Isles: but I find it impossible. Scores of learned and unlearned men, lay and ecclesiastic, have, centuries ago, preceded me in this work. They have written it in various species of prose, and in poetry of the epic kind. The facts of common acquisition to them all have been swelled by some of them into gigantic exaggerations, and this untruthful nucleus they have buried under a crust of new conjectures, suggestions, hypotheses, and statements, most or all of which they owe to their own heated brains, and to their anxiety for the fame that attends even upon presumptuous originality. These fantastic and sinful writers have been followed by others, lazy rather than imaginative, who have worked after the eclectic mode. They have chosen a pretty theory from one ancient, a monstrous lie from another, a ridiculous assertion from a third; and, with a certain labour, have moulded the whole into what they were pleased to call a history. The amount of nonsense in the Canarian bibliography is therefore prodigious. A man might sift his wits away in the effort to extract the grains of sense from the piles of nonsense.

At least, however, I will give a brief common epitome of the conceived origin of the name, the inhabitants, and the very bulk itself of the islands: for nothing has been taken for granted about these petty spots in the Atlantic. The Abbé Viera, who wrote in the last century, is the Canarian classic historian. I rely upon the 1,700 octavo pages of his four volumes for my wisest words.

The Canarian Archipelago consists of seven inhabited islands and five uninhabited islets, all ranging between latitude 27° 30' and 29° 25' north, and between longitude 13° and 18° west of Greenwich. Their nearness to the north-west coast of Africa is therefore apparent.

The islands, in the order of their size, are Tenerife, 1,946 square kilometres; Fuerteventura (with Lobos), 1,722 kilometres; Grand Canary, 1,376 kilometres; Lanzarote (with adjacent islets), 741 kilometres; Palma, 726 kilometres; Gomera, 378 kilometres; Hierro, 278 kilometres. Their present population is nearly 300,000—of which Tenerife and Grand Canary provide more than half.

But whence the name Canary, which, late in the middle ages, superseded the title of "Fortunate," applied to them by King Juba, and recorded by Pliny? Ah, whence indeed? Here are a few solutions for the amusement of philologists.

Antonio de Viana, a native of Tenerife, printed, in 1604, an epic poem in blank verse, beginning,

"I sing the origin of the name Canary."

The poem contains sixteen cantos, each averaging twenty-four pages, and thirty-six lines to the page. But it must be confessed that he does not give all the 13,000 lines of the epic to the single subject. He is responsible for the hardy and unscriptural plea that Noah, late in life, had two children, Crano and Crana, who put to sea, sailed into the Atlantic, and landed on the Canaries. Once here, the rest was easy. They peopled these solitary rocks by their own unaided efforts. The islands were also named after them—Crana or Crano. For the sake of euphony, their descendants decided to transpose the letters of their great ancestors' name. Hence arose Canar—whence Canaria.

This thought of deducing from Noah the generic name of the group seemed to subsequent writers so brilliant that they hesitated not to expand it. Thus that credulous old simpleton, Nuñez de la Peña, ascribes Gomera to Gomer, a grandson of Noah, by Japhet, and Hierro, the most westerly isle, to Hero, a great grandson.

Again, it is assumed by some people that in the Canaries there is a never-ending chorus of song from the little yellow birds, which, it is also assumed, have given these islands their name. Both assumptions are wrong. As for the first, were it so, the brain-sick wanderer to Tenerife, in search of tranquillity, might as well take rooms in Cheapside. As for the second, though there were not wanting those who derived Canaria from the Latin *cano*, with reference to the canary birds of the islands, others, with more intelligence, have pointed out that it is the birds who have taken the name of the islands, and not the islands a name derived from an attribute of the birds.

A third source of strife is hardly less absurd. Is it not clear, asks Ambrosio Calepino, that the word Canary comes from the Spanish *caña*, or the Latin *canna*, which means a cane, and especially a sugar cane? The islands grow sugar cane—that settles it. But this dull gentleman did not perceive that he had laboriously harnessed his cart to the horse. The aborigines called Grand Canary, Canaria (whence the distinctive name of the group), long before the Spaniards conquered it. And it is simple knowledge that the conquerors first introduced the sugar cane into the islands.

Thomas Nicols, an Englishman, whose travels, early in the sixteenth century, appear in the Purchas' collection, agrees somewhat with Calepino. He says he was informed by the natives that their land was called after the euphorbias, or cardons, which abound in it. But the root of the matter is as insecure as Calepino's. The euphorbias were called *cañas* by the Spaniards, and Nicols did not see that a Spanish word could not explain a name that existed ere Spain influenced Canary.

A priest broaches the theory that Canary and Canaan are identical in origin. The Canaanites who fled before Joshua when he invaded Palestine took to the sea like the children of Noah, and reached the Fortunate Isles. Again, the Canarians are the offspring of the tribes of Israel, dispersed by Shalmaneser. But, it has been well asked, what was there in common between the luxury of Tyre and the extreme simplicity of the Canarians, alike in food and clothing?

The adjacent mainland of Africa offers a sixth elucidation. Ninety miles east of Grand Canary is the cape we call Bojadore or Mogadore, but which Ptolemy and others called Chaunaria extrema— whence Caunaria and Canaria. This derivation is not to be despised.

But here comes Pliny, with an authoritative claim in the christening. Writing about the Fortunate Islands, and drawing his material from the manuscript of King Juba, who had visited them in person, he says explicitly that the island of Canary got its name from the multitude of huge dogs in it—two of which dogs Juba took back with him to Africa. Viera holds to this as the most rational of all the theories; and, indeed, it sufficiently accounts for the name given to it by King Juba. It were, however, a curious problem for an antiquary to show why Canary in after ages retained this Latin name, while five of the other islands, then known respectively as Ombrios, Junonia, the greater and the less, Capraria, and Nivaria, lost completely their old designations. The dogs of Canary are certainly a distinct breed. Even Nicols notices them; and he accuses the natives of eating them.

A last reckless surmise is the association of the

island peopled by Elishah, the son of Javan (Genesis x. 4), and quoted in Ezekiel xxvii. 7, with the Elysian Fields of the ancients, which again have been identified with the Canary group.

But the subject is bewildering, and I am glad to turn my back upon it. There are they who doubt if Tenerife and its six companions are the Fortunate Islands referred to by Pliny. Great Britain is preferred: in which case, of course, King Juba carried home a couple of bull-dogs for the improvement of his African kennels. In short, nothing but impudence is needed to support the thesis that the Canary Isles have no fellowship whatever with Tenerife, Grand Canary, and the others of this Archipelago.

From the name we fall to a consideration of the structural history of the islands. Were the Canaries at one time a part of the continent of Africa? Was it due to Noah's flood that they first became insulated? Are they identical with the Atlantis of Plato? Or are they comparatively modern additions to the landed property of our globe, by submarine upheaval?

There is no lack of evidence for the support of these various notions, and so the dilettante may pick and choose at his leisure. The sandy soil and the camels of the eastern islands are held as conclusive testimony that they and the continent were formerly one. The flora of the islands and the continent is almost the same. The language of the Berbers, the nearest uncivilized race of Africa, has been proved to have close affinity with the individual languages of the islanders before the conquest.

Everything indicates therefore that the islands are

merely accidental parings from the mainland. If a thousand fathoms of water intervene, it is nothing to the point.

Similarly, in the words of a modern, "everything indicates that this whole island of Tenerife is, in its entirety, but the summit of a half-risen mountain." (Piazzi Smyth.)

After this, one cannot be surprised to learn that for several centuries the Spaniards did not know exactly how many islands they ought to include in the number of the Canaries.

The history of the "enchanted island" of San Borondon is indeed a most singular geographical romance. For nearly three centuries after the conquest, the authorities were frequently puzzled by reports, having every apparent mark of truth, of the observation of an island in the neighbourhood of the Canarian Archipelago, and which was believed to be the eighth member of the group. This island could never be found by direct search; but, when it was least looked for, then, to the wonder of the mariners, its strange high mountains were wont to loom in sight. No one could account for such coquettish conduct. Nevertheless, the island was duly registered as a property of the Spanish Crown.

Among the articles of the treaty of Evora, in 1519, between Spain and Portugal, in which treaty Portugal ceded to Spain its claim of seignorage over the Canaries, San Borondon is included as the island "Non Trubada" (not found). It was, however, fancifully described as 87 leagues long and 28 broad; as being 40 leagues distant from Palma, 100 leagues from Hierro; and 40, 15, 10, or 8 leagues (according to the diversity of opinion) from the island of Gomera.

The name of this mysterious island was derived from a certain Scotch monk, Saint Brandon, or Blandon, or Borondon, who, in the sixth century, with a fellow monk, Saint Maclovius, and eighteen companions, is said to have set out on an evangelizing tour from the north, and arrived in the Canarian waters.

Sigeberto, a mediæval chronicler, gives the details of what followed, with quaint circumstantiality. The monks had been long at sea without a sight of land. Easter Sunday arrived, and they were bitterly distressed that they were unable to celebrate the Holy Eucharist. In their sorrow they all went upon their knees on the deck of the little ship, and prayed to God to create some land in the middle of the ocean, available for the Paschal services. Hereupon the island of San Borondon or Brandon made its first appearance, and, in a transport of joy, the monks went ashore, and built an altar.

Another version of the story says that the Saint Maclovius whose name is associated with Saint Brandon, was not a companion, but a gigantic native of the island, whom Saint Brandon found dead in a cave, resuscitated, and baptized. But the amazed giant was not altogether satisfied with his involuntary resurrection. Fifteen days after the event, he begged that he might be allowed to return to his grave. His request was granted; but, before his second death, he informed his benefactor (*sic*) that his contemporaries had been acquainted with the mystery of the Trinity and the Pains of Hell.

Then the monks sailed away, and left the island to itself.

It has been suggested that this temporary altar in the sea was only a whale, miraculously controlled. But this does not explain the constant reappearance of the island, with its proper equipment of mountains, wood, and water. Four times between 1526 and 1721 the Spanish officials of the Canaries sent expeditions in quest of San Borondon. Chaplains and artificers, as well as warriors, were on board these boats. But each expedition returned discomfited. The pilots and mariners who had told such unprofitable tales never omitted one feature pertaining to the island. A storm invariably drove them away from it, when they had watered the ship, and had had time to admire its beauty and fruitfulness. For centuries, however, though San Borondon was truly an Aprositus, or inaccessible island, no one seems to have doubted its existence. It was somewhere, but its day had not yet come. So late as 1730, two fathers of the Church, " the one very short of sight and the other of intelligence," while with their bishop in the Isle of Palma, thought they saw San Borondon, and immediately wanted to go thither to preach the gospel. One precise historian even endows it with an archbishop and six bishops, seven wealthy cities, harbours, rivers, and a Christian people, blessed with all the blessings of prosperity. After this, one may excuse Gautier, the French geographer, who, in 1755, boldly set down the island of San Borondon on his map. According to him, it stood 5° west of Hierro, and in latitude 29°.

It were a thankless task to attempt to explain how an error like this held the popular understanding for so long a time. Where there is little knowledge there is much credulity.

The Abbé himself, one of the most enlightened Spaniards of his age (1731–1813), tried to explain San Borondon as a freak of refraction; but Humboldt soon afterwards demonstrated that this explanation was as unsound as its predecessors.

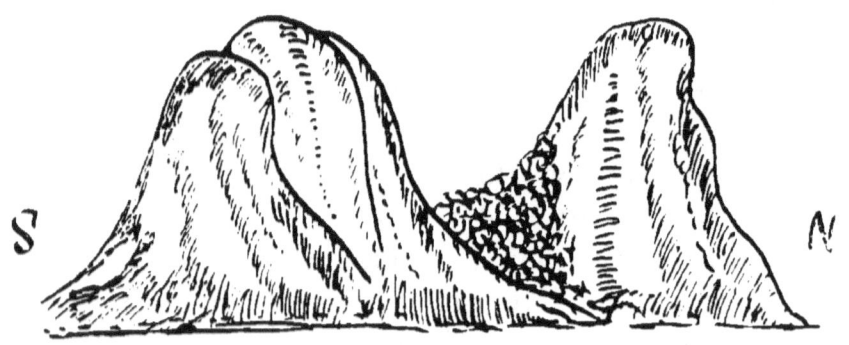

The island of San Borondon, or San Blandon, or San Brandon, or San Brandan, according to Spanish belief in the fifteenth to the eighteenth century. (From a drawing made in 1730 by a priest of Palma.)

I must add a few words about the mythical first inhabitants of these islands, before I describe the actual people whom the Spaniards, in the fifteenth century, crushed into subjection to the Peninsula. It may be thought that this question has already been sufficiently debated as part and parcel of the puzzle of the origin of the word "Canary." No such thing. It has involved distinct treatises of awful length, complexity, and weight, and the subject is still open to discussion.

We have seen that Canaan, Gomer and Hero, the grandson and great grandson of Noah, and Elishah the son of Javan, also a great grandson of the same patriarch, have been made responsible for the peopling of the isles. So also has the Phœnician Hercules (from Harokel, a merchant), who, in a naval battle with the King of Mauritania, drove certain of the Africans into the archipelago, where they stayed from that time forward. Others give the early parents of some of the isles a low origin. They were a band of criminals whom Himbric, king of the Vandals, exiled from the mainland, having deprived them of their forefingers and thumbs, and abbreviated their tongues. This seemed to account for the thick pronunciation which characterized the native speech when the Spaniards came upon the isles.

Then they are regarded as autochthones, the fortunate few who clung to the high lands of Atlantis, when the greater part of that island—of which the present Canaries are the survival—went down into the sea.

Again, Herodotus tells us of Egyptians who, in 616 B.C., sailed round the Cape of Good Hope, from east to west. It were natural that, in their return home after this long voyage, certain of these brave fellows should be tempted to land among the verdure of the Canaries. Egypt, therefore, has a claim upon the stock of the country.

These two or three of the possible progenitors of

the Canarians will suffice for my purpose. I do not wish to enter upon controversy, whether ethnological or etymological—especially about a group of islands whose united superficies is less than the area of a single English county. But I willingly admit that these islands may be "the Elysian Fields at the extremity of the world," whither the happy Menelaus was to go for the endless winter of his life —" where men live sweet and tranquil days, where there is no snow, nor rain, nor severe winters; but a never-changing balmy air, breathed from the sea."

There is, in truth, so little rain in the island that a poet may be forgiven when he says that there is none at all. But is it not odd that the island of Tenerife—a component part of this heaven on earth—should have been called by the Guanches of the middle ages, Hell? and, therefore, also styled "Infernus" in the early Bulls issued by the Popes of Rome in ecclesiastical matters that concerned the Canaries?

CHAPTER V.

Tacoronte—Its museum and miraculous crucifix—The Guanches—Their mummies and method of embalming—Their polity—Coronations—Ceremony of ennobling—Religion—The vestal virgins of Grand Canary—Education—Morals—Trial by smoke—Punishment of crime—Dress—General character—Food—The Palma mode of dying—Dwellings and furniture—Inscription of Belmaco—Strength and agility—Reflections.

A VISIT to the pretty village of Tacoronte, on the breezy slopes between Orotava and Laguna, gives me a fit opportunity to say something about the Guanches of Tenerife, and their barbarian brethren in the other Canarian islands.

Tacoronte has only four or five thousand inhabitants among its palm trees and red and white villas; but it boasts a museum of native antiquities not to be matched in Tenerife.

Here, in pleasant disorder, one sees the mummies, the weapons, the unguents, the spices, and clothing of these ancients, who, three centuries ago, were still talked of by the Spaniards who had suppressed them as ideals of "Arcadian innocence" and gentle simplicity. The kingdom of this world is for the strong: the poor dispossessed Guanches were welcome to poetic excellence. Besides, those of them who had not died in the process of civilizing, were so degraded that it cost nothing to praise their forefathers. It may be remembered also that, in spite of this laudation, the governors of the six great colleges of Spain made it a bar to the admission thereto of a boy, that he had Guanche blood in him.

This ancient town, the seat of "the proud Acaymo," one of the nine kings, who, after Tinerfe, divided the island between them, contains other objects of interest, as well as the museum. Its women are beautiful: but what is one to say about the ladies of a land, each little village of which claims to surpass all the others for its beautiful women! There is an extraordinary sameness about black eyes, viewed in the abstract; and yet, putting in retrospect the women of one place against those of another, I recall such sweet varieties of charms as baffle all cold comparisons. In its church there is a silver chandelier, weighing a quintal, or about a hundred pounds avoirdupois; and also a wonder-working crucifix, which the sacristan shows with a dubious glance of appeal, as if imploring it to withhold any miraculous proof of wrath which it might feel inclined to manifest, to punish him for his sins. A record is kept of the attested miracles wrought by this ensanguined figure; but they do not differ from other miracles of the kind. A freak of the marvellous that met us in Tacoronte, and made more impression than these tales, was a mule walking up the street at a demure pace in two pair of sackcloth breeches. "It is because of the flies, señor, the cursed flies!" said the muleteer, with a smile of sympathy. I fancy the animal would rather have had his red wounds exposed to the flies—venomous though they are—than be pent in such a stiff unnatural style.

The mummies of Tacoronte have none of that cheerful picturesqueness with which an Egyptian mummy in his case invariably charms the eye. They are indeed very gruesome. There is a queen with a fine set of white teeth, and thick curly mouse-coloured hair on her head. She is wrapped in several sheepskins, the wool being inside, and tied up with parchment thongs. But her attitude and general appearance give her the look of a large cat that has been done to death through much agony, and mummified while in the last convulsive paroxysm. A still more ghastly object is a loathsome dishevelled old man with his tongue out. But one notices with interest, that almond-shaped finger and toe-nails were the fashion even among the Guanches.

The Guanche method of embalming differed from the Egyptian. The embalmers were a despised class of people, but very skilful. They took charge of the dead man, drew out his entrails through the mouth, washed him with salt and water, paying particular attention to the ears, the nose, the fingers, nails, and other tender parts, and then rubbed the body with an ointment of goat's butter, aromatic herbs, turpentine, bark, pumice dust, wood ash, and other absorptive materials. Afterwards, it was placed in the sun for fifteen days, during which time the funeral ceremonies lasted, with much lamentation and weeping. Then the mummy was a finished work of art, dry and light as paper. It was lastly swaddled in sheep or goat skins (sometimes as many as ten or twelve), tied, ticketed for future recognition, and buried in a cave. Monarchs and the nobility were put in coffins of hard wood, and either set upright against the side of the cave in regular order, or laid horizontally, about two feet from the ground, on crossed pieces of pine or tilo timber.

But although we can give such circumstantial details about their process of embalming, we could no more practise the art with their success than we could preserve the dead in all the freshness of life, without the secret of Ruysch or Swammerdam.

Let us now turn to the polity and manners of these people.

The Guanche government was a kindly despotism. Their theory of the creation of human beings was perhaps the most aristocratic ever conceived. At first, they said, God made an equal number of men and women, and provided them all with sufficient means of subsistence. After a time, however, He created others, whom He omitted to endow with worldly goods. And when these applied to Him for sheep and goats, He bade them serve their elders, who would then give them food and raiment in return for their services.

Thus originated the three orders of Guanche society—the kings, the nobles, and the common people or servants. The king, as the individual representative of the nobles, owned all the land, the usufruct of which he gave to his people, in proportion to the size of their families. At the death of these vassals in chief (as they might be called) their estates reverted to the sovereign, who then dispersed them anew among the survivors.

The kingship in Tenerife was hereditary. Until about a hundred years before the Conquest, there was but one monarch for the whole island. The great Tinerfe, at his death, however, left nine sons, and the realm fell into nine petty kingdoms or principalities. In each kingdom the skull of the first sovereign of that realm was preserved. A new monarch convened his nobles in the place of assembly, and, having kissed his ancestor's skull, solemnly placed it on his head, saying, "I swear by this bone, which once wore the crown, to follow the example of him to whom it belonged, and to study the happiness of my subjects." The nobles then one by one took the skull, and, respectfully holding it on their right shoulder, kissed it and said, "I swear by thy coronation day to guard our realm, and the king thy descendant." The crown assumed by the king was a garland of laurel, palm, and sweet flowers, and the sceptre the thigh bone of the monarch upon whose skull the oaths were made.

The ceremony by which the son of a noble Guanche was himself at a ripe age enrolled among the aristocracy was curious. The Faycan or high-priest (the second person in the realm, and generally the king's brother) received the aspirant in the presence of the people—the youth's long hair marking the legitimacy of his claim to nobility. The Faycan then addressed the assembly, " In the eternal name of God (Alcorac), I conjure you all to declare if you have ever seen N——, the son of M——, enter into the cattle yard to milk or kill the goats: If you know that he has prepared food with his own hands: If he has made raids in time of peace: If he has been uncivil or spoken amiss, especially to a woman." A favourable reply having been given by his hearers, the pontiff then cut the youth's hair below the ears, and gave him a lance to use in the service of the king.[1] Thenceforward, he was a noble. But were he convicted of soiling his hands by such ungentlemanly deeds as those mentioned, his hair was all snipped from his head, and he was condemned to be a villein for life.

In the island of Grand Canary, a noble would never wound or kill any one, except in a stand-up fight. And in time of war, when he had his enemy at his feet, he would not kill him. This chivalrous scrupulosity was such that it was held a most marked insult if raw meat of any kind were cut in his presence.

It must not be supposed that the religion of the Guanches was an elaborate theological or ceremonial system. They called the Deity by synonyms meaning—the Preserver of the World! The Sublime One! The Great Lord! Even after the Con-

[1] This lance was only a long piece of pine wood with a pointed extremity, hardened and blackened in the fire. The Tacoronte museum has specimens on its walls.

quest, when the Spaniards introduced Mariolatry, they could not be persuaded to honour the Virgin save as the mother of the Preserver of the World—of the Sublime One, &c. They had no idea of a Divine revelation, except the revelation of nature. Nor did they attempt the impossible by moulding images in conceivable likeness to Him they called the Preserver of the World. Only in times of drought they all betook themselves to a high hill with a number of kids and lambs; and thence their petitions for rain, commingled with the plaintive bleating of the motherless little animals, were supposed to ascend to the heavens.

In Grand Canary, on the like occasions, the people, with palm leaves and sticks in their hands, went in procession, headed by the Vestal Virgins, carrying vases of milk and butter. They danced and wailed on the mountain top, and left the milk and butter as a propitiatory offering to the Deity. Their subsequent conduct was extraordinary. Working themselves into a rage, they descended to the sea-shore, with angry shouts and gestures, and flogged the waves with their palm canes and sticks until they were tired. Perhaps they had a vague idea of the principle of evaporation; but surely not even the spectacle of Canute in his throne upon our Kentish coast could be more ridiculous than this stern castigation of the in-coming tide.

The religion of the islanders of Palma was very primitive. In each of the twelve kingdoms of that country was a pile of loose stones, which served them for divinities. The Caldera, however, was peculiar in its possession of a natural isolated rock about one hundred feet high, with which the destinies of the people of the district were thought to be allied. It was therefore periodically approached with offerings of the entrails of pigs, sheep, &c. "Are you going to fall?" one of the priests would say. "It will not, if you give it what you have got," was the reply from another priest. The offerings were then flung against it, as a sacrifice.

It is doubtful if the hierarchy of the Guanches included the Vestal Virgins who were so greatly reverenced and so important a part in the religious ceremonies of the Grand Canarians. These women (admitted at a tender age, and absolutely chaste), called Harimaguadas, attended upon newly born children, poured water upon their heads, and gave them names. Unlike the Aztecs, however, who had the same form of ritual, they did not regard this lavation as in any way concerned with the inherent sinfulness of human nature. Among the Aztecs, again, a youth or a maiden on the threshold of adolescence was subjected to serious and formal lectures on the depravity of the heart, the evil that is in the world, the beneficial aridity of the paths of virtue, and so forth. The moral education of the Guanches, on the other hand, was very simple, and judiciously casual. "Look, my boy," an elder would say to his son, "at those two men: the one with a cheerful countenance, respected, possessing abundant flocks, and of a healthy body; and the other, living like a dog, doing good neither to himself nor to others, and held in contempt by the rest of us. The one is a good, the other a bad man. You would, of course, like to resemble the good man, therefore follow his example." The Guanches really offer the bracing spectacle of a people whose enjoyment of life was quite untinctured by the fancy that they were not as good as they might be. Their Faycan, indeed, was more of a temporal than a spiritual dignitary.

In such a state of society, morality is likely to be a matter of convention only. A Guanche marriage was completed by the consent of the father to the applicant for his daughter's hand : her consent being previously obtained. But, according to some writers, before the consummation of the marriage, the bride had to keep a recumbent position indoors for thirty days, during which time she was required to do nothing but eat to the best of her ability ; and if at the end of the month this process had not fattened her to the bridegroom's satisfaction, he repudiated her. In a land where all worldly pelf was the king's, a suitor was not despised for his poor circumstances. But the melancholy practice of prelibation kept the husband aloof until the king, or a Faycan, or one of the nobles, relieved the bride of her virginity. In the eastern isle of Lanzarote, at one time, a woman was allowed to have three husbands. She maintained them in a sublime state of dependence, receiving them into her house, month by month, in due rotation. This custom did not prevail among the Guanches. With them, however, divorce was as easy as marriage. A Guanche king, who could ally himself with none but royal blood, was at times obliged to marry his mother or his sister. But this habit cannot be imputed to licentiousness in a country where it was criminal in a man to address a word to a woman whom he did not know.

The early history of Lanzarote has a singular illustration of the value ascribed to legitimacy in the regal line. A Spanish vessel visited the island in 1377, and the captain was amicably entertained by the king of the country. Nine months later the queen gave birth to a child which, from its fresh colour, rather mystified all except its mother. The child grew up, and in time became the wife of Guanarame, an undoubted son of the king's. Guanarame succeeded his father on the throne, and died, leaving a child as his heir. Certain of the nobles now accused Ico, the widow of Guanarame, of illegitimacy, whereby the child would be disinherited. She was condemned to a trial by smoke. Three plebeian women were chosen to be her companions in a tiny chamber which was so rigorously enclosed that no air could enter to mitigate the effect of the smoke from fires of straw kindled within it. If she died, it was proof of her impure birth. The plebeian women soon succumbed; but Ico was saved by the intervention of a friend, who had given her a damp sponge through which to breathe for her salvation.

In the punishment of crime, the Guanches were very lenient. Disrespect to women ranked high as a criminal offence. A homicide was merely ousted from his lands. When the sentence included corporal punishment, it was administered with the royal sceptre—the thigh bone of a king. But it was also customary, immediately after the flogging, to apply healing ointments to the bruises inflicted by such a hard rod.

House-breaking was a capital crime in Fuerteventura and Grand Canary; and also theft, rape, perjury, and homicide. The felon in such cases was laid flat on the ground, with a rock under the shoulder-blades, and the professional butchers beat in his breast-bone with stones, so as to crush his heart into his ribs.

In Hierro, moreover, the "lex talionis" applied to bodily injuries.

But perhaps the humanity of the Guanches is best shown by their method of punishing certain Spaniards whom they took prisoners during the war of the conquest. They set them to wash the goats, and kill the flies that worried them. Such menial offices were a supreme degradation. This intolerance of bloodshed also made them keep their butchers as a clan apart, ostracized by the nature of their work, but fully provided with all the necessaries of life.

Though the islands of the archipelago are so near each other, the islanders held remarkably divergent opinions about the same action. Thus, while in Hierro a thief was deprived of one eye for the first offence, the other eye for a second offence, and so on, until the rogue had nothing but a sentient trunk remaining, in Palma, as in Sparta, the man was most esteemed who could lift cattle with the greatest dexterity. I am indeed disposed to think badly of the natives of Palma from first to last. They did not resist the Spaniards very valorously; they were reputed a melancholy people, in uncommon subjection to their women, who were, to the eye, as well made and capable as the men.

It has been said that a man is known by his dress. In truth, however, the climate rather than the character is betrayed by a study of national costume. Thus we find among the Canaries that in Lanzarote, the most easterly island, nakedness, except as to the shoulders, was the fashion; whereas in Tenerife, the inhabitants of which were habituated to the look, if not to the sensation, of snow, no one went out of doors unattired in the *tamarco*, a species of mantle worn over the sleeveless chemise reaching to the hips, and common to men and women alike. Viera attributes the morality of the Guanches in a measure to the length of their skirts. Strangely enough, a certain tribe of Central Africa, among whom immorality is very rare, explain this by the fact that their unmarried women go about in a state of nudity.

The natives of Grand Canary were the most ostentatious in their attire. They dyed their goat-skins, and worked them into helmets, as well as long-fringed and decorated gowns. In Fuerteventura, feathers were worn in the caps. Sheep-skins, unshorn, were the fashion in Hierro; the woolly side served for the winter, and in summer the coat was reversed.

Pedro Bontier and Juan le Verrier, the two chaplains who accompanied Béthencourt in his invasion of the Canaries in 1402, have left us a record of their comparative opinion of the islanders. As a whole, they considered them the finest people in the world;

but doubtless they wrote with a very limited knowledge of the world. The natives of Lanzarote and Fuerteventura were compassionate, though stern; friendly and sociable; and fond of dancing and music. Those of Gomera were clever at feats of skill and the chase. Hierro shared with Palma a people of melancholy temperament. The Grand Canarians were lively, brave, and amiable, though, according to European judgment, treacherous. The Guanches were strong, active, warlike, modest, generous, and honourable.

Fuerteventura boasted of a giant twenty-two feet high, and in Tenerife a Guanche of royal blood was said to be fourteen feet in height, and furnished with eighty teeth.

Lanzarote and Gomera were singular in certain matters. The women of the former island were said to be without bosoms: they gave their lips to their children to suck, which much deformed their appearance. In Gomera, moreover, it was civil to offer a stranger refreshment of women's milk.

Physically, all the Canarians were robust and long lived. They fed simply, and were abstemious in their medicines. *Gofio*, the national food (flour of maize, pease, barley, lupins, beans, &c.), and the meat of their flocks, gave them all the solid nourishment they needed. In Tenerife they used to roast their meat until it was almost black—when, in their opinion, it was most nutritious and palatable. Rancid goat's butter was the foundation of most of their medicaments. Whey served as a cathartic. They combated with honey the colics and diarrhœa which were troublesome then as now in the islands. Surgical operations were performed with knives of obsidian. Sosa, writing in 1678, says that in his day the same rude knives were used, and used successfully, in the country districts of Grand Canary, for letting blood, and for chirurgery in general.

Thus the islanders lived happily to the age of a hundred, or thereabouts. Only in Palma do we hear of them anticipating the summons of nature, near the close of life. Here, when an invalid came to the conclusion that death was preferable to life, he convoked his friends and relatives, and told them that he wished to die. They seem to have regarded such a wish as unalterable; for the sick man was promptly carried to a cave, laid on a pile of skins, with a jug of milk by his head. The mouth of the cave was then blocked up, and the invalid was left to die in solitude.

The dwellings of the Canarians were as simple as their manner of life. Caves abound in the volcanic tufa of the islands, and they were largely inhabited.

To this day, on the south side of Tenerife, and elsewhere in the other islands, thousands of the people make these caves into commodious homes, delightfully cool in the summer heats. Small huts, thatched with straw or boughs, and centring round a natural palm-trunk, were also used. In Lanzarote and Fuerteventura, the portals of the dwellings were sometimes fancifully chiselled; but their entrances were so diminutive that it was necessary to crawl through them; and the smell within, from deficient ventilation, and their habit of curing meat in the living apartments, was disagreeable. In Hierro they built round houses of stone, roofed and thatched with boughs and straw.

The furniture of these primitive abodes was not luxurious. A hand mill for the *gofio* was essential. This consisted of two round stones, such as are still in common use among the Canarian peasantry. The beds were of straw, and they and the stone seats which served them for chairs were bespread with skins. Sea shells made capital spoons. Fish bones or palm spines were worked into needles. The horns of goats made rude but strong small ploughs. Splinters of pine were natural torches—still much in request. Earthen pots of an uncouth kind were easily made. Add to these trifles, the kid skins for holding the *gofio*, cords of gut, and the various weapons of the country (clubs studded with flints, lances and javelins with fire-hardened points, shields of dragon-wood, axes of obsidian, &c.) and the household furniture was complete. It is doubtful if fermented liquor was known to them. The Guanches at any rate drank nothing but water; and, to preserve their teeth, they took this, not at meal-times, but half an hour afterwards.

The Guanches, strange to say, seem to have had no method of expressing their ideas or thoughts in writing, glyphical or otherwise. The solitary discovery of anything of this kind in the archipelago was made in 1762, when some inscribed basaltic rocks were found over a cave in Palma. Here in Tacoronte is a copy of these hieroglyphics, which will probably remain a puzzle to antiquarians to the end of time.

A modern Spanish writer sees in them "the general epitaph upon the sepulchre of the entire extinct race of the primitive Palma people." This is conjectural,

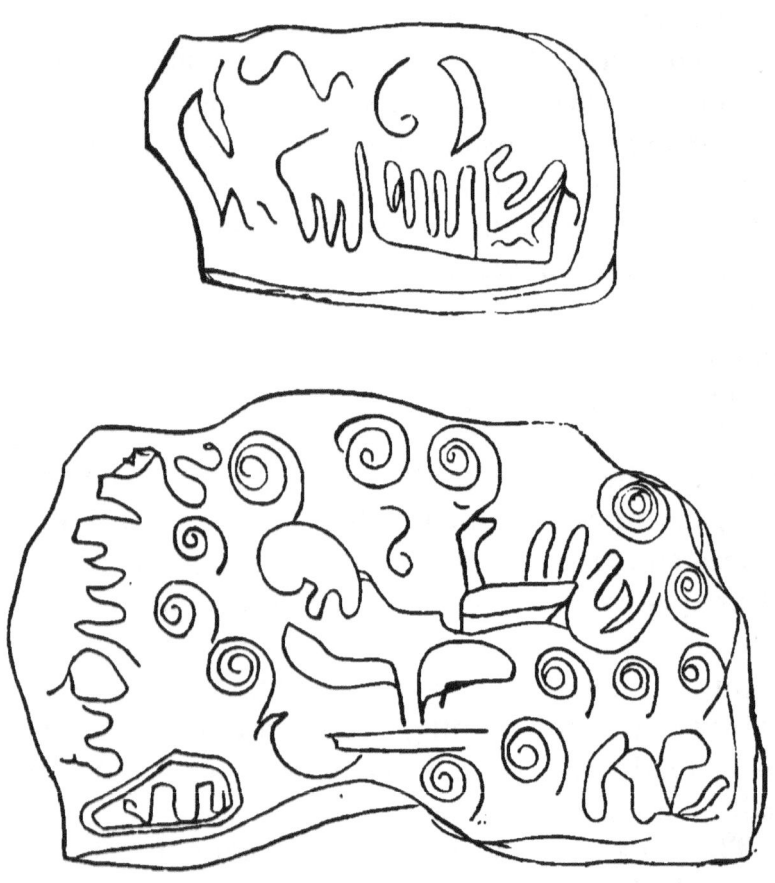

Facsimiles of the inscriptions on the basaltic stones over the cave of Belmaco, in the island of Palma; assumed to have been the dwelling-place of the princes of Tigalate, one of the twelve royal provinces into which the island was divided. The stones were found in 1762.

of course, and it is more than possible that their true purport is not of so exalted a character.

In concluding this concise record of the manners

and life of the old Canarians, two or three illustrations of the muscular force and agility of these people may prove that the Spaniards were likely to find the acquisition of the Fortunate Isles a task less easy than they, not unreasonably, expected to find it.

The Grand Canarians were trained from babyhood to be brisk in self-defence. As soon as they could toddle, they were pelted with earth balls, that they might learn how to protect themselves. When they were boys, stones and wooden darts were substituted for the bits of clay. In this school they acquired the rudiments which enabled them, during their wars with the Spaniards, to catch in their hands the arrows shot from their enemies' crossbows.

After the conquest a Canarian was seen at Seville, who, for a shilling, let a man throw as many stones at him as he pleased, from a distance of eight paces. Without moving his left foot, he avoided every stone.

Another Canarian used to defy any one to hurl an orange at him with such rapidity that he could not catch it. Three men tried this, each with a dozen oranges, and the islander caught every orange. On the same understanding, he hit his antagonists with each of the oranges. Thus disciplined, would not the Canarians have made the best cricketers in the world?

In the eastern islands, the natives were so agile that many of them could achieve a high jump of not less than seven to eight feet.

Athletic exercises were as much favoured by the Canarians as by the Greeks. They held periodical games, which were esteemed so important that a truce suspended any wars the nation might be engaged in. Guests were invited, and the popular attention was wholly devoted to the dances, wrestling matches, races, stone throwing, jumping, and weight lifting, which were their favourite tests of strength and nimbleness. The games were enlivened by music, which varied in the different isles. Sosa says "the melodies of the natives of Hierro affected the bowels of hearers in a singularly sympathetic way." In Grand Canary, on the other hand, the style was light and cheerful.

These games were interspersed with a certain number of tournaments, between individuals, which had first to be licensed by the Faycan or high priest. The combatants were rubbed with fat and the juice of herbs, and, for the improvement of their muscles, hugged the trunks of trees. In due time, they entered the arena, attended by their respective friends and relations, and took their stand on a small circular platform about a yard above the level of the ground. Here they were visible to all the surrounders. Then, each taking a staff with a nob at the end, three smooth flint pebbles, and some sharper bits of stone, they began their duel. Their skill in avoiding the stones and blows aimed at each other was extraordinary, and it is credible that the spectators were the first to weary of the monotony of their futile attacks. When this was so, or when one of the combatants broke his club, the chief warrior who presided at the tournament cried, "enough! enough!" and the contest ended with lasting honour to both of them.

I suppose there is a certain amount of affectation or insincerity in the common phrases used to express regret for the extinction of this or that race of noble savages. The weakness is sentimental and momentary. But if ever it were worth while to wish for a revival of an uncivilized state of being, methinks one might welcome a resurrection of the Guanches.

As it is, however, they are hopelessly dead. These uncomely mummies; the messes in jars and bottles, covered with the dust and congelation of ages; the black clubs upon the walls, ludicrously trivial by the side of the repeating rifles and revolvers of this century; and the jars, skins, and grindstones of their simple domestic life: these trifles in the Tacoronte Museum, and the myriads of bones littering the caves of the land, are the sole remains of them.

They have been reproached for their feudal form of society and government—at the same time that they have been praised for their Arcadian simplicity and happiness. It is only among such races as the Guanches that feudalism and happiness can co-exist.

CHAPTER VI.

The Gardens of Acclimatization—Eccentric trees and shrubs—The dragon tree—Orotava Villa—The private gardens of the Villa—The Castillo monument—The Villa Church de la Concepcion—The Dominican nuns and the Jesuit fathers—Periodical eruptions of Teide—Philosophy of life in the Villa.

From Puerto I rode again and again up the steep, slippery, lava-paved highway to the Villa of Orotava. In two miles we rise two thousand feet. By continuing past the Villa to the top of the *faldas* or slopes of Tenerife's backbone, in six miles the rise would be six to seven thousand feet.

It was reckoned a feat of fair endurance to walk to the Villa on a bright afternoon. The sun then made nothing of the attempts of the palms, eucalypti, and fig trees to throw shade upon the road; and one envied the lizards that slid like quicksilver to and fro about the crannies of the walls, charmed with the heat. White dresses and parasols could not save the ladies from evident exhaustion; and gentlemen, with green umbrellas and pith helmets, were commonly to be seen resting heavily here and there at different stages of the ascent.

The famous Botanical Gardens—or Gardens of

A SCENE ON THE ROAD TO THE VILLA.

Acclimatization—stand between the two towns, about 650 feet above the sea-level. They are enclosed within palings fit for the Brobdignagians, but their cool luxuriance of shade was always welcome with suggestions of a halt amid the strange trees and flowers which have given them a world-wide reputation.

These gardens owe their origin to the Marquis de Villanueva del Prado, Governor-General of the Canaries late in the eighteenth century. It was thought that, by judicious transplantation from zone to zone, the vegetation of the tropics might eventually be brought to so robust a condition that it would thrive in Norway as in Brazil. Tenerife offered an excellent preliminary stage for this experiment. At first there was lively hope. The plants of the Equator took kindly to the climate of Orotava. But, subsequently, the visionary nature of the scheme became evident. Transfer after transfer was made from Tenerife to Spain, apparently a step of less consequence than from latitude 0° to latitude 28°; but these transplantations were unsuccessful. And it is now acknowledged that such acclimatization is only possible along the same isothermal lines. The Botanical Gardens of Orotava are therefore merely a picturesque failure. The Spanish authorities think they are doing enough in maintaining this chimera at a cost of about £40 per annum to the clever botanist who has it under his care. A sum of £200 annually is voted towards it, but of this the bulk goes in expenses which do not benefit the gardens or the gardener. Thus this unique place is neglected; and in the hands of a man less enthusiastic than M. Wildpret, it would soon become a jungle.

What curious and magnificent specimens of the world's trees and flowers one sees here! March is not the time for fruit, else I might have eaten custard apples and mangoes as if I were in India or the Sandwich Islands. Each hot country of the world seems to have contributed a different kind of palm to the gardens. There are trees with fruit and flowers germinating in the most erratic manner. One, a single trunk about ten feet high, terminates skywards in a spiral salmon-coloured blossom. Others extrude flowers—crimson, blue, yellow, purple, &c.—in impossible places like the tips of the leaves. The Australian fig tree (*Ficus imperialis*), a giant fellow, has clusters of hard figs round the base of the trunk, where it rises from the ground. The caoutchouc is as much at home here as in the East; and the banyan tree, with its bevy of connected saplings, sheltering under it like chickens under the hen. As for the eucalypti and pines of various kinds, the difficulty is not to induce them to grow, but to prevent them from injuring other plants by their exuberance.

These gardens are a true banquet of the senses. To the Spaniards of the district, however, they are, perhaps, more interesting as a rendezvous for occasional concerts. At such a time one may admire, under brilliant conditions, the grace of movement of the Spanish ladies in full toilet. But conceive how one is likely to be blind to the charms

A DRAGON TREE.

of the brightest of eyes, when the cheeks beneath them are smeared with powder! Under the garish noontide sun, these girls, in spite of their actual innocence and beauty, impressed me like a troop of unfortunates patrolling between the London lampposts. The peasant women, in their bright-coloured silk head-dresses, and natural brown, were, on the other hand, attractive enough. And it was delightful to watch their excitement when, at intervals during the afternoon, common paper balloons were, with immense fuss, filled, and sent into the air by the public functionaries.

But of all the odd trees in the Orotava Gardens, if not in the world, the dragon tree (*Dracæna draco*) is perhaps the oddest. It is common in the islands, but uncommon elsewhere. Early in this century, in the garden of the Marquis de Sauzal, in the Villa, there stood one of these trees measuring 60 feet in height, $48\frac{1}{2}$ feet in circumference at the base, and $23\frac{3}{3}$ feet nearly five yards from the ground. Humboldt computed its age at 10,000 years. No doubt he spoke at random; but, as there exists a little dragon tree known to be 400 years old, and as this tree is not yet a foot in circumference, it is clear the veteran had lived through many centuries. Since Humboldt's time, however, the tree has died of old age and storms, and only the memory of it remains.

Many are the legends begotten of the dragon tree in the Canaries. It is supposed to have a close interest in the country and people round about its trunk. When it blossoms (which it does but seldom), a good harvest and myriads of common flowers are anticipated. When it bleeds, misfortune threatens the community or individuals.[1] And when it falls, I suppose the impending ruin is prodigious.

Even as the Canary Islands are said to be the Gardens of the Hesperides, so the dragon tree is identified with the dragon that guards the golden apples of these happy realms. The golden apples are somewhat tamely associated with the modern orange.

One antiquarian discerns the outline of a dragon in the pulp of the fruit of this tree. A French writer goes further, and avers that the tree is no tree, but a congregation of living animalculæ, 6,000,000 of which go to a cubic inch. Such *bizarre* tricks will the imagination play even the best controlled of intellects!

But, in truth, the tree seems to be merely a mammoth breed of asparagus, gifted with extreme longevity. As for the dragon's blood, that is the reddish sap of the tree. This resinous exusion, which oozes easily from a knife-cut, was for long one of the most valuable of the island exports. European apothecaries—attracted by the name—had as strong a fancy for it as for the Guanche mummies, which they beat with their pestles into various disagreeable medicines of price.

In appearance, the dragon tree is a symmetrical candelabra. The corrugated trunk rises free from branches until it attains a certain altitude. Then the boughs diverge with extreme regularity, and in

---

[1] " Cuando la sangre del drago salta,
 Llegar la desdicha nunca falta."

their turn beget symmetrical twigs, tufted with sharp olive-coloured leaves. In justice to the tree, and in the face of its fabulous credentials, I ought to add that toothpicks made from its timber are reputed to be good for the gums.[1]

From the Acclimatization Gardens it is a steep but beautiful stroll to the Villa. M. Leclerq, in the pleasant account of his impressions of Tenerife, writes of this part as "une débauche de végétation." It is truly a debauch of the most enjoyable kind. Not even Corfu, with its high hedges of roses, can compare with the road beneath the Villa of Orotava for the luxuriance of its blossoms.

Orotava—the Arautapala of the Guanches—was the place in all Tenerife most favoured by the Spaniards. The noblest of De Lugo's followers received allotments here after the conquest: Trujillo, Joven, Valdés, Viña, Gallego, Medina, &c., are some of the names that have helped to raise Orotava in its own and its neighbours' esteem. So early as 1522 the town had a reputation for good blood, and thereafter it continued to keep its celebrity by the magnificence of its residents and the number of conventual establishments it erected and supported.

Nowadays, to the visitor who goes through its steep grassy streets, mindful of its past fortunes, Orotava is hardly less forlorn than Laguna. Its monastic houses have fallen to ruin, or been turned to secular purposes; many of its ancient nobility

[1] The dragon's blood was also one of the ingredients in the dye used by the Venetian ladies in the production of their famous *golden* hair.

have vanished; others have fallen in the world like the monasteries, and, though they still live in their ancestral houses, with imposing armorial bearings over the portals, they have perforce put aside the exclusiveness of the grandee, and turned their attention to trade and the science of money-making.

Among the few nobles still in Orotava are the Marquis de Sauzal, whose name will long be coupled with the phenomenal dragon tree already mentioned; and the Marquis de la Candia, whose family name of Cologan shows that Ireland has a prior claim to him. To the transitory visitor, these gentlemen are merely the proprietors of beautiful gardens, which, with a large generosity, they open to strangers as freely as to themselves. But the man who is privileged to make their acquaintance in domestic life will remember them for other reasons. I hope I may not soon forget the dark eyes and sweet expression of Donna Eustachia, the younger daughter of the house of Cologan, or the wit and vivacity of Donna Beatrix, the elder. These ladies themselves acted as bright cicerones through their gardens. There was much to see, and notably the famous chestnut tree dating from the conquest, which has died twice, and twice has renewed its life from the heart of the ruin. The bulk of its timber is immense, and so graciously contorted that the artist who sees it, and does not immediately want to make a drawing of it, is reckoned to be a very insensible creature.

The garden of the Marquis de Sauzal is even more interesting, as a garden, than that of the Cologans.

But methought the liberality of its owner was somewhat abused by the invasion of it, through the marble halls of the dwelling-house, by a knot of ragged little boys, who sought for pence by showing us its treasures, and who picked nosegays of rare exotics, and offered them to us with as much courtesy as impudence.

One more of the many gardens which make the Villa so enchanting must be mentioned. This is really a beautiful terrace of flowers looking down to the sea, all devoted to the embellishment of a single tomb. The tomb is of Carrara marble, dome-shaped, replete with exquisite detail, and approached by a stately tier of steps. But the occupant does not yet inhabit the monument, though he died five years ago. The work is said to have cost $100,000. The dead man, however, was a freemason; and the Church withheld the licence necessary for an interment of this kind. The bitterness of the inscription on the tomb may be forgiven to the mother of the man it commemorates—

> "Mater ejus Domina D. Sebastiana del Castillo
> Hoc monumentum vovet, velut tam cari capitis
> Desiderio solatium datum et compensationem injuriæ
> Quam hinc Christiano benigno prædito ingenio nobilique
> Iam mortuo conata est inferre intolerandia religiosa.
> Anno MDCCCLXXXII."

To my mind, the church of Orotava is the most pleasing in the island. Its exterior, thanks to the dome and turrets, and the elaborate, if rather gross, sculpture on its façade, is more imposing than the

Cathedral of Laguna; and its proportions are good throughout. The old frescoes in the dome are curious—especially the one symbolical of the washing away of the sins of the world through the blood of Christ. The Virgin holds the child Jesus, while crimson streams flow from His hands and feet and side over a blue globe beneath Him. The virtues and vices are also boldly depicted in allegory. Near the pulpit—itself a gem of simple design, there is some graceful originality in the sculptor's work. The base of the columns is chiselled into banana leaves and pods; they are so good that an acanthus would make but a poor figure by the side of them. In the Sauzal Chapel, to the north of the building, moreover, there is some woodwork, richly gilt, behind and over the altar, which makes one think highly of the Spanish artificers of the sixteenth and seventeenth centuries. The life of the Virgin is depicted on this screen, wholly in carved work—the annunciation, conception, circumcision, &c. The church is dedicated to the Conception, and dates from the beginning of the sixteenth century. Proclamations of rejoicing for the accession of Charles V. to the throne were made here on the 22nd June, 1516, as well as in Laguna.

Viera tells a story about the conduct of some Dominican nuns here, which gives a curious picture of earlier life in Orotava. These ladies migrated from Laguna to Orotava in 1632, and lived in monastic ease in this fair valley for the term of their lives. Their successors had the misfortune to be burned out of their convent in 1717. For the ensuing year, they accepted temporary quarters, though their distaste for these unconventual walls waxed stronger every day. It happened that there was in Orotava at that time a house of Jesuits which had lost its old importance, and, though commodious and healthy, gave lodging to but two men, the Rector of the house, and his assistant. Upon this building, the nuns cast their eyes, and early one day a band of forty of them advanced against it, determined, if they could, to appropriate it. By strategy, they induced the Jesuit brother to open the outer gate, and then they all trooped into the courtyard, and fell upon their knees, to thank God for this preliminary success. Vain was it for the Rector to join his subordinate in earnestly representing to them what a scandal they were likely to cause by their behaviour. The nuns for the time put aside their more sacred character, and appeared merely as very resolute women, strong in the knowledge that they were as twenty to one in the trial of power that was at hand. "Father Andrew, this is a large cage for so few birds!" they exclaimed. A few, more reasonable, calmly explained that they were in real need of a house to hold forty or more, and that they hoped Father Andrew and his colleague would not refuse the "spouses of Jesus" this asylum that seemed meant for them. The Rector then fled to the sacristy, locking the door behind him. From this safe retreat, he exhorted his colleague to be of good cheer. "Patience, brother, and do your best to extricate yourself from those ladies." The unsupported and harassed brother, however, with difficulty saved himself from the nails of the excited nuns.

This lasted for three or four hours. The town knew all about it, and bands of young men watched the proceedings from the bars of the outer gate, studiously neutral in their sympathies. But eventually the Jesuits had to yield, and abandon their building to the ladies, who continued to occupy it until a new convent to their taste was duly erected.

The Villa has endured many worse experiences than this revolt of its nuns. Conflagrations have lowered the pride of its buildings. Locusts have swarmed upon it, and eaten the vicinity as bare as a new-born babe. And, worst of all, earthquakes and volcanic eruptions, above or below it, have sent its inhabitants flying over the fields in terror; and neither our Lady of Candelaria nor the Holy Eucharist, though with priestly pomp brought into their midst, have been able to comfort them, or avert the evil. For it can never be forgotten that Orotava lies at the foot of Teide. Whether the mountain be visible, or screened by clouds, one feels that it is near. About once in a century,[1] it breaks forth in eruption. From such perils, Orotava is fairly shielded by the great bar of mountains which enclose it. Else it were a sublime sight to see the lava fall in a fiery cascade over the lip of the rocks. As for the likelihood of the upheaval of another mountain in the valley itself, though it might burst up in the heart of the town (even as in Lanzarote, in 1828, a volcano abruptly rose in the middle of a field of barley), no sensible resident will vex himself by

[1] 1390, 1430, 1492, 1603, 1605, 1705, 1706, 1798.

THE VILLA.

entertaining so very disquieting a fancy. A dweller on the thigh of an active volcano has no concern with the future. Thus the placid souls of the Villa fly kites against each other from the roofs of their houses, attend mass and the cockfights, love, eat, sing, and sleep, without a thought of what may at any moment come down upon them like the crack of doom.

CHAPTER VII.

A tour round Tenerife—The boys and the bell-tower—The configuration of Tenerife—Barrancos—Zones of temperature—Realejo, Upper and Lower—Bencomo and Realejo—The Church of Rambla—Icod—The dragon tree—The sad citizen—Garachico—The story of 1706—The drunken prisoner—Sunset on the Peak—Playing the pedagogue.

WHEN first I projected my tour of the island, I had decided to go alone. It seemed both unwise and unnecessary to encumber myself with a guide—who was sure to be ignorant of the country he professed to know; who might fall ill by the way, and require careful treatment; and who would certainly be hampered by scruples, religious and otherwise, to deter us from entering a town or village at festival time. But Lorenzo Despacho, from whom I hired the mare, put pressure upon me.

"It is fifty leagues, Señor. The mare is a good mare—Caramba! though it is her master that says so. But suppose she lose a shoe?"

"In that case, my good Lorenzo, if she cannot proceed without it, we must replace it," said I.

"Without doubt, Señor; but how? And who will look after her corn? How will your worship know that she gets more than half what you pay for? Not by the aspect of her stomach, Señor; for it is a world not wholly good, and there are many bad ways of swelling the mare, without properly nourishing her. And perhaps—if I may be pardoned for saying so—you do not talk Spanish sufficiently well to relieve yourself from a difficulty when you are among strangers."

"Well, in effect, what am I to do?"

"Take the boy José with you, Señor. He will be a comfort to you. Ave Maria! I should think so. Whenever you are in trouble, with perhaps a broken leg or an arm, he will shout; and the boy can make his sister, at work in the fields, a mile off, hear him quite distinctly. He will call to some one, and ask, and all will be well. As for the mare, she has an affection for José, and will do at his bidding what I do not think, Señor, she would do for you and the stick—good quiet horse that she is! And for the cost, it shall be only a shilling the day the more, which is, of course, nothing."

I did not want the boy, as I have said; nevertheless, he came. He was not quite new to me, for a day or two before, in visiting the parochial church of Puerto, I had seen him, in company with other little boys, amusing himself at the altar with a number of candles as long as his body. One of these boys, a child of twelve, had told me that he was the sacristan of the church, and in that capacity he showed me all the ecclesiastical treasures of the building, from the monster "Maria" behind the altar, already being robed in sad-coloured velvets for the stately processions of Holy Week, to the little glass flagon, silver-topped, containing the residue of some sacramental wine, much bescummed, which had been used I forget how many years ago. When I had seen the church and its dull old pictures to my contentment, we all ascended to the bell tower, to look down upon the town. Here were three bells, the largest bearing date 1671 ; and I was so interested in this large bell that when the boy José suggested that I should sound it, I did not hesitate to swing the tongue against the sides in the common way. The tone was loud and mellifluous; but on hearing it all the boys, headed by the sacristan, fled down the steps, gasping with mirth. However, as it was nothing to me if I had given untimely warning of some holy hour, I stayed among the bells until I had seen enough of the town, and then descended, and went off to my hotel. From this experience, I fancied that José might prove a rogue. On the contrary, however, for in the matter of separating his hours of business from his hours of play, he was a boy singularly gifted.

We started betimes on a sunny March morning. The mare took kindly to me from the outset, and I shall have nothing but praise to say of her. José carried my knapsack : for it was unbecoming in a *caballero* to be burdened with aught save a bit of stick tufted with horsehair, to use in warfare with the flies. The boy wore his yellow leather boots until we were out of the town. Then he slung them over his shoulder instead, and chanted disturbing madrigals at the top of his voice. I learnt to know that whenever I wished to depress the boy's spirits, I had but to tell him to get into his boots. Instantly there-

LOOKING WEST FROM PUERTO.

after his lip fell, and in glum silence he trudged in the track of the mare, with the nerveless swing of a south country tramp who has seen all his bright days. But as on such occasions he became also very thickheaded, failing to understand the simplest remark, however well accented, I was generally as willing to have him barefooted as he was glad to be so.

A few additional words about the configuration and natural scenery of Tenerife are, I think, here needful for the better understanding of the scheme and pleasures of our little tour. The importance of the Peak is already made plain. Some geologists say indeed, that the Peak is all the island, that from the shoreline of the entire fifty leagues of circuit, the land moulds itself upwards simply and solely to help in the achievement of the Peak, its pinnacle. But this is a disputed point, soluble only by a very minute investigation into the nature and age of the various mountain masses of Tenerife. The Peak is thought to be a very steep hill. In fact, however, the average angle of its acclivity from the sea-level to the summit does not exceed 12° or 13°. The ascent begins at Puerto, about twelve miles distant from the sugar cone, which is the top of it. It is this cone that one sees from the Atlantic, fifty or a hundred miles away. The rest of the island is usually mantled in the clouds which Teide draws around its loins during the greater part of the year. And it is the aspect of the abrupt isolated cone, suspended between heaven and earth, that makes one think the mountain must be a very complete test of the pluck and tenacity of a climber.

The scenery of Tenerife is uniquely varied. You may choose your climate on this small island in the Atlantic as emphatically as if you had a continent at your disposal; and of course the vegetation varies with the temperature. In Puerto, for example, we lived amid palms, bananas and flowering oleanders. Here the heat, even in March, after early morning, made movement laborious. Not that the thermometer marked a high register. But the air is so dry, that one's strength seemed to evaporate from the body in quest of the moisture it would like, but cannot get. We lived under sub-tropical conditions.

But at an altitude of 3,000 feet above Puerto, the climate is, of course, colder and more bracing. From potatoes and apple orchards, one looks down at the sunlit rocks and sands of Orotava, a singular contrast to the grey gloom of the cloud which up here hangs motionless and indissoluble for days at a time.

In this zone of country, the goats of Tenerife live and thrive. They descend daily to the coast towns to be milked, and then again climb the weary hills to feed themselves fitly for the morrow's milking.

Above this zone of chestnut and apple trees is the zone of laurels. After the laurels come the heaths, growing gigantic at a height of from four to five thousand feet above the sea. The bright yet low Canarian pines (*Pinus Canariensis*) follow the heaths, and struggle into life among the arid disintegrating lava and powdered pumice which here cover the hot rocks.

But when we have left the red roofs of Orotava

about 7,000 feet below us, and have also overtopped the very cloud which girdles the island, there is no vegetation to cheer the eye save the silver-grey bushes of the retama (*Spartium nubigenum*). The Peak rises from the centre of a parching infertile plateau of yellow pumice sand about twenty miles in circuit. In the whole of this elevated expanse, there is not one habitation. The solitary traveller who, from fatigue or other disabling cause, here chanced to die, might, by the action of the sun, and the pure desiccating air, be transformed into an excellent mummy, ere a wandering goatherd, a *nevero* (snow-gatherer), or a sulphur worker discovered his body.

One other characteristic of the country must be noticed — the *barrancos*. These deep cuts in the body of the land radiate from the old crater or plateau from which the cone of the Peak ascends, and they terminate only at the coast. I do not know how many dozen of them there are on the north-west and south sides of the island, with depths to be bottomed by the traveller varying from about fifteen hundred to two thousand feet. Some are dug with sides nearly perpendicular. In such cases, the track of descent and ascent is a perilous zigzag path scratched in the rock walls — a path moreover which the prickly pear trees do their best to expunge by the persistency with which they mat their formidable arms across it. It is prudent to leave horse or mule to itself in these *barrancos*: one's own feet are a sufficiently onerous responsibility. And, that the stranger may have his blood upon his own head, if he determine to be reckless in these ravines, sundry rude little crosses appear in awkward places, to commemorate this or that fatal accident; and the peasant whom destiny has given you for a temporary roadfellow, will enumerate those of his acquaintance who have fallen over the rocks into the dry blue river bed six or seven hundred feet down—just as you might fall if you slipped to the left that self-same moment. When I had made acquaintance with two or three of the *barrancos* of Tenerife, I began to bless Lorenzo that he had given me José to hold the mare.

But we were spared these particular trials on the first day of our journey. We were to sleep at a little town called Icod, whither the high road goes nearly all the way. For the most part, we kept about a thousand feet above the sea, with a wall of rock many hundred feet high on the left hand, and, on the right, a jungle of useful vegetation to the shoreline. Maiden hair and other ferns grew large from the midst of a hanging garden of brambles, wild vines, scrub fig and caroub, and the water drops dripped from the leaves into a careful canal which dispersed the precious liquor among the beans, potatoes, and bananas on the other side of the road.

There are two *pueblocitos* or small towns, between Orotava and Icod—Realejo and Rambla. Realejo is built well up a steep slope, with a ravine crossing the slope, and dividing the town into two parts. It is a pretty place, with its white church tower rising above the houses, and the eccentric branches of its dragon trees one over the other. Its warm climate is shown in the wealth of its greenery and magnificent trees. The church of the lower town is interesting for the queer carved heads on its portal, and for its very extraordinary picture on the ordinary subject of the world to come. In this picture, men and women are seen up to their girths in the fires of hell, looking as much at home with each other, and the element to which they are condemned, as a group of French people in the sea at Boulogne.

The two villages of Upper and Lower Realejo are built on the site of prime incidents in the history of the conquest. Bencomo, the king of Taoro, and chief prince of Tenerife, had retreated before De Lugo and his Spaniards, to this the extremity of his principality. For two years he had held the Spaniards at bay. But the terrible pestilence of Laguna, which carried off thousands of Guanches in a few weeks, made the rest of the natives weak, and an easy prey to the scientific blockade which, later, the leader of the invaders instituted. After the pestilence, and thanks to it, the Spaniards held the land at their mercy. But, for a crowning combat, the two armies—of Guanches armed with clubs, obsidian axes, and fire-hardened javelins of wood; and of Spaniards in coats of mail, leathern jerkins, and with all the weapons of contemporary European usage—put themselves into position on this slope, about 800 feet above the sea.

Realejo is the Spanish for "camp." And it was here, where the spire of the church of Upper Realejo marks the land, that poor old Bencomo determined to arrest further slaughter of his people by resigning his realm to the king of Spain, on condition that the Guanche natives were not despoiled of their property, and by accepting the baptism that the Spaniards pressed upon him as one of the chief articles in his bond of surrender. But it is very absurd of Viana to make the Guanche king express joy in his abdication of sovereignty, and a humble acknowledgment of the superior claims of Ferdinand of Spain to the island of the great Tinerfe—" Though I lose in temporal things, I gain in eternal glory. . . . Ferdinand alone is worthy of being king here; and though I am unworthy to be his vassal, I am more honoured in obeying him than in being king of Tenerife. . . ." In fact, however, the generous monarch paid the penalty for his confidence in the words of the Spaniards. They took him to Europe, against his wishes, where he graced the triumph of De Lugo, and afterwards died. If Viana, in his eccentric epic, narrating the love of Dacil, Bencomo's daughter, for Castillo, a lieutenant in De Lugo's army, had been able to tell us the real history of the end of the king of Taoro, I doubt not the pathos of it would have been in singular contrast to the inflated cantos in which he describes the king's gratitude for and appreciation of his baptism.

Once only on our way to Icod did we descend to the sea-level. This was at the cheerless little town of Rambla. It is built on a black promontory of lava, the rough edges and scoriæ of which are dismal to behold. Nevertheless, it is not wholly a place of gloom. For the blue sea was breaking into white foam upon its distorted rocks, and the industry of

BALCONY IN SAN JUAN DE LA RAMBLA.

the townspeople had erected gardens in the middle of this small wilderness; so that the bright verdure of vines, maize and potatoes, with the dull red roofs of the houses, and the olive and grey balconies, made a show of colour. Inland, we could track the lava flow up the mountain side, until it was lost to sight among the spurs of the Peak. But, in fact, the two leagues of coast between Rambla and Garachico, which is beyond Icod, is a tract of land terribly ruined by the outflows from Teide at one time or another. The road winds between monster cinder-heaps, which recall the banks in our own Black Country. But the heat of this unshaded expanse is hotter than Staffordshire at its hottest ; nor can our Black Country show the prickly pear and aloes which grow between the charred and decomposing boulders of this forlorn part of Tenerife.

I visited the church of Rambla, but with no lively expectations. As a rule, the church architecture of Tenerife has little originality. It is the ambition of every small town to have a fine bell-tower, in which the boys may stand to knock the bells at their convenience. After the bell-tower, I think an altar to the Virgin " de la Concepcion " is most fancied. I wonder how many of these figures I have seen in the Canaries, all modelled upon Murillo's beautiful Virgin in the Louvre Gallery, but with such variety of execution and adornment ! S. Lorenzo is another famous subject for a local altar, and the statue is sometimes provided with a large gridiron that could only have come from a Birmingham factory.

Here at Rambla, however, I was suddenly immersed in an atmosphere of perfume, when I pushed aside the heavy wooden door. It was the Friday before Palm Sunday; and in preparation for the day the pavement was littered with the petals of roses and red geraniums, and the many little altars of this little church were bedecked with boughs of bloom of various kinds. A number of women were kneeling among the rose leaves, and, in the far end, by the altar, there peeped from the eave of his confessional the round head of a priest, who was listening to the murmur of a penitent at his feet.

Of course the ladies for the moment forgot their devotions when they saw a man in riding dress and heavy boots come crushing amid the flowers on the floor. They fell a whispering and fanning themselves, and those of them who were very far gone in worldliness touched their faces, to ascertain if the powder still lay upon their cheeks in a comely manner. But, in justice to them and the father in his confessional, who peered forth several times with an unamiable expression on his broad countenance, and in justice to myself also, I did not stay long in the little church. Such a curious, unreal, mannikin place of worship I never saw before. From the *coro* in the west, with its banisters spotted with white mould, and its rafters a dull scarlet, green, and gold, to the flash of the same colours in the east of the church, with a little blue added to the prevalent green and gold, the whole seemed to me like a somewhat stale old dolls' house of a large size, with groups of eccentric moveable dolls set about the pavement. The very lintel of the porch, and the crossbeams within the church, were coloured with dry rot, and the flags under my feet oscillated as I moved from one to another. The dust of the early Spaniards who lay under the loose stones of the nave must long ago have evaporated among the congregation, and got re-incorporated with them.

It was one o'clock before the mare set her hoofs upon the slippery grass-grown cobbles of the streets of Icod. Though we had done but half a day's work, we were all tired—the animal of the rough dusty track and the flies; I of the heat of the sun, and the labour entailed in freeing her from the more venomous of the flies; and José of an empty stomach. To the Plaza de la Concepcion, where there is an inn, we therefore made our anxious way, for the time heedless of the beauty of the town and its surroundings.

The landlady proved to be a kind soul, and a little more resolute than a Spanish hotel-keeper is wont to be in the welcome of a guest to the bare boards of his building. A bedroom was at my disposal. It contained nothing in the world save a couple of small beds, and a coruscating chromo of the Virgin; but, as she said, what more was wanted? And, while my breakfast was being prepared, I might choose between the salon adjoining the bedroom, where was a dusty sofa on unsound legs, some chairs, and a large mirror covered with tinsel to protect it from the flies, and the roof of the hotel, a promenade renowned for its splendour.

Indeed, once I was on this roof, I was ready to vie with any one in praise of Icod. It has a wonderful situation, on the actual northern slope of the Peak. Imagine a glacial mass proceeding straight from the summit of a mountain to the sea, between high precipitous rocks, and with a town built on it, half-way in its course. Such, in some sort, is the aspect of Icod. In a direct line, the cone of the Peak cannot be more than six or seven miles from the houses of the town; and, from the white roof of the little inn, I looked at the broad swelling mountain, with its snowy cap closing the upland view, all in the full glow of glorious sunshine, and pronounced Icod divine. And this was the place to which the old inhabitants of Taoro used to banish their criminals! Here, too, in the last century, the Spanish Government for awhile kept the Marquis de la Villa de San Andrés in exile, pending an inquiry into the guilt that was imputed to him!

Close to the inn, among the onions and potatoes of a useful patch, is a huge dragon tree, from which, while examining it, under the guidance of its owner, I was allowed to cut off a shoot. What pain I caused to it I cannot of course tell. It did not shriek like the mandrake. But when, afterwards, from sheer wantonness, I plunged my knife into its side, there trickled forth, one, two, three thick drops of red blood. "Oh, yes; it lives," remarked its owner, "without doubt it lives!" Then I retired, not without a fancy that there was a dim but horrific menace in the myriads of its spear-shaped leaves.

I bore a letter of introduction to a rich citizen, who was also the doctor of Icod. He came to see me while I was engaged with the *puchero*. Many years ago he had lived in the American States, but his English had rusted from disuse; and he was a man of so humble a turn that he chose rather to speak little than to speak ill. I praised the glory of the place he had fixed upon to cheer him in the autumn of his life. His humour, however, was melancholic, and he retorted about the trials of life, and its sufferings. He was a kind man, of whom others spoke well; but also, I am afraid, one of those who learn wisdom and acquire pelf only through much travail of experience. In the evening, lit by the moon and the white beacon of Teide, I visited him at his house, and I shall long remember him as I saw him, immured in his high well-filled library, reading by the light of a single candle. There was a skull on his table, and, when my friend came to meet me, all else was so dark that I saw nothing distinctly except the skull. For the moment, he affected a mood of levity, and talked of billiards and whist at the club, but nature asserted itself by and by, and he made many distressful remarks as we paced up and down the moonlit streets.

This worthy but sorrow-stained man gave me a card to the Alcalde or Mayor of Garachico, whither I walked on the afternoon of our arrival at Icod.

Garachico is a sad town. Three centuries ago it was rich in noble and conventual houses, and ships from many countries came to its port. The green cliffs of the land fell close to the sea. It was a local vaunt that a man might shoot and fish thereon at the same time. But in 1706 Teide ruined Garachico. A volcano suddenly appeared on the high ground several hundred feet above the town, but perilously near to it. Then came the lava. It surged over the cliffs, and step by step surrounded and tried to destroy Garachico. Monks and nuns, hidalgos and peasants, hastened from the doomed place to Icod. Nor did the lava rest when the town was burnt and in great part submerged. It ran on into the harbour, and choked the best port of Tenerife. Thus Garachico got its death-blow. It was despoiled of its commercial importance. Its cultivable land was buried under the lava, and the convenient cliff which had been its glory was scarred into ugliness by the congelation of the molten cascade that had streamed over it. Tenerife has had to lament many scourges since it fell to the Spanish crown; but the destruction of Garachico most of all.

The path from Icod led me down through a lovely valley beset with orange groves, *nisperos*, tall maize, sugar-cane, vines, and fig trees. Groups of feathery palms stood from its lower slopes, with the blue sea beyond them. The verdure of the precipitous rocks that hedged the valley was astonishing. Vines and brambles hung in unbroken trails, scores of feet long; crimson and yellow flowers bloomed in the crannies; and the persevering *verode* a circular evergreen that seems to have no stem, stuck like a plaster to as much of the cliff sides as was otherwise unappropriated. The water that causes this verdure was carried from side to side of the valley in a thin spidery aqueduct of pine trunks, from the many leaks of which the lower lands enjoyed a perpetual shower-bath.

A great rock stands by the road where Garachico's red roofs begin, and a crucifix surmounts the rock. In the contracted bay, which is now Garachico's apology for a harbour, there is another rock rising perhaps two hundred feet out of the water. On this also a wooden cross meets the eye. Elsewhere are other crosses, scratched on the lava boulders which have rolled from the heights, or set by the sea in the black volcanic sand, beyond the reach of the tide. Thus Garachico seems to plead with heaven that it may be spared future devastation like the flood of 1645, the fire of 1697, and the eruption of 1706.

The Alcalde told me the story of 1706 with as much feeling and exactitude as if he had been an interested witness of the wreck; and from his roof we traced the current that had sped from Teide. Anon we visited the parochial church, the pillars of which show the mark, fifteen feet from the ground, reached by the lava. In the streets are the shells of many fair buildings with Corinthian portals, chiselled balconies, and dainty heraldic work; but there is nothing behind these imposing façades. The remains of Garachico's *casa fuerte*, or guardhouse, still stands by the sea, with two or three unlimbered guns by its battlements. But it is now a purposeless fort, since the harbour it protected is gone.

The duties of the present recalled the Alcalde from his kindly retrospect. A sound that was half howl and half sob broke upon the still air when we were passing the Municipal Buildings. The Alcalde was at first puzzled to explain it. But his memory did not long deceive him. With a smile and a shrug of the shoulder, he called to a slipshod man, and sent him to the town clerk for a key. He then entered the overgrown garden of the inner courtyard of a deserted monastery, and, unlocking a wicket, stood in a little square of grassy ground with a stone seat in a corner, the sky for a ceiling, and a wailing red-faced woman sitting on the seat. The woman sprang towards the Alcalde's knees with a torrent of words and tears, appeals to the Virgin, promises to amend, &c. She was the one prisoner in this the gaol of Garachico, and was sentenced to three days' incarceration, with bread and water, for being drunk and disorderly. This time, however, the Alcalde remitted her punishment; and, having picked up a crust that lay among the grass, the woman shuffled away with many grateful adjectives upon her tongue.

In the evening, from the *azotea* of the Icod inn, we watched the sun set. The Peak was at first quite free from cloud; its black lava streaks, its snow, and its rosy cone, were alike bathed in the warm yellow light of evening. But after a while a burly cumulus crept round its shoulder two or three thousand feet from the summit, and broke into fragments that hung to all appearance motionless about its tremendous body. As the sun sank, these fragments were dyed a light amber colour, through which the purpling mountain slopes shone divinely where they fell to the Canarian pines, yellow as buttercups, at the head of the Icod valley. Later,

ICOD AND THE PEAK.

the clouds, and the spurs of Teide where there was no snow, grew abruptly black. There was an air of indescribable awe about the towering phantom that thus brooded over the town so nearly, and was yet so majestic that nothing could seem more remote from the intrusion of restless mortals. All the world was by this time in cool shadow of hurrying twilight—the mountain flanks, the pine woods at their base, the fields of tobacco, barley, and potatoes about the town, and the reddish roofs of the houses, interspersed with palms and dragon trees, all sloping gently towards the sea—all the world except the Peak of Teide. As for the Peak, it glowed with crimson light until the very moon over our heads was lustrous enough to read by.

When this scene had passed, we descended to dine. The company was scant but courteous; the dinner Spanish yet excellent, and the wine of the best native growth. It fell to my lot to settle a dispute about the comparative worth of English and Spanish wines. An elderly gentleman was surprised to find that in defending the vintages of England, which he confessed he had never tasted, he had been whipping a dead horse, or rather a horse that had not yet been foaled. Probably he mistook the pale ale of Burton, which is in every Canarian wine-shop, for a strain of the British grape.

Towards bedtime, new diversion offered. The hostess remarked that she had a daughter, and upon such a possession I congratulated her. "Moreover," continued the good woman, "she is learning the French, and speaks it a little; not so well as the señor speaks Spanish, but better than not at all."

"Then," said I, "the poor girl must have few words at command."

"No, it is not so," rejoined the landlady, laughing civilly. "Would the señor like me to fetch my daughter?"

She was a well-grown girl of eighteen, and she brought her grammar with her. There was nothing for it but to sit side by side, and test each other's acquirements. The mother meanwhile produced her lacework, and, with a pleased expression of face, composed herself on the other side of the table, now and then proffering a word of encouragement when her child's wits were wool-gathering, or centring in her smiles and blushes. For, though her cheeks were bepowdered (ay, and her very ears!) so that she was pale as a corpse, the blood showed through the powder, and her large dark eyes put these foolish artificial modes of adornment much to shame. Occasionally a citizen sidled his head into the room, but I fancy the student's mother told them with a glance that their presence was not then desired. Thus we spent an agreeable hour, and at the end I wished Dolores sweet dreams.

"I did not think the English had so much patience!" said the hostess, in comment upon our labours. But I of course had to assure her that patience was needed rather to help in bearing the cessation than the continuance of such gracious tasks.

CHAPTER VIII.

A trait of Icod character—A fair morning—Pumice plains and lava beds—Gomera—On the Cañadas—A *volcaneta*—The Peak at its toilet—Palm Sunday service—Garachico from above—A valley bivouac—Santiago—A severe mountain—Chia—Guia—Excitement in Guia—Hospitality of Guia—For and against country life.

AT ten o'clock the next day, José and I set out for the Cañadas, or lower and ancient crater of the Peak. We were to ascend whither so many grievous torrents of lava have flown over the west and south-west of the island. For it is on this south-western slope of Teide that most of the recent *volcanetas* have arisen, and the great mouth of Chahora, which belched fiery fluid day after day for several weeks in 1798, adjoins the Peak on this side, being only about 2,300 feet lower than it.

José ingenuously confessed that he did not know the way to the Cañadas on this side. For six pesetas (5s.), however, I procured a responsible youth, who gave me an insight into Canarian character by bargaining with another youth to relieve him of the work for three pesetas. To this arrangement I did not object, as the latter guide was a merry fellow with a simple and honest expression. He spoke an iniquitous dialect, but insisted that his bargain compelled him to carry the maize, bread, eggs, wine, &c., with which my boy had duly girt himself. From the time of this betrayal of his simplicity, José lorded it over him with patronizing kindliness.

The day was perfect, and the mountain magnificent in the morning light. Swallows circled about us in the clear warm air. The blue smoke from the fires of the charcoal burners, two or three thousand feet above us, hung in straight firm columns. The very goats browsing amid the lower scrub and bracken seemed full of elation on this glad invigorating day; they skipped from hillock to hillock with a lively ringing of bells, and laughed to scorn the superintendence of the goatherds in long white smocks, and the stones which the goatherds threw at them. In this rather populous region we met many a countrywoman descending to the town with admirable poise of her shapely body, and a basket of eggs upon her head, muleteers clad in cool linen, with their scarlet vests loose upon them, and foresters laden with pine trunks that would have crushed you or me to the ground.

Thus we passed from the infamously rough rocky lanes of the lowlands, which kept my mare in a sweat of anxiety, by woods of flowering gum cistus and tall heaths, into the cheerful and odorous zone of pines, the droppings from which lay so thick that our footfalls were inaudible. Our progress was indicated by the growing nearness of Teide on the left hand, and the appearance to our right, one after another, of sundry scarlet hillocks, which shone like blood through the gold of the pines, and, one after another, were left behind and below us.

At a height of about 5,000 feet, we were out of the pines. The extreme dryness of the air, the heat of the sun in a cloudless sky, and the toil, had made the boys almost intolerably thirsty. But neither for them nor the mare was a drop of water obtainable, for we were close to the lava-beds, which, within the last century, have scorched the bowels of the land, and whence no springs fall to the valleys. Thus we trod into the midst of the weird but fascinating evidences of volcanic work. The mountain of Chahora seemed very near. But we could not have climbed the broad slope of primrose-coloured pumice dust, studded with retama, which led to its summit, in less than two or three hours. Its rounded peak, seen from below, is not, however, very attractive. Viewed from Teide, it is vastly more interesting, for the great mouth of the new volcano is there seen to admiration.

For many minutes we now kept to this yellow pumice, with a wavy bed of light-brown lava to the right of us. Nothing could seem more impracticable than this rugged iron stream, with its surface rising into twisted pinnacles, humps, and chilling edges, and sundered by crevices as deep as the fancy cared to make them. Here were no signs of disintegration. As the iron band had unrolled itself upon the country some score of years ago, so it lay, rigid and inflexible. Not even a hardy retama could find a fissure capable of nurturing it. The desolation was absolute.

But by and by the pumice sand ceased, and we

were face to face with a wide inky current which had run from the lip of Chahora down towards the brown lava, intersecting it at right angles. This was the last lava flow in the island—the outcome of 1798. It lay like a long coarse blot upon the land.

At this point the delicate toil of the day began. For, though the stuff looked so impassable, we had to cross it and much more ere the Cañadas could be reached. In preparation, José straightway put on his boots; his epidermis was no doubt thick, but the keen points of the lava, unblunted after a century of life, were too much for him.

How we laboured over this awful tract! I left the mare to herself, of course. Even then the poor beast did not know where to put her feet. It was the work of an acrobat to step from point to point, and, withal, to avoid slipping into the painful crannies between the points. A fall from the animal would have brought me in peril of an impalement.

Thus we struggled along for a couple of hours, rising all the time. Lava bed succeeded lava bed, with brief spaces of level dust or easier rocks between the different beds. We were so high that we could see the island of Gomera lying close to the south-west. Its appearance was charming. We looked down upon its mountains in such a manner that they had the form of an irregular shadow cast upon the placid silvery sea. Gomera is little visited, in spite of its "Valley Beautiful" and the best harbour in the Canaries. It was from this harbour that Columbus sailed west. After Gomera, he had done with Europe, and the outskirts of Europe. The old inhabitants of this island were, among other derivations, thought to be allied with the Cumri of Cambria, and their fellow Celts: Gomera was held to be an expansion of Gombri, which of course had affinity with Cimbri. But, whatever their origin, these islanders, whether as aborigines or Spaniards, were a brave race. Drake could do nothing against them in 1585, when he purposed sacking the chief town, and carrying off a thousand skins of wine for the enlivenment of his voyage to Peru. Nor had Windon, in 1743, better luck when he threatened to ravage the island unconditionally if his demand for provisions was not acceded to. He shot five thousand balls into the town, killing two men and a woman, and then withdrew.

We were 7,000 feet above the glittering sea round Gomera, when a sudden clap of wind buffeted us in the face. Immediately afterwards, a surge of mist swept with a roar across the great plateau of the Cañadas. The mare was terrified, and began to plunge. She had got used to the stillness of these upper regions, which have nothing to do with life or death. In time, however, she got used to the mist also; and it was enveloped in this dry hurtling vapour that, at three o'clock in the afternoon, we sat on the sharp edge of the Cañadas crater, and ate our dinner with much appetite. Now and then the mist parted, and showed us the serrated peaks of the Cañadas mountains which fringe the crater. Some of them are 9,000 feet above the sea level, and they are boldly contorted. The snow still lay thick on their sides, in fine contrast with the brilliant reds and browns of their rocks, and the yellowish stretches of sand at their base, studded, like a great leopard's skin, with many light spots—the clusters of retama. There was snow, too, within twenty yards of our dinner-table; and, in fact, neither our wine nor our noses lacked the property of coolness.

On the return journey, we made a detour to examine a little volcano which uprose about forty feet from the midst of one of the brown lava streams. Familiarity had bred in me some disrespect for the dangers of the lava: as a result, I lost blood and skin ere we were at the base of the hillock. This proved to be a dainty excrescence, in shape like a conical lime-kiln. In its side was the rift whence the lava had seethed upwards to join the stream that was already pressing past it. I suppose the teeming flank of Teide, which had burst primarily higher up, was here glad to get another vent. This little bubble of stuff was extended as a tap subordinate to the main outflow. Within the *volcaneta* were traces of sheep and goats. They had probably rested here on their way to the retama of the plains. But what a temptation to Dame Nature to cook their mutton while they slumbered in trustful security within one of her ovens!

Leaving the *volcaneta*, we dropped gaily down the slopes of Teide, with the full evening light upon the yellow pines. The boys sang, very much in dis-unison, but with exceeding heartiness. For my part, however, I was a willing victim to the charms of Teide, and nothing but Teide. The mountain seemed to come nearer as the sun went west. Its snowy

THE PEAK IN MARCH: FROM ABOVE ICOD.

pyramid, and the pink cone cresting it, with soft inward curves, were dazzling to look at. Anon, a purple shadow fell upon the base of the mountain, and crept slowly upwards. And in this stage of the day, with a sky of the purest blue above, and never a cloud in the heavens, Teide wove gossamer veils one after another for the tiring of her head, and discarded them as fast as she put them on. They were the most patent of shams—absolutely transparent; but how they enhanced her beauty! And one by one they stole from her, and lay in glossy horizontal strata, until they dissipated into nothingness. To speak more exactly, the sulphureous vapours, which are at all times exhaling from the cone of the Peak, now became visible in the chilling air.

The third day of our travel was Palm Sunday—a festival of great honour in Tenerife. While I dressed, I watched the populous gathering of town and country folk on the greensward in front of the church, and in the Plaza beneath my window. The women wore silk handkerchiefs of gay colours, bound round their heads, and tiny straw hats, fit for a large-sized doll, poised upon their crowns. Otherwise their attire was not singular; clean prints being the common material of their gowns. There was more actual dandyism among the men. One young buck, for example, in a tight-fitting white and black cotton jacket, a large crimson neckcloth, and snowy pants, pranced superbly into the Plaza, twirling his moustaches while he managed his horse. Like most of the others, he carried a broad palm-leaf in one hand.

When the hour of mass was rung, I entered the church with the rest. Every foot of standing room was soon occupied. The women went to one side, and very lively was the effect of the hundreds of kerchiefed heads—purple, yellow, crimson, and blue—from which the small straw hats were removed. The men were hardly less reverent than the women during the function. The two or three exceptions were spruce adolescents who leaned against the columns, and chattered at their leisure, with their eyes upon the ladies. But even they held palm-leaves. The flutter of the fronds in all parts of the church cooled the air amazingly. Drawn from side to side of the choir was a thin veil of gauze, to symbolize the veil of the Temple. On the ensuing Friday this would be dramatically rent in twain, and afterwards the dolorous effigies of the crucified Christ, and the tear-stained, heart-broken Virgin, would proceed down the aisle, and through the streets, towards the Calvary where, amid much sobbing, the burial scene in the cave of Arimathea would be enacted. But to-day the veil seemed to cool the heated church, like the palm-leaves.

José attended mass, like the rest of Icod, and after the service confessed himself ready for the twenty miles of roadway which I proposed for the day's stage. Dolores came to the door to see us off. She had powdered her fair young face again, so that there was no divining whether her expression was one of sadness or relief. I, however, at sight of her made a resolution that has not been kept. I vowed that when next we met I would put into irreproachable Castilian that "beauty unadorned is beauty at its best," and whisper it insidiously into her receptive mind. But I fear fashion is omnipotent, even in Tenerife.

Bearing across the valley, we at once struck upwards by a path, which an hour later brought us to the summit of the cliff that overhangs Garachico. Here we halted, under a torrid sun, with nothing around us but the grey lava which in 1705 sped hence down to the town. We looked below. A few red specks, with a hand's breadth of green turf between them—this was all that Garachico appeared to be. The black rim framed it all too closely. At first it seemed odd to find, in two or three places, this upland lava sufficiently decomposed for the growth upon it of some small fig trees, a few square yards of potatoes and vines, and some sprigs of flowing gorse; whereas elsewhere it was unyielding. But this material is very capricious in its surrender to time; a recent outflow not seldom breaking up before an earlier one.

The morning passed in uneventful labour. The previous day we had been where water of any kind is not. This day we struggled through the hottest hours seeking in vain for drinkable water. The soil was a moist vermilion sort of loam, and acres of potatoes stretched to the eyeline on both sides of us, at an altitude of about 3,000 feet above the sea. We were, in fact, in the midst of English greenery and English hedgerows; larks sung over our heads; and the air was damp. But we tried puddle after puddle in the red earth, and rejected them all.

At length a valley opened at our feet, and the thin glistening line that meandered through it was hailed as "sweet water." Thither we descended briskly, for it was long past the hour of lunch ; and then, by the side of a stream, secluded from the outer world by smooth, rounded hills, mottled with gorse and heath, we spread the contents of the saddle-bags, and let the mare bury her nose in a sack of barley. Two or three huts like pigsties held the population of the nook; and ere long we had a wondering throng of savage little faces within hail of our meats and bottles. The hill scenery of this valley, and the large, staring eyes of these grimy children — fresh from play with the pigs and poultry—alike reminded me of Marathon. By and by a man appeared, leading a cow by the horn. He sat at a distance that he might not disturb us by his presence. When José marched up to him, with his hands full of food, and the conventional, "*Hagáme el favor*" ("do me the favour"—to eat something), he declined, but with a bow down almost to the ground. Afterwards, however, he joined the youngsters in appropriating the fragments we left.

It was cruelly against the grain to forsake this grassy Eden for the hard hillsides, when our meal was done. Even the mare feigned to be mightily stiff. Maybe she had presentiment about the state of the road on the other side of the hill. We ascended to the brow of a ridge, and looked down at the large village of Santiago, embosomed in a plateau on the other side, and with the peaks of two or three soaring red mountains casting shadows over its low, rude houses. These conical red hills to the left were the same which, yesterday, on our way to the Cañadas, we had kept to the right hand. The descent into Santiago was detestable. It was all the mare could do to keep on her feet—so slippery were the broad inclined planes of naked rock which led by degrees into the valley.

Santiago is a *poblacion* of about 2,000 inhabitants, very rich in fruits and cereals, and picturesque from the irregular shape of its environing mountains; but else uninviting. The citizens and their wives were so much astounded at sight of us that I thought the church bell would be rung in our honour. But the houses had a dilapidated air very dissonant with comfort, especially in a place nearly 3,000 feet above the sea, nor was I sorry when, at some cost, José had thrown off the last of his interrogators, and we were stumbling over gray lava pebbles towards another upland track. The whole of this country is volcanic, and the very basin in which Santiago stands must, in remote ages, have been repeatedly deluged with lava from the volcanoes around it.

From Santiago we climbed the face of a mountain by a monstrously steep trail. For my life's sake, I would not have ridden down it. But these Tenerifian horses go at the severest ascents with surprising pluck, and I had rather to curb the good panting mare than to stimulate her.

We rose until we were a thousand feet or more above Santiago and another like village in a green plateau nearer the sea. A trick of vice or terror in the mare would here have sent us both rolling down the abrupt declivity. Where the ledge was narrowest, moreover, we met a muleteer with an ass so laden with brushwood that it took the space of three asses. José was a little anxious, but contrived to give the ass the outside berth, where it passed with two of its feet considerably lower than the others.

But when we had done with the ass, we had done with the hard work of the day also. Thenceforward, until five o'clock, we gradually lowered towards the town of Guia, to which I was recommended for the night.

Hereabouts, we said goodbye to the Peak for four days. Its tiny cone just looked over the hither thighs of the vastly-broken country which intervenes between it and the coast in this part of Tenerife. Thin woods of pine shaded the higher of these intermediate hills, but ere we reached Guia the clouds had settled upon the ridges in a long, steady, black bank of vapour.

In the meantime, we passed through the village of Chia, where the inhabitants seemed as degraded as those of Santiago. Ancient crones, squatting on the thresholds of ramshackle houses, thatched loosely with maize stalks, were taking snuff out of small tin boxes, or smoking cigars in social knots, their brown breasts exposed to the air, and chaffering with each other in loud, unfeminine tones. The men, however, were fine fellows to the eye, in their red waistcoats and Sunday finery. They and the lads of Chia greeted us with a running fire of questions and ejaculations, and acknowledged José's proud record of our feats of travel (for so they were regarded) with many an Ave Maria! and Caramba! of stupefaction. But we hastened past them all, and on across the desiccated lava fields, in which the barley grew miserably, but the prickly pear and the fig-trees attained a hugh size. José had an uncle born at Guia, and he boasted the salubrity and scenic charms of the place with such a flourish of superlatives that I looked forward to our arrival. It promised little, however, in appearance. A coterie of low, flat-topped, white houses, with but scant greenery among the houses; all set on a naked slope of mountain, surrounded by stony fields and unprotected from the sun—such was Guia. Fortunately, it stands about 1,800 feet above the sea, visible at the base of its long slope. Otherwise, its heat were like to rival that of Timbuctoo.

The excitement we provoked here was greater even than at Chia. The citizens, with their wives and daughters, flew to the roofs of their houses, and with telescopes, opera-glasses, and their own dark eyes subjected us to a very critical ordeal. There was no evading it, for the mare aroused loud echoes by her clatter over the rough stones of the streets. The windows were filled with faces, and at the door of the Casino, or club-house, a crowd of young men stood with billiard cues in their hands to see us go by. Thus we reached the house that was *longæ finis viæ*. José had of course donned his boots for the occasion; but his feet had swelled, and this, with the tormenting cobbles, made him limp lamentably. Nevertheless, he prated with glee of the mare's performance to any that would listen to him.

Here, in Guia, as elsewhere in the Canaries, I learnt to love the Spanish nature. With much merely external courtliness, it includes an earnest desire to be hospitable towards a stranger that is as winning as it ought to be. The town lacks an inn, but, thanks to Dr. Montez and his family, I was fain to be glad of it. The ordinary English person would not (perhaps because he could not) "give himself away" to a stranger with the absolute *abandon* of kindness which makes this house memor able to me. At dinner, for example, with a grace that barred all thought save of gratitude, the ladies (of whom there were five or six) vied with each other to put tit-bits of this viand and that upon my plate. It was a bright meal, illumined by black eyes. My friend's mother sat at the head of the table. In the drawing-room, she also held the place of honour, in the middle of the sofa. So manifest a rule of the mother-in-law would agree well with but few English wives. Here it seemed to go with admirable smoothness.

Late in the evening, the doctor armed me through the quiet, moonlit streets of the town. "There is nothing to seen in Guia—nothing at all," he said. He had migrated to Tenerife from Seville for family reasons, but found the contrast between Guia and Seville hardly supportable. Speaking professionally, however, he admitted that the climate of Tenerife was marvellously healthy: "Drier than Madiera, and better than Madiera." The cheapness of living in Tenerife was also in its favour. Upon an income of 2,500 pesetas (£100), it was possible to keep an establishment of seven or eight human beings, besides horses and dogs. The common necessaries of life cost little. The supply of fruit is infinite. Partridges and rabbits represent the game of the neighbourhood.

Yet, putting these positive advantages against the isolation of life in Guia, for a man of ardent temperament, my friend pronounced it a terrible trial. This no doubt it is; for though Tenerife is but a speck on the ocean, he could not make the journey to the capital of the island in less than two very hard days work.

CHAPTER IX.

The hot south side of Tenerife—the Euphorbia—José's bragging—Adeje—Its *Casa fuerte*—Its population—Ascent to Chasna—Chasna of the clouds—The doctor and his daughter—A morning outlook—Flower customs—The Eve of St. John—Granadilla—Its oranges—A sturdy gentleman—Granadilla's church, club, and tobacco factories—Rio—*Barrancos* and cave dwellings—Flies—Arico—The ex-dockman—Fast life in Arico.

LED by a new guide, we left Guia at 8 a.m., and reached Chasna, high in the mountains, at 7 p.m. We were in the sun all the day, with not an inch of shade about us on this burning south side of Tenerife. The scant vegetation was largely African. Barley, however, stood up, yellow, thin, and stalky, among the grey lava stones. Cornflowers and poppies beat the grain on its own ground. No potatoes grew here. Tobacco, in patches, took its place; and jungles of low fig-trees, loaded with purpling fruit. But the chief shrubs of all were the euphorbia, or cardon, of both kinds — the poisonous and the harmless. The *barrancos*, which here clove the land with tremendous energy, were thick with the olive brown-mottled organ-pipes of the poisonous euphorbia, eight feet high, and with roots extended over many square

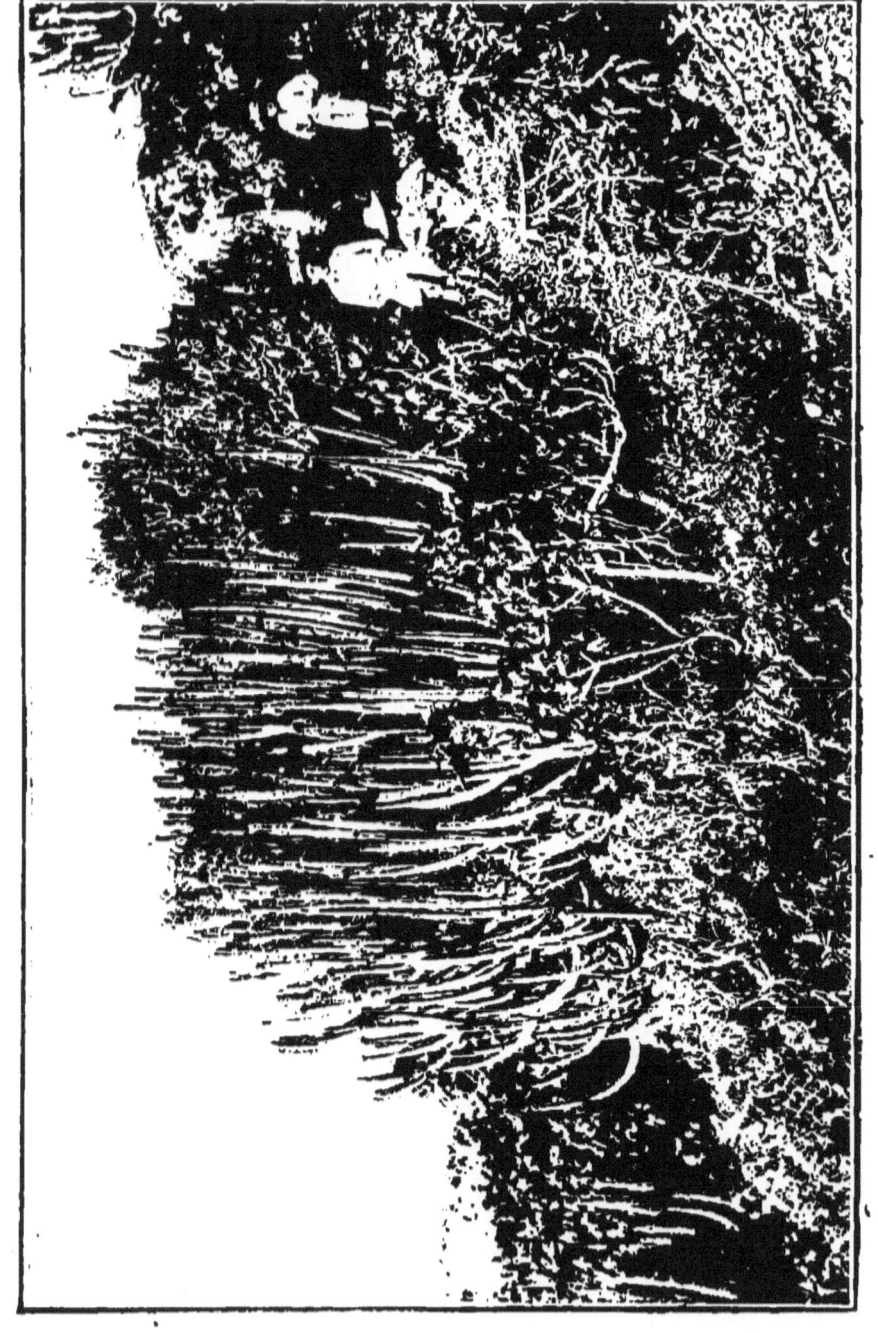

A CLUMP OF EUPHORBIA.

yards of surface. Both the good and bad cardon, and the prickly pear (bearing crimson and lemon-coloured blosoms, and myriads of ripe fruit,[1] were woven with webbing of the Tenerifan spider, which claims to be as venomous as the bad cardon itself. It was by no means a pleasant land. The thermometer tarried at 120°; the *barrancos* held no sweet water; and it was necessary to dismount from the mare two or three times hourly for the passage of the ravines.

A few words may be acceptable about this euphorbia, which is so constant a scenic addition to the rocks of the Canaries. The good kind is said to have been named by King Juba after his physician Euphorbio, who discovered its valuable properties. Both kinds, when cut, exude a milky liquor: but the poison of the one induces a convulsive movement of the lips, and, in some cases, death; whereas the other is even an antidote to it. Viera associates the fatal cardon, when read as çardon, and the " sardonic" laughter which it causes. Pomponius Mela, in his essay on the Fortunate Isles, mentions two fountains, the one poisonous, " making a man to die of laughing," and the other its antidote. The expression " fountain " might readily be used in error by a compiler who did not write of the euphorbia from actual knowledge.

We halted in the heat of the day at a wretched little *venta*. The boys could not resist the muddy wine in its dirty bottles. Besides the wine, this

[1] Called *lingua tinta*, because the juice dyes the palate and tongue.

poor place offered for sale nothing except some reels of cotton, a button or two, and some oranges and lemons. The delight of the dame who sold us the wine was so great at seeing us that she wished to present us with our entertainment. "*Madre de Dios!*" she ejaculated many times when she understood the scheme of our tour; "to think that I should live to see such a *caballero*! Such courage!" You see, José had a knack of exalting our performances most unduly; but his eyes sparkled with rapture while telling his fibs, and he so enjoyed what renown he got by reflection, that it was impossible to bid him check his ever-ready tongue. Indeed, considering that the poor boy was afoot all the while, he deserved what satisfaction and praise he could get for his pluck in the journey.

How heartily glad were we all when the happy hour of bivouac arrived! It came late, however, for we had first to victual at the old town of Adeje, and then proceed until we found water in a *barranco* fit for the mare to drink. Above Adeje the ravines are terrific, notably the one called Infernal; and it was in the lower part of *barranco* Inferno, under a brooding pile of black crags and crag-riven clouds, that we lunched upon cheese and comfits and wine, while the mare paddled in the snow water, and munched her beans.

Adeje is said to have been the royal abode of the great Tinerfe. He did not live in a palace; nor are there any remains of his court and puissance. The Spaniards also took a fancy to the place, which, with its frame north and east of giant mountains, and its fertile, because well-watered, slopes towards the sea, no doubt appeared an ideal settlement. Here the best tobacco of Tenerife is grown, and acres of tufted sugar-cane. Indeed, the sun is concentrated upon this naked incline so intensely, that nothing in need of heat ought to fail in Adeje.

For the protection of his estates here and in the adjoining island of Gomera, in 1568, the Count of Gomera built what he called a *casa fuerte* or stronghold, close to the mountain wall, in a position commanding the town. This castle still stands, as pregnable as ever it was, and a wonder in the eyes of the people. It has a drawbridge spanning a moat that one may take at a jump, and its battlements are guarded by a number of toy cannon. But though one may now laugh at this nursery fortification, probably in the sixteenth and seventeenth centuries it did good work in frightening back to their ships many a piratical bluejacket or turbaned Moor, who had been drawn towards Adeje by the rumour of its wealth and accessibility.

The modern town is one long street of red and white houses, with sweet water from the mountains running down its gutters. Its people seem rough and unsophisticated; and the gathering of bronzed and wrinkled crones, half-naked children, and bright-eyed girls whom we attracted, made such a clatter with their tongues that they frightened the tired mare into a wild irresponsible canter through the borough.

Our five hours' labour after lunch were an unceasing ascent. Adeje is only a few hundred feet above the sea; Chasna is 4,270. We had panoramic views of the valleys towards the sea south-east of Adeje; of Arona and its orange trees, girt with russet volcanic hills; and of San Miguel, in a similar valley. The country became more and more impoverished, colder, gloomier. The barley was miserable. The prickly pear were but just budding; the lupins only a few inches above the ground; the fig trees hardly in leaf. The rare countrymen we met were cloaked from chin to knee in the heavy white ponchos which Witney makes specially for the highlanders of Tenerife.

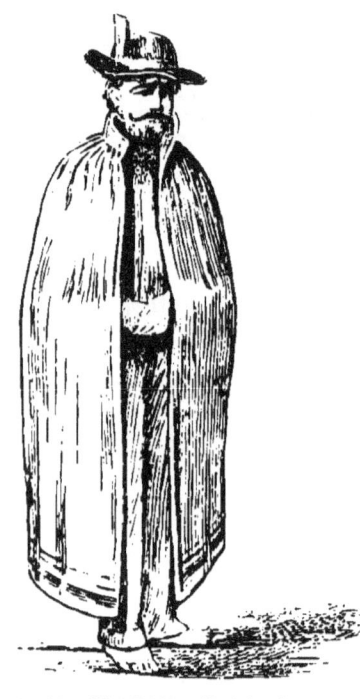

A TENERIFAN IN HIS MANTA.

By and by we got into the clouds, and for a couple of hours plodded on in chill, wetting mist, much in contrast with the dry heat of Guia and Adeje. There was nothing in view, and we seemed to be ascending nowhere, over a red, stony soil. But, with a suddenness that had a brisk effect on our laggard energies, the mist fell away as we turned a hill side. Above, we could see the graceful shading of thick forests of pines, and the outline of eccentric mountains dim beyond; while, below the pines, in a bower of greenery, red roofs and white blossoms appeared. We hurried on, for this was Chasna, the renowned summer watering place and hygienic resort of the island; and soon we climbed its stony streets through orchards of pear, apple, and cherry, all in a blaze of flower, and sparkling in the twilight with the drops left on their leaves by the fleeting clouds. Groups of men in white cloaks stood at the doors of the houses; and high, time-stained, and carved buildings bespoke the importance of this, the most elevated of the towns of Tenerife. To me it seemed that I was in Gloucestershire, breathing the air of a moist April evening. Yet I doubt if even Gloucestershire in the best of seasons could match Chasna, 4,270 feet above the sea, for the luxuriance of its grass and its blossoms.

It fell dark while we were yet in the streets of this town, and the inhabitants withdrew to their houses, barring their windows with heavy wooden shutters. I feared we were in a quandary, for the doctor to whom I bore a letter had left his former house. But it came right in the end, though neither the mare nor ourselves tasted dinner before 10 p.m. In the meantime, I sat, unkempt and unwashed, *vis-à-vis* with my host in a large bare upper room, shot with draughts from all its sides. He plied me with questions, commented somewhat cynically on the answers, and took snuff. He was pleased to think that the English were likely to be periodical visitors to Tenerife, and hoped those who stayed through the summer would pay him a visit at Chasna. Medically, the place suited stomach and renal affections, dyspepsia, &c., but it was agreeable for the sick and the well alike.

Among the pretty faces of Tenerife, I shall long recall the doctor's little daughter. She was but twelve or thirteen, but quite angelic. Her features were regular, and not so heavy as with most Spanish girls. But the beauty and brilliancy of her eyes were incomparable. And when, with her mother's help, she had laid the supper table, and came and stood by the one candle which lit me and the room, her small hands folded one in the other, she was loveliness incarnate. Yet, though so young, she had the dignity and grace of a woman, and was self-possessed to a marvel. Her small brother, a baby of six or seven, brought his picture books, dolls, and go-carts for me to see; and with bright eyes of interest she interpreted his childish lingo, adding explanations in a charming manner. Three years hence, this little one will be a Hebe worth the winning. "God go with you, señor," she said, in customary farewell, when she gave me her hand the next day; and the conventional rejoinder, "May He guard you, too, señorita," could not but be spoken with peculiar sincerity.

This night in Chasna (or Villaflor, as it is more often called) was cold for Tenerife, and I used all the bed-covering I could get. But how delightful was the morning outlook when, aroused by a sunbeam through a chink of the window, I opened the shutters! Such glowing verdure and scent of blossoms in the cool, moist, sunlit air! The vegetation so various: from cacti, aloes, lemon and orange trees, and budding figs, to cherry and apple and poplar trees! In the Plaza below was the shell of a decorated stone building. Grass and fig trees grew dense within its walls; and by one side of it stood a tall cypress, healthy and strong as an Oriental tree. This was a ruined conventual establishment: the expulsion of the Jesuits in 1767 suspended its completion. Beyond were the red-roofed houses of the town, their white bodies looming through the greenery which enwrapped them, and blue smoke soared in spiral columns from the chimneys into the still, fresh air. The lowing of kine, the chirping of birds, and the crowing of cocks, sounded in cheerful tumult from all parts of the town.

Chasna is remarkable in that its inhabitants live most of their time above the clouds. From my window, the gay pine-clad hills (being the southern side of the Cañadas, with the conical Sombrecita as the dominant and most striking of the cliffs) which frame the town at from one to four thousand feet above it, were visible in detail: a charming study of purple and gold and crimson; but, below the houses, where the land falls abruptly seawards, nothing was to be seen except a mass of woolly vapour, with here and there a dark shadow upon it. The clouds were about a thousand feet lower than us, while we were under a blue sky and a warm unmitigated sun.

We left Chasna (which boasts of no antiquities) soon after 7 a.m., equipped with a gigantic bouquet of boughs of orange, pear, and apple blossom, and one little violet from the doctor's daughter. The last is now dry and scentless, but I keep it as an amulet of value.

This giving and taking of flowers, so common in

Tenerife, is a kindly and gracious custom. In England, I suppose a lady would hesitate ere she offered a gentleman a sprig of orange blossom. But here it is an every-day civility. It is also more than this. Thanks to the embargo that Spanish etiquette places upon intercourse between unmarried girls and the rest of the world, the young of both sexes have established a very adequate code of signals expressible by flowers. The language of flowers is in fact a language very much alive, and not a mere sentimental fiction. The hapless lover, in the heat of his passion, may not be able to sit by the side of his mistress in her father's house or elsewhere. But it is permissible and easy to take a loose nosegay in his hand, and, stationing himself in a plaintive attitude on that side of the street which affords him the better view of the girl's fair face, as she sits sighing towards him, weave pretty messages of admiration and love with the roses and jasmine and heliotrope.

The maiden, too, depends on flowers as a means of divination. When she yearns to know who shall marry her, she throws a bouquet into the street. He who picks it up has the claim upon her. But no doubt she will not resort to this hazardous method of inquiry, unless she believes her heart's lover to be near at hand. If a pig touch the flowers with his snout, it is a sign that the lady is doomed to a Portuguese, and not a Spaniard.

The great season for these experiments is the 22nd of June, the eve of St. John. It is the custom then to light bonfires at the doors of those who bear the saint's name—Juan or Juana. A maiden listening at her window to the chatter in the street is wont to give credence to the fancy that the first male Christian name which she hears spoken after the lighting of the fires is the name of her future husband. Another plan is to break a new-laid egg into a glass of water, and let it stand through the night. By rising at dawn the next day, the votary may distinguish marks in the commixture of egg and water, indicative of the trade or profession of her beloved. Another less cheerful superstition belongs to this St. John's Eve. A dish of water being set out on the eve, may be looked into at daybreak. If the reflection be clear, the augury is good; otherwise, the dimness forebodes death to the experimentalist within the year.

From Villaflor we rapidly descended in the bracing atmosphere, to the town of Granadilla, some two thousand feet lower down. The tract was broken but distinct, bordered by asphodels, and red and yellow poppies; now leading us into a steep gulley coated with scrub, and now by rough barley fields and down broad steps of slippery white rock. As we proceeded, the sun melted the clouds at our feet. Thus the lowlands were gradually uncovered, and rounded hills, green basins, and inclined reaches of uncultivable lava came into view, to the water's edge. Ere we neared the orange groves of Granadilla, the atmosphere had cleared so that the mountains of Grand Canary, fifty miles away, stood forth boldly.

The entrance to this balmy town was by a series of awkward rock slabs, which brought the mare upon her haunches twice or thrice. At its outskirts we came to a lava monument, surmounted by a monk in the attitude of preaching. Then a bountiful fountain testified to the supply of that best commodity of a Tenerifan town. But Granadilla is more famous for its oranges. Not Florida has its trees weighted more profusely. The perfume of the blossom was too sweet. Oranges lay in piles in the gutters. A beggar woman, sitting by the roadside, was making her breakfast from them. She did but squeeze out their juice, and the heap of indented carcasses by her toe-less shoe marked the measure of her indulgence.

At Granadilla, I made the acquaintance of a type of Spaniard new to me. The Guia guide carried my introduction to him, while I waited in the large inner quadrangle of his house, watching the brisk movements of the milkmaids and ostlers, all by their activity betokening a master of no common kind. Such, in fact, Don Ramon Garcia proved to be.

He was a little man, preternaturally broad, with a full round red face, and a minute moustache neatly waxed and turned at the ends. José winced at the sight of him; and the thunderous bidding of Don Ramon to take the mare to a stable and do all that was necessary, seemed to be no more than his intuition made him expect.

With me, of course, Don Ramon was less authoritative, until breakfast was served. We sat in his drawing-room at the window, and he talked loud, so that the people in the street gathered at the corner to see what was happening. He offered me Madrid journals six weeks old, discussed the telegrams about Castillo, and bade some one fetch the *cura* of the parish church. His reverence duly appeared—a sheepish, dirty, blushing young priest, who, it was clear from his obsequious demeanour, was in most things my friend's very obedient servant. In two words, Don Ramon told his business. He was to have the church unlocked and everything on view for us in an hour's time. " Yes, sir," said the *cura*, who with a bow and a new blush, withdrew like a domestic.

Breakfast was soon ready; and then Don Ramon, with generous hospitality, enrolled me among his slaves. He plyed me with his best wines till my head thickened, and made a feint of emptying his glass at every toast, so that he might have excuse for refilling mine. While we ate, a maid whisked the flies from our head with a peacock's feather. She was alert enough, but not to Don Ramon's satisfaction. " The señor's head! Caramba! Do you not see there is a fly upon him? *Dios mio!* what a simpleton!" Thus he bullied the girl, while he fêted me. Once he caught her smiling, and abused her so that she replied, and then he stormed her out of the room. José, the Guia guide, and two or three others, stood in the quadrangle, on the other side, smiling and shrugging their shoulders ; but whenever Don Ramon turned his head that way all such levity ended. I never saw such a domestic tyrant: He was a bachelor to tame a Xantippe.

After a cup of chocolate of unrivalled excellence (" you would not get such chocolate in the house of a married man," said my friend, with elation), we went out to view the town. The church came first ; a building newly restored, with white walls, and green railings in its white bell-tower. Don Ramon would not enter the church. He committed me to the *cura*, and himself stood outside with his back to the porch, his short legs wide apart, smoking a stout cigar from his own factory. As for the priest, he was a very ignorant person. He guessed at the meaning of the daubs on the walls, and guessed wrongly. To show the date of the ancient missals still in use, he put his unclean thumb on the epoch of the enunciation of a certain canon. The silver candlesticks, monstrances, figures of the crucified Christ and the Virgin being decked for the festival of the week, the bier for the dead, draped with festoons of dusty paper flowers—these things, however, he took pride in showing me; and in dilating upon their intrinsic worth and magnificence.

Don Ramon was more anxious to show a stranger the town club than the town church. In its establishment he had been prime mover; and the billiard room, library replete with old periodicals, and theatre, were all deducible from him. The drop scene of the stage of the theatre was a particular wonder. The blinds of the room had to be drawn, the lamps lit, and the day turned into night that I might admire the artist's ingenuity, and guess the subject his genius had evoked for the joy of Granadilla. The perspective was shocking, and it was not without an effort that I recognised the church just visited, and the orange trees which proclaimed Granadilla itself.

After the club, we visited a tobacco factory, one of Don Ramon's own. The fields were within hail of the town, and here, in the different rooms of two small houses, their produce was dried, sorted, rolled by the deft fingers of three men, and finally packed and labelled by sundry girls. At Don Ramon's kind command, an embarrassing cigar, a foot long, was made and presented to me, and others of various brands—the most costly selling in Madrid for 40s. the hundred.

By this, it was time to say good-bye to my odd good friend. At parting I was rude enough to express the wish that he might soon change his state of single blessedness. But he received the wish with a hard smile that told how ill it fitted with his aspirations. "No, no, señor, *soltero siempre*" (always a bachelor!) he said, with decision—"á Dios!"

The Guia guide was eager to gossip about Don Ramon as soon as we were out of the town. "Rich! I believe it, señor," said he, "Why, Don Ramon owns houses and lands, and mills for tobacco, sugar, and *gofio*; and only one mouth to feed with it all! Ave Maria! that is a rich man, without doubt!"

In the nine miles of track from Granadilla to Arico we passed over much hot stony land, divested of trees. The red and white rocks were in some places picturesque, and the clouded mountains to the left were so throughout. At the entrance to the village of Rio, six miles on our way, we had to cross a yawning *barranco* of the most tiresome kind. A man might throw a stone over it, and yet we spent nearly an hour in descending its precipitous walls to the stagnant yellow puddles in its bed, and then toiling up the light-brown rock on the other side.

In the neighbourhood of Rio, where the surface is formed of singularly even strata of hard grayish tufa, are several hundred troglodytes. They may be regarded as direct descendants of the Guanches, who, five hundred years ago, also lived in caves on this side of the island, and may be, in the same caves. The holes run in regular streets, and vents cut in the upper layer of rock serve as chimneys. At the invitation of a proprietor, I entered his house. It was in two parts, the sleeping-room divided by a natural wall from the stable and kitchen, where an ass lay among the pots and pans. The ceiling was certainly low, but had been chiselled smoothly. But the chief charm of these dwellings is their coolness. The Governor-General at Santa Cruz, with a bower of orange trees and tropical shrubs enclosing his palace, cannot enjoy so exhilarating a temperature as these poor troglodytes, who depend for their livelihood upon the one little ass they let for hire when an occasion offers, upon the roots of this hard ungenerous soil, and the rare opportunities of manual labour. This particular cave also held a weaving frame of a rude kind, and the swarthy housewife controled it while watching her various children, and calming the squeals of her baby. The *gofio* mill, besides, is an essential in every household.

It is difficult to say whether travel has an enlarging or a repressive effect upon the human sympathies as a whole. But, in some respects, I am afraid it tends inevitably to harden the heart. In this cave the flies were upon the walls in clots. Outside it was worse. My mare was in an agony.

They stung her where she could not protect herself. The consequence was that she kicked methodically as some relief for her pain. How many of the flies I killed with the handle of my fly-whip, prone upon the neck of the mare, I should shudder to conjecture did I think that retribution awaited whomsoever deprived a living being of its life. In fact, I learnt to pity Nero that, by the ignorance of those who live in temperate regions, and know little of the pests that appertain to heat, he should have been gibbeted in the minds of so many well-principled boys and girls as the very king of cowardly tyrants, because he found pastime in the massacre of flies. How should you like to be eaten alive by these industrious little creatures? Yet this is the fate of numerous asses and horses that are prevented from using the means of protection supplied to them by nature. The animal does not disappear in infinitesimal morsels, all at once, in the midst of a swarm of countless house-flies. Hardly. But this is true, that many a one begins the summer with a stout, unfractured hide, and ends it covered with red wounds and holes, due more or less to the flies. A weak animal may readily succumb to this incessant torture, and thus be the victim, absolutely, of these same flies.

Having drunk a little of the yellow water which was the best these poor cave-dwellers could offer us, we went on to Arico. We were in the aridest part of Tenerife—a land scorched by the sun throughout the year, and with little or no soil over its rocks. The outer fringe of the Cañadas falls steeply here, intersected by vast ravines. The entire slope is veined with lava deposits; and the blue sea that washes its shores breaks into foam upon the sharp edges of caves which at one time were undisturbed cells (gaseous bubbles) in the stream of scoriæ from the Cañadas. On this torrid incline, among some patches of languishing barley and beans, are a few white houses—the majority dilapidated, not one imposing. This is the village of Arico, a forlorn place; and thither we went, with but dim assurance of a reception, still less a welcome, from any one.

But here again the Guia guide proved his discretion and thoughtfulness. He went straight to the house that seemed in best repair, and stated our case with homely eloquence. And, after a brief confabulation between two or three burgesses and their wives, I was installed in the upper room of a house, approached by an outside wooden ladder. The master of the house, a stout, sly, sleek man, was effusive in his welcome, and unduly apologetic.

"*Casa de campo* only, señor," he said. "But the heart is as warm in a poor cottage as in a king's palace." He had migrated years ago to Havana, and there been so uncivilly used by fortune that he had served as a dock porter. "And my health suffered. I was glad, therefore, to come home again. And now here I am with a wife, several little children, and an old mother, all upon my hands. I do my best, but it is hard, señor, and *me not much money*."

These last words were in English, he having picked up shreds of the language by intercourse with English dockmen and others. Out of compliment,

I suppose, he continued to afflict me by remembering other unpleasant phrases and adjectives, and proferring them with a whine. I am afraid it is fair to assume that the man who harps on his own misfortunes is either soft of wit, or devoid of principle.

In Arico I met a brother of Don Ramon of Granadilla, a gentleman with fewer prejudices than the Spanish grandee commonly possesses. He was stupefied at the idea of English ladies ascending the Peak; but, on the other hand, he admitted that if the Canarian girls were allowed to run about and play like their English sisters, unrestrained by rules of etiquette, it would be better for them than their present confined life. Señor Garcia, unlike his brother, was married, and he too was very rich. Later in the evening, I found him in an outhouse tossing dice with half a dozen ill-looking men. Such condescension costs a Spaniard but little. He avers that gentility is of blood, not money; and where is the Spaniard whose blood is not as blue as he would have it to be?

After dinner my landlord thought to amuse me with a little of life behind the scenes in a country village of Tenerife. He summoned two or three of the gilded youth of Arico, and we all walked to the outskirts of the place, to a little cavern cut in the rock. It was a comfortless hole, with the rain that chanced to be falling filtering through the tufa of the ceiling in our midst; but I sat on a stool, willing to be entertained. An ancient hag kept this den, and, being bidden, put before us a dish of salted water, raw beans, and a bottle of wine. The young men fillipped the beans at the nose of the old lady, and as her nose was large and red, it was a mark easy to hit. But this was not proper usage for the beans. They were to be eaten from the salted water with the wine. Later, in came three girls. They were very alluring by the faint light of our one tallow candle. But they were not modest girls, and when the bean fillipping was extended to them they accepted the challenge with such vigour that in a few moments the place was like a battle-field. The worst of it was that the boldest (indeed she was also the prettiest) of the girls asked me point blank if I was not in love with her black eyes. Having given her the admiration she wanted, I found myself yawning with such determination that there was nothing for it but to wish the merrymakers "good-night" and go off to bed, leaving behind, no doubt, a desperately low opinion of English gallantry.

CHAPTER X.

A dilemma—Spanish generosity—The *Barranco* de Herque—Fasnea—The genial householder—A downpour—Escobonal and the *carretara*—View of Guimar—The procession of Holy Thursday—Fanaticism—Candelaria—Rude burial—The camel—Santa Cruz—Strategy—Laguna—Orotava.

MUCH rain fell during this night at Arico, and the country looked very lowering early the next day. The clouds hung in slow-moving masses over the mountain sides, and their big shadows embraced us and the town, and reached even to the shore. Here, however, the sparkling blue of the sea, lit by the sun, was in brilliant contrast to our gloom. The rain had had a wonderfully freshening effect upon our surroundings. The close atmosphere reeked with the perfume of wild mint and thyme, and the lean yellow barley, and the poppies thick among it, were strung with water-drops. This rain was also the talk of the town. Everyone out of doors was wrapped to the mouth in his white *manta*, and, while speaking, held his hand before his lips for fear of the damp. "Of course you will not go on to-day!" they said to me. And then they told dubious tales about the perils of the *barrancos*, and the roaring torrents that the mountain downpour would cast into them. José, too, sidled up, with a straw in his mouth, and said the mare could not do more than she could.

Little as I cared to stay in Arico, a deterrent worse than the weather was like to have kept me there for a time. The worthy ex-Havana dockman presented me with a bill out of all proportion to reason; and as I had no inordinate supply of money with me, the payment of it would have left me penniless for the two days hence to Santa Cruz. Expostulation did but make the man whine about his duty to his family, and the few travellers who came that way ("it is therefore necessary to make the most of one when he *does* come," said he): he could neither abate nor trust me. But in the midst of the turmoil appeared Señor Garcia, the brother of Don Ramon. He was no sooner enlightened about the matter than he sent a servant for a roll of dollars, and put them into my hands. "Take what you want," he said, and turned his back. I was rejoiced, of course. But the good Spaniard, on his part, would not even receive an acknowledgment of the loan. Nor was this the limit of his benefaction. He summoned a weatherwise man, and by the side of a well held solemn debate about the clouds and the *barrancos*, until the danger of our way grew tenuous and even visionary. Then he procured a guide towards the next village, and, everything being in order, I mounted the mare and left Arico. I have been thus prolix in the narrative of our trouble in this place that I might the better portray the kindness and courtesy of this typical Spanish gentleman.

To know such a man is more educative than an octavo volume of solid moral maxims.

The new guide did not stay with us long. He went off to his goats, bequeathing to José so verbose a description of his duties and the country that the boy wrinkled his forehead with anxiety. It was in truth a frightful tract of land. But for occasional puny little parallelograms of barley, growing miserably in the red, stony soil, I should have said it was absolutely sterile. The heat, too, got suffocating. Both of us, and the mare, panted for breath as we climbed wearily over the whitened rocks towards the town, high up in the hills, which was to be our first stage that day. The flies were insufferable. But towards noon even they seemed overmastered by the close atmosphere, and we three creatures struggling upwards were the only movables in sight. In spite of the prognostications of Arico, we found no water in the ravines until we reached the clouds, about 2,000 feet above the sea.

On our way we were confronted with the *barranco* de Herque, celebrated as the site of the catacomb or Pantheon wherein Viera saw a thousand Guanche mummies. It is a gigantic rift, with sides so nearly perpendicular that we had to proceed to its very mouth, where it debouches upon the sea in a cove of fine smooth sand, before we could cross it; and then follow its hot stony bed inland until a feasible incline of its brown walls, clumped with euphorbia, is perceptible. This inviting little cove has doubtless been often visited by English and other sailors in search of Guanche mummy medicaments. But it would try the nerve of the most skilful mastheadman to climb to the caves of this *barranco*, which, from their position and aspect, were most likely to reward the explorer for his pains.

We reached the village of Fasnea and the skirt of the clouds at about 2 p.m. Fasnea is only a league from Arico, yet it had cost us four hours of our time! We were glad to have done with the repellent vicinity of Arico. The sun had scorched and blistered us like the near flames of a furnace. If such were the case early in April, one might well perspire at the mere thought of the same country in July or August, with the added charm of a south wind blowing hot from the Sahara upon the shore. Below Fasnea we stepped into a water flood that soon soaked us to the skin. José wore nothing over his brown body but a thin cotton jacket, and this now adhered to him like a new skin. For an hour we fought against the downpour; then the apparition of a pleasant house, with blue and green paint upon it, drew us to a pause. It was lunch time, moreover. But what was the housewife likely to say to such sopped rats as us? José, however, did not give her much chance of objecting. He even treated the matter so cavalierly as to offsaddle the mare, carry her gear into the reception room, and set it down, all slobbering with rain, under an engraving of the patron saint of gardeners (St. Fiacre). "It is nothing, *caballero*—nothing at all!" exclaimed the housewife. She was a stout, hearty young matron, with a dark moustache; and she laughed at our proceedings. She did more: she gave us dried figs from her own garden, wine of her own pressing, and hunches of barley bread, the material for a sound meal; and she uttered monosyllables of satisfaction in a deep bass voice while she stood with her arms in her fat sides, watching us eat. During the feast the mare, with all her grace of deportment drowned out of her, put her head into the room through the window. It was a pretty scene, this cheerful apartment, with its mirrors and pictures of uncommon saints, adorned with tinsel paper: the portly, dark-skinned lady filling the foreground; the tender face of the good mare bending over the señora's shoulder to get the bread with which she tempted it; José, showing his teeth with spasmodic grins; and the dripping foliage of the fir trees and shrubs in the garden behind the mare! But the lady marred the romance of the situation by accepting, in conclusion, about four times as much money as the worth of what we, including the mare, had consumed. Probably, after all, the wetted boards went to her stout heart.

The rain continued to swill from the clouds in spite of our tarrying. Once again we went into brief shelter. This time we were on the edge of a *barranco*, but, at the invitation of a countrywoman, with a cock in a basket on her head, we joined her under a slab of rock. Here we saw the rapid growth of a torrent in the ravine. At first the *barranco* was hardly more than moist. But while we crouched, numberless brown frothing streamlets drained down from its sides into its bed. We did not delay long; for an hour later it promised to hurl about the immense bluish boulders, which are ordinarily the only litter of these dry, hot crevices.

From Fasnea to Escobonal, still in the mountains, is only about half an hour; and here, with mixed feelings, we clambered up from the old track we had followed for the last four days, and attained the *carretara*, or coach road, which is completed from Santa Cruz thus far in this direction. José sighed with contentment. Thenceforward, he would have much less care for the mare's shoes, and it would be impossible to lose the way. But to me it was not so pleasant thus to come plump upon the methods of civilization after our rough but happy shifts for nearly a week. However, it is one thing for a National Board of Works to make admirable roads, and another for the people to use them. Between Escobonal and Guimar (about five miles) we met not one vehicle of any kind. But now and again we saw an agile man or woman, who, in following the old, more direct, though steeper, path, had to climb over the walls of the new road. This and the grass on the excellent highway were somewhat insulting to the authorities; but what could be done in remedy? An innovation so serious probably affected the country folk here much as the railway affected our own peasantry fifty years ago. As a spectacle it was superb, but rather demoniacal.

A sudden turn round a cape of rock in the vicinity of Escobonal gave us an impressive view of Santa Cruz, about twenty-eight miles away. The capital was in sunlight, while we were in black shadow. It stretched from the mainland as a dazzling white line, with the Anaga peaks behind it. Hence, also, the island of Grand Canary—about thirty-five miles distant—was very clear.

We now crossed the grandiose *barranco* Badajos, and mounted gradually, to descend into the Vale of Guimar. The *barrancos* were no longer a trial, for they were all spanned by the blue and white lava-stone bridges, which are so creditable a feature of the *carretara* of Tenerife. But José, like the natives, shunned the *carretara*. I constantly thought he was lost, and was only reassured by seeing him appear in front, dropping down the sides of a red or purple bluff of rock, heedless of the nopals and euphorbia which threatened him on all quarters. Thus it happened that the Vale of Guimar burst upon me, all unprepared, with another abrupt turning round the edge of an immense mountain wall. It was a satisfying sight. Humboldt affirmed that the Vale of Orotava is the most beautiful in the world. To my mind, Guimar is more beautiful than Orotava, although it lacks the Peak itself as an element in its picture. But Humboldt did not see Guimar.

I was about a thousand feet above the valley or amphitheatre when it was unfolded to me, the road being cut in the side of a precipitous mountain. The town lay below, a brilliant congeries of white houses, dotted with palm trees, and set on a slope of the *cordillera* running from the Cañadas towards Laguna. The mountains of this *cordillera* are 6,000 to 7,000 feet high, and so steep from Guimar that the sharp vermillion and olive summits are little more than a league from the houses of the town. Angular shoulders fall from the range into the valley, shaded with pines on their crests, and with thickets of wild fig, quince, and other fruit trees, and myriads of prickly pear lower down. The background to Guimar is therefore much bolder than that of Orotava, from which its amphitheatre of mountains is several miles distant. At Guimar, as at Orotava, the country between the town and the sea in the foreground is diversified by volcanic ash humps, monstrous mementoes of the troubled past that may at any time be repeated in fresh trouble.

But it is the singular broad scene of devastation that makes the valley so much more impressive than Orotava. Viewed from above, the area of decomposing lava south of the town seems prodigious. It is mapped out into hundreds of little paddocks, where vines and fig trees are gradually thrusting their roots into the soil underneath the crust of ruin which has covered it for scores of years. Yet, in stern and most emphatic proof that all this labour may at any time become labour lost, are two wide lines, intensely black, permeating the valley, and running seawards. They proceed from one of the hinder peaks, and are the lava streams of 1704 and 1705, when the hapless residents of Guimar experienced ten or twelve earthquake shocks every day for three continuous months. These inky scores give grand colouring to this extraordinary landscape. The glory of the crimson mountain tops, the vivid greenery of many tints where tobacco, sugar-cane, maize, and every vegetable of common use, dye the fields recovered from the old lava, the white houses, the wisps of cloud floating about the hill slopes, and the red-brown walls of rock, west of the valley, studded with a various garb of shrubs, cannot reconcile one to the fatal significance of these two dark still rivers of destruction. Nature is here distinctly " a fearful monster, for ever devouring her own offspring."

With such thoughts in my head, and listening to the sweet tones of the Guimar bells, the mare and I slowly descended into the valley. It was the eve of Holy Thursday. We were just in time for the ceremonies of Holy Week.

Guimar is a town of some importance, with about 5000 inhabitants, and daily coach service connection with Santa Cruz. It has, therefore, an inn—an inn Spanish to the backbone. At the outset, José had to stand for a few minutes, cap in hand, pleading earnestly with the innkeeper to give us a lodging. The man was of great size, and eyed me and the mare for some time, questioning José about both of us, ere he proferred any sort of an invitation to enter his house. Moreover, as he kept a shop as well as an inn, and customers were numerous, during this period of uncertainty he vanished now and again to attend to his clients. This apparent neglect seemed to send the mare to sleep, and whilst she slept I smoked cigarettes upon her stalwart back. Perhaps, in the end, it was our common affectation of indifference to the shocks and slights of fortune, that made the man at last order the boy to lead the mare to the stable, and bring out a three-legged stool for my use.

" A bed, señor ? " said he, like one solving a problem; "why, without doubt! But it is my wife's affair: she will arrange it. What I want to know is what your worship (*su merced*) would like for dinner. Afterwards, tell me what you think of the country."

It was a comfort to know the matter was settled. I had heard hard tales about this Guimar inn. But the truth is that its master and mistress were people to be approached with tact, and rather flattered into complaisance than forced into anything. It was only after delicate manœuvring that I contrived to make the lady of the house understand how grateful I should feel if she gave me clean sheets to my bed. But when I put the request before her so as to cast no slur upon her establishment, she humoured my eccentric tastes in this and other particulars. Later, she served the dinner with her own hands, in a masterful but kindly way. It was an excellent meal, with fair wine. Her face shone with pleasure when I praised it, and I believe I made her completely happy for an hour when, over the bananas and oranges, I questioned her little boy about his studies, and complimented him upon his erudition. The youngster could not, I am glad to say, devote much time to this sort of cross-examination. The tolling of the bells made him run away to church, where he was to join the procession as a scarlet acolyte.

"He has a sweet voice," remarked his mother, "and the *cura* thinks much of his singing. But for my part"—she added, with a sigh—"I wish the poor boy did not squint in his left eye. He might have a voice like a crow, but I would be happy, Ave Maria! if he could only see straight also." It was true that the lad squinted, but he was so intelligent that the misfortune seemed lost upon him.

From my bedroom, with a saint on each of the walls, I soon followed the boy towards the church of Guimar. The people of the town are reputed to be the most fanatical in the island in religious matters. Their priests are omnipotent. A word from them would almost suffice for an *auto da fé*: and he were a bold person who dared to air an heretical or liberal notion within their jurisdiction.

Unluckily, I did not learn that Guimar bore this character until I had left it. I thought it no wrong to go into the town in riding attire and a white hat. To be sure, it was soon evident that the citizens and their families at the windows of the houses and on the roofs, were all in black and bareheaded. But, as a stranger, methought I might be excused for only partial conformity to their customs. It was not so, however. For a time, all went well. I joined the throng who followed the statues of Christ bearing the cross, and the Mater Dolorosa in purple velvet, as they were carried through the street by a file of crimson-robed ecclesiastics, boys with lamps and candles, and a band of musicians who marched with inverted muskets, and played sad, moving melodies. But the scene and its surroundings, with the dull, unintelligent faces of the men and boys of the crowd, soon depressed me to such a degree that I left the procession and went to the side path of the Plaza, through which the images were being borne to the church at its extremity. Here I caused displeasure by putting on my hat. I did wrong, no doubt, in forgetting where I was; but I am sorry to say that the harsh, insolent, and even savage cries of the bystanders acted upon me like an irritant. The consequence was that for the length of the Plaza (about a hundred and fifty yards), I ran the gauntlet of gibes, sneers, and even menaces, to the very door of the church. One youth approached to unbonnet me, but he forbore to do so. It was a wholly discomforting and merited humiliation, and I wished myself far from this parish church of Guimar. The very priests, who ought to have poured oil on this public exhibition of ill-feeling, did but scowl on me where I stood within the porch, while they all passed by towards the sanctuary; and men, women, and children were not slow to follow the example of their spiritual rulers. The little acolyte of the inn, with a gilded lamp in his hand, seemed no better than the rest. He stared with horror, as if I had nothing in common with the person to whom he had so recently discoursed, in calm mental unrestraint, about the countries of Europe and their respective capitals. But perhaps the poor lad's affection of the eye made his looks discordant with his feelings.

However, as I had no mind to humble myself in public after these various slights and insults, I stayed in the church as long as I pleased, and then retraced my steps through the Plaza, to all appearance, I hope, oblivious of the existence of the hundreds of Guimar citizens and youths who still kept at their doors. They, on their part, did not hesitate to continue their coarse and derisive remarks, which I allowed to enter at one ear and go out into the air by the other. But when I reached the inn, and had well considered the matter with a cigar, upon the roof of the building, aided by a mild, bright moon, and a sweet aroma of cut sugar canes, I passed judgment upon myself. It was certain that I had met with my deserts. In Guimar, as in Rome, one ought to follow the fashion.

Early on Holy Thursday, we left Guimar for our last stage but one. The day was warm, and the scenery, for Tenerife, tame. For the whole twenty miles we followed the *carretara*, now almost touching the sea, and again bending inland, until the coast was screened by intervening hills.

We halted but once during this brisk journey. It was at a lowly wayside wine shop, nearly as full of children as flies—"and all mine," said the countrywoman who kept the shop, referring to the children. I counted nine, and others were with their father, pelting stones at the goats on the hill sides. In Tenerife it costs little to rear a large family. *Gofio* is the common food, as in the days of the Guanches. It is taken dry, by mouthfuls, with glasses of wine or water to wash it down; or it is made into dough, and so eaten; or, if the peasant can afford to be luxurious, it is mixed with honey, milk, or coffee. For the man unused to *gofio*, nothing is more apt to induce death by choking. But it is a nutriment well suited to the Canarians. They will walk all day upon the strength of a couple of handfuls of it.

A few miles from Guimar, nestling by the coast, is the ancient port and shrine of Candelaria. This little village used to be the holiest place of pilgrimage in the islands. Here, in the time of the Guanches, the Virgin appeared and consented to dwell in a lowly cave which the troubled natives prepared for her. Of course the Guanches did not identify her as Maria Santissima; but the legend says that they so revered her (although she severely punished the ignorant goatherds who on first seeing her threw stones to frighten her away from their flocks) as to regret nothing so much as her removal by the early Spaniards, who were astounded to discover the image in a land they thought absolutely heathen. Afterwards, the Virgin was restored to her original cave, which grew into a grotto, surrounded by monastic and other buildings for those who came to do her honour. When the island was disturbed by war, pestilence, locusts, floods, or volcanoes, it was to the Virgin of Candelaria that the people ran as a supreme resource. The statue was then ceremoniously paraded through the stricken district, and the wonder was worked. But, in 1705, when the locality was shaken by numerous earthquakes, the image itself was transported, for safety, to Laguna. This Virgin of Candelaria, the main theme of Viana's epic, was in 1826 washed out to sea by a flood in the *barranco* which held the grotto. The present glory of Candelaria is therefore posthumous glory. But if, as certain irreverent writers aver, the original image was only the figure-head of a ship, driven ashore, the sea did but receive its own again.

The country between Guimar and Santa Cruz is thinly populated. We passed two or three old churches or hermitages, but at considerable distances from each other. This explained the presence of a black and yellow coffin in a certain rock hole near the road side. The coffin contained an occupant lying under a loose lid, fast decomposing in the lime which had been heaped over it. It may be that nothing except bones will remain when a convenient opportunity for burial arrives; or burial in consecrated ground may be avoided altogether.

Another trivial incident of our journey may be mentioned. We were nearing the capital when the ungainly form of a camel came swinging along the high road. There are but two or three of these brutes in Tenerife, though Lanzarote and Fuerteventura have them by hundreds. The mare could hardly be expected therefore to take kindly to the apparition. A brace of paniers were hung across the camel's backbone, and on each side sat a peasant woman, rising and falling as if she were on the sea. The beast approached: the mare stopped still, set her ears back, trembled, and then bounded off at a tangent, almost transfixing me upon a hedge of aloes. Here I kept her until the grinning countrywomen had slouched uneasily by: but for the rest of the morning she saw camels in every gate or building by the highway.

Thus we descended into the white city of Santa Cruz, on the afternoon of Holy Thursday, in time for a surfeit of religious processions, and to hear so incessant a clapping of muffled church bells that one's head revolted against the noise. Most of the shops were shut. The ships in the harbour carried their flags at half-mast. Citizens, with their wives and children, all in sleek black, walked about the streets with an air of depression, or entered the churches at intervals, to kneel with the crowd that covered the pavements throughout the day. Now and then, the precise step of a body of soldiers sounded heavily at the church porches. Headed by their officers, they marched up the aisle to the altar rails, knelt for two or three minutes, and then, with military clatter, retraced their way into the street.

On the following day, Good Friday, we had to use strategy to leave the town. An official order forbade other vehicles than the mail coach to pass through the streets. It was thought that the mare would be included as a vehicle. Accordingly, by tortuous ways, we avoided the viceregal palace, on the high road, where a military cordon was stationed to prevent such desecration of the day. The same trouble threatened us at Laguna, and might have kept us between the two towns for four and twenty hours. It was therefore with some trembling that we trod the grassy streets of the old capital. The mare made a pitiless uproar, poor beast, irritated by flies and the slippery stones, and many a citizen turned a hard eye of condemnation on us both as, wrapped to the nose in his cloak, he bent his steps towards the Cathedral. However, we got safely through, and a good gallop carried us far from the fringe of danger.

After Santa Cruz and Laguna, we were careless of the knots of villagers in their best clothes—at Tacoronte, Matanza, Victoria, and Santa Ursala; though they muttered, and tried to make the mare shy. The road between the various churches and the Calvaries, whither the statues of the dead Christ were taken for the night, was bestrewn with rose and geranium leaves, and palm fronds were set in the ground in avenues. We caught glimpses of these processions here and there—priests in red robes, acolytes, lamps, banners, and images, and heard the dirges which went with them. But neither the mare nor I were disposed to stop for anything during this ride to Orotava. The flies goaded the poor animal so that she was almost beside herself. She found no relief except in brisk movement. As for José, it was vain to think that he could keep up with us on this road worthy of Macadam. He did not reach his stable in Puerto until the mare had been warmly embraced and welcomed by Lorenzo, her master, and had rested for two full hours after the various labours of the past week.

CHAPTER XI.

Easter morning—A Guanche festival—Benromo—The city of Laguna—Its history—The romance of Dacil and Castillo—The pestilence of Laguna—Ecclesiastical appropriations—Public festivities and mourning—The miraculous sweat—Some governors of the Canaries—Bishop Murga's injunctions—The expulsion of the Jesuists—Laguna as it is.

I RODE from Orotava to Laguna on the morning of Easter day. The air was fresh and moist from nocturnal rains. The vines were beaded with waterdrops. Canaries and thrushes carolled from amid the blossoms of the roadside trees. The sea to the farthest promontories of the land was quiet and glistening. The white head of the Peak uprose through the clouds, against the blue. Nature was gay, as if she too were celebrating a resurrection; and she was calm, as if she were content with herself.

According to Viana, the Guanches held a festival which in the calendar corresponds nearly with the Christian Easter. The last nine days of April were holidays. If the kings of Tenerife were at war one with another, they then established a truce. It was the time of harvest. And when this was got in, games, feasting, and jollity were the order of the day until the truce ended.

These joyous festivities were ushered in with certain feudal ceremonies. The king sat in state, and received the annual homage of his people. The nobles bent the knee to him, kissed his right hand and said, " I am thy vassal." The more considerable of the commons followed their example, kissing the left instead of the right hand of the monarch. Lastly, the multitude of plebeians humbly presented skins and flowers, and, prostrate, kissed the king's feet, in token of their abject obedience as well as their vassalage.

If there were any privileges to be confirmed or grievances to be ventilated, no doubt such business followed this acknowledgment of fealty. But it is probable the Guanches neither had nor wanted a Magna Charta. From their Westminster Hall, they all flocked gaily to the sports which then were celebrated. The king sat on a scaffold shaded by boughs and leafage, with his grandfather's thigh-bone in his hand, and gave the word for the troops of his realm to deploy before him in the sight of all the people.

Would you have a sketch of King Bencomo as he was on this occasion, in 1494, while the ships of the Spaniards were already on the sea approaching the island? He was a gigantic man, with a fabulous number of teeth in his head (*sesenta muelas sin los dientes*), broad and brown of face, with a wrinkled brow, loose hair, piercing black eyes, thick prominent eyebrows, a large, widenostrilled nose, heavy curled moustaches, fat lips, a white beard down to the girth, brawny arms, covered with scars, sturdy legs, and small feet. His clothing was of the finest skins. He was choleric and fierce; but otherwise he had every kingly virtue. Thus he sat, with his son and daughter (the fair Dacil), and his chief captains around him, and scrutinized his ten thousand warriors as they marched before him.

Suddenly, this placid review is disturbed. Two captains, smitten with love for Dacil, disagree and fight, and their men join in the quarrel; so that the hurly-burly of battle brews in a twinkling. In a rage the king leaps from his throne, and is about to speak and act with severity, when the combatants, at sight of him, draw apart. The enamoured captains ask pardon. It is granted, and straightway the next scene in the Easter festival begins.

Tables are spread, and weighted Homerically. We see *gofio*, or flour of barley, milk, butter, honey; among fruits, red strawberries and black cherries; mushrooms and other fungi; kidlings and lambs, goats and sheep roasted whole, and dripping with gravy; cheese, old and new; and other toothsome food. The feast continues merrily until the stars are out. Then there is singing and dancing, until it is time for sleep.

The next day and the next are devoted to athletic games; and thus, amid wrestlings and tournaments, eating, drinking, and all manner of junketing, the nine days of holiday draw to a close.

It was at such a time as this, when the fun was at its height, that a hapless augur dared to forewarn

Bencomo that his kingdom was in peril from certain "white wings" then sailing over the sea. "By the bone of my grandfather". .... swore the king; and, as we know, for his candour, the augur was strung to a tree, to die ignominiously. It was a sad Easter for him, and the first of other sad Easters for the king and all his men.

These picturesque events occurred in the neighbourhood of Laguna, which has since seen many curious sights, and now has an English hotel in its midst.

This city of Laguna, or, to give it its full name, San Cristóbal de la Laguna, is a very solemn place. It stands on a delicious plateau in the mountains, nearly 2,000 feet higher than Santa Cruz, and five or six miles distant from it. In the sixteenth and the two following centuries, the Spanish colony with a capital on the seaboard, was doomed to suffer much at the hands of foemen. But Laguna, safe in its mountain nest, could laugh at Drake and Blake, and defy them to burn its records, or ravage its church plate from the sanctuaries.

So early in the history of the Spanish occupation as 1561, Laguna had 7,220 inhabitants. Santa Cruz then numbered but 770. In 1670, Santa Cruz had risen to 3,728, and in 1706 to 6,847. This increase continued; though Laguna still held the lead. In 1797, however, by its successful resistance to Nelson, Santa Cruz gained the pre-eminence in Tenerife. Thanks to this, it was in 1803 declared to be "*Muy leal, noble è Invicta Villa*," much to the rapture of the citizens; and in 1821 it was made the capital of the province of the Canaries.

In vain did Laguna plead its age, its salubriousness, gentility, holiness, and central position. In the intensity of its hatred for Santa Cruz, it even begged that the seat of the capital might be transferred to the island of Grand Canary, since the honour had gone from itself irrecoverably. This was very currish; but it was in vain. The democratic seaport had triumphed, and Laguna began to decay in earnest.

This old city had, like all cities, a very small beginning. At first it was but a coterie of native huts, set amid the woods bordering the small lake which gave it its name. Its stragetic value was recognized even by the Guanches, and as soon as the conquest was finished, the Spaniards chose it for the seat of Government. The land rises from the north and south shores of Tenerife, and forms an intermediate plateau about ten miles long and two broad, fertile and healthy. Here the city is built, surrounded by orchards and orange groves, with red volcanic hills cumbered east and west of it, and, twenty miles away, the cone of the great Peak soaring over the nearer mountain shoulders. The lake has now been drained away, and vines, grain, beans and potatoes have supplanted the woods of the plain.

It was in the neighbourhood of Laguna, that Dacil, Bencomo's pretty daughter, and Castillo, one of the chief captains of the invading Spaniards, romantically met and loved. The augur who foreboded the ruin of the king, told the king's daughter that her husband was to come from across the sea, but that a thousand disasters of war were to happen ere they were married. The girl believed him, though her father believed him not ; and, clad in her native skins, with her long golden hair over her shoulders, a string of beads round her fair neck, and bright eyes of expectancy, she wandered about the wood of Laguna, awaiting her fortune. Then came the ships, and, by a gracious accident, Castillo was commissioned to reconnoitre the land. Thirsty, he drew near to a spring, in the boughs of the laurel overhanging which lay hid the princess, fearful yet exultant. Her reflection in the water met his eyes, and, heedless of its source, he fell fast in love with it. Later, he looked for the reality thus brightly mirrored, and, having with difficulty discovered her amid the leaves, he gives her his heart at once. His eyes alone bear witness for him ; and he freely curses that " proud tower of Babel," which, by confusing the tongues of the earth, makes it impossible for him to speak what he feels. In his sweet despair he offers her his hand, which Dacil, having from the outset been favourably moved towards the soldier, takes as if for guidance. Then Castillo vows that he is hers for life—" I live in you, and without you I die," and the first act in the drama is ended. Their love being reciprocal, let it go forth for the satisfaction of all romancers that the hidalgo and the savage were eventually united by Holy Church.

The cruellest scene of all in the history of the Guanches, was also enacted here at Laguna. In the beginning of the war, the Spaniards were crushed by Bencomo. They had to withdraw to Santa Cruz to recruit and regain heart. In the meantime, the Guanches mustered in great force by the lake where now stands the city of Laguna. Here, while they tarried in arms, a pestilence came upon them. In ten days, 6,000 of them died. The dead bodies lay corrupting in heaps, adding to the mortality. Dogs preyed upon them, and grew so used to human flesh that they dared to attack the living Guanches as well as the dead. Thus, while the reinforced Spaniards on the coast were timidly speculating about the wisdom of an assault upon the strong position of the natives, these were dying fast by "the visitation of God." At length, an old woman enlightened them about the state of affairs on the plateau. "What keeps you from going into the land?" she asked, bitterly, "since every one is dead of the plague." This was exaggeration. Nevertheless, the scourge was fatal to the native army. The Spaniards advanced, and, with a loss of only forty-five, killed seventeen hundred of the sickly and enfeebled Guanches. Within little more than another year of desultory skirmishes, the island was formally surrendered to Spain, Bencomo deposed, and the Princess Dacil baptized and married to Castillo.

The later annals of Laguna have at least been free from bloodshed of this kind. With the founding by De Lugo of the Church "de la Concepcion," the city grew apace, so that in a few years thousands of stout Spaniards and their wives were established on its lands. So early as 1500, we find the city a municipality, enforcing the erection of houses in the plain, by ostracizing those people who built on the slope or "the upper town," and inflicting a heavy fine upon whomsoever supplied them with bread wine, vegetables, and the other necessaries of life.

The clergy soon asserted themselves among these superstitious, blustering freebooters, who were now content to live and die in a state of civilized peace. They acquired grant after grant of property. The city became an assemblage of monasteries and convents —absolutely church-ridden. But, just as in later times Laguna was perpetually quarrelling with Santa Cruz, so, in the sixteenth century, it was ever full of intestine discord. The churches of the Concepcion and "los Remedios," both built soon after the conquest, disputed for the privilege of the Corpus Christi processions. The municipal authorities decided in favour of "los Remedios," because it was the better building in finish and situation. The clergy of the Concepcion then laid the matter before Charles V., who, in 1523, decreed that the two churches should respectively have charge of the procession in alternate years. But even this great king's order had no permanent effect; for, in 1746, the same question is brought before the sovereign, who again ruled "that the church " de los Remedios " do not call itself the principal, since the two churches are of equal eminence."

Never was a city so promptly made amenable to the clerical yoke. For example, in 1526, it chanced that an important citizen married a certain woman, in disregard of the prohibition of the Bishop's Vicar-General. He was at once put under an interdict for his contumaciousness. It transpired then that, in spite of this, many of his fellow-citizens held intercourse with the spiritual outlaw. The city itself was therefore excommunicated. Public service was suspended. The dead were buried in unconsecrated ground, &c. In their esteem for their fellow-citizen, the stalwart worthies of Laguna bore this awful penance for a while. Finally, however, it was arranged that the cause of the calamity should temporarily go into exile.

Laguna ever professed to be a city of extreme loyalty. The king's accession and marriage, the birth of his offspring, and his death, were all celebrated with great earnestness. The words "Let God be thanked, with bulls, illuminations, and other testimonies of joy" were often heard in the City Council chamber. Thus, in 1527, on the birth of the child who afterwards became Philip II., there were jousts and sports in abundance. Races were run for lengths of satin and damask (six yards for the first, four for the second, and three for the third); wine was set flowing in the streets; twelve bulls were devoted to the amusement of the people; and a sixpenny lottery was instituted. All the blue-blooded Spaniards who had left the old country, and found rich settlement in Tenerife, were convoked to join in the celebration; and they were bidden to deck themselves and their horses with all the splendour of apparel at their command.

Seldom, however, has Laguna been so aroused as, in 1648, by the miraculous sweat on the picture of St. John the Evangelist in the church of the Concepcion. The face of this painting was one morning found bedewed with what appeared to be common human sweat. Dignitaries, lay and ecclesiastical, hurried to see the miracle. To convince the doubting, and to confirm the faith of believers, the picture was wiped, the church closed, and every means of ingress officially sealed. Notwithstanding this, the painting continued to sweat, and so for forty days. It is easy now to explain this wonder as due to the separation (from sun, bad air, &c.) of the mercury and sulphur which composed the vermilion used in colouring the face of the picture: and, therefore, to identify as the sweat the little globular points of quicksilver which would naturally trickle down the canvas. But it is not so easy to understand the excitement caused throughout the whole island by what in those days could not fail to be regarded as a most conspicuous and local revelation of Divine power and favour.

The many governors of the islands who lived at Laguna have provided some strange characters and suffered some curious vicissitudes. One governor embarked at Garachico for the island of Palma, on an official visit, and was transported as a fat prey to the Netherlands, then at war with Spain. The ship was a disguised Dutch privateer. Another governor spent six months as a prisoner among the Moors, who captured him and his vessel on their way to Spain. Don Miguel de Otazo, again, is memorable for his quaint exit from the world. Though almost at the last gasp, he chose to be dressed and armed from head to foot, set in a chair of state, and allowed to brandish his sword with his dying arm. "Michael! Michael! what are you doing?" expostulated a father confessor who was present; "remember that you are but dust and ashes." A few minutes afterwards he died. Don Luis Mayony Salazar, a septuagenarian when he began his rule, was as obstinate a dying man as Don Miguel. The doctor wished to give him a narcotic. "Take it yourself!" retorted the invalid. Excuses did but increase the governor's determination to be obeyed, and so from his death-bed he had the satisfaction to see his medical man swallow the dose, and fall fast asleep instead of himself. The old gentleman then died at his ease with a smile on his lips. Don Diego Navarro, another governor, by his arbitrary measures, wrought the mild Canarians into such hot hatred of him, that one night a multitude assembled under the moon, rang the church bells, took the obnoxious man out of his house, mounted him on a horse, accompanied him to Santa Cruz, and did not leave him until he was safely on board a sailing vessel just about to lift anchor for Europe. Don Andres Bonito, on the other hand, gained innocent fame as the first governor who climbed the Peak.

Of the long line of bishops who have governed the islands in spiritual concerns, perhaps Don Cristóbal de la Camara y Murga made the liveliest stir. He did not use brute force to gain the respect or at least the fear of his flock, like another Canarian bishop. This latter summoned the people together, and then, taking a cheese, cut it in half, and excommunicated one half—which half, to the popular alarm, was seen to be black, while the other half was of the common colour of cheese. Don Cristóbal choose rather to reform abuses than work wonders. Thus no sooner did he set foot in Grand Canary than he issued a pastoral, convoking a diocesan synod, " for the reformation of manners, and the establishment of a spiritual polity in the church in harmony with the decrees of the Council of Trent." Some of the institutes here ordained are singular and instructive of the state of Canarian society in the year 1629. The clergy were to teach the Christian doctrine " at least every Sunday, and during Lent and Advent," either in class-rooms, or by chanting it in the streets. They were to adapt their sermons to their hearers, and avoid eccentric, subtle, dubious, scandalous, and the like subjects. The confessionals were to be in the most public possible parts of the church. Women were not to be shrived in the chapels nor in private houses; but in open confessionals, separated from the confessor by a screen, grating or net; and not before dawn or after vespers. Privilege to receive the Holy Communion daily was rarely to be granted, especially in the case of girls of doubtful virtue. The Eucharist was to be denied to felons under sentence of death.... In treating of the clergy, it was ordained that their beards should be different to the beards of the laity: low and rounded, "to facilitate reception of the Body and Blood of Jesus Christ." They were to wear the biretta, except when it rained, or the sun was hot, or at night, when a hat with a broad brim was allowable. Their gowns were to be of serge or cloth, black, and reaching to the instep. Their underclothing was to be clean, and their shoes were to be properly tied. Except for a journey, they were not to go abroad in short clothes, and then in gray, violet, or black stuffs. In travelling, they might carry a sword, but no other arms. They were not to use a cloak in the streets, squares, or markets. It was forbidden them to play at ball, to gossip, indulge in festivities, take part in politics, follow the chase, or keep dogs. They were not to take snuff before saying mass, nor for two hours afterwards, &c. On the important subject of images, it was properly decreed that "old and misshapen ones, provocative of laughter rather than devotion," were to be destroyed.

In this elaborate work, Bishop Murga's energy was admirable; but it was not universally appreciated, and many rejoiced when, in 1635, he was translated to Salamanca.

In dwelling thus largely upon the clerical element of Laguna, one is historically just. It was the defect of the city that it was dominated by priests and priestly influences. It was also its ruin. In 1767 came the expulsion of the Jesuits, and from that day Laguna, with its many churches and monastic establishments, lost ground. There was brief congratulation when, in 1817, the city received royal sanction for a provincial university. But in 1846 this was degraded into a mere provincial institute, and now its spacious buildings, library of rare old quartos, and overgrown gardens, are the lounge and resort of barely half a dozen schoolboys.

Laguna is a place to dream in. Its narrow, cobbled streets, are bordered by high, old mullioned houses, many with Corinthian portals, and exquisitely chiselled marble heraldic bearings over the doorways. Empty

A LAGUNA PORTAL.

palaces meet the eye, with cobwebs thick across their upper windows, fractured escutcheons, and basements now given up to hucksters who sell pimento and salt fish. Nor can the perfume of orange blossom, which blows from the tangled gardens of these mansions, charm away the melancholy that clings to them. The tiresome streets are as empty as the palaces. The echoing click of his horse's shoes upon the stones is the only sound the traveller hears; though he may be suddenly startled by the clashing of bells from one or other of the tall dark church towers peering above the houses. This riot perchance sends his horse pelting through the silent thoroughfares, with a noise apt to wake the dead that lie dense under the pavements of the churches. But however it may affect the dead, it does not disturb the living of Laguna. Two or three *postigos* move on their hinges, and as many pair of black eyes look forth with mild inquisitiveness. That is all. Apparently, this old city is under a witch's spell, or some horrific ban of the Church, which still holds it inert and speechless. And no sooner is the traveller out of its depressing radius, past the final one of its many wayside crosses, and again between the cheerful hedgerows of the red volcanic fields, than he looks back upon the sombre place, its tall grey houses, touched with dingy green, and studded with mould, and its dark church turrets, with feelings of wonder almost akin to awe.

CHAPTER XII.

The Laguna Churches—Social difficulties—Scheme for the emancipation of women—A working men's club—Ecclesiastical Treasures—The library—The Professor and his pamphlet—Superstitions—The burning of Judas Iscariot—A diocese without a head.

HERE in Laguna I fell among friends, and for five pleasant days lived like a Spanish knight successful in the lists. The large drawing-room of the house was littered with velvets and silks, lent to the church for the recent processions, and now to be stored out of sight. The sadness of Passion Week was over, and on this Easter evening, like Indians home with victims after a raid, we danced amid the silks and velvets.

The next morning we went from church to church, to see the silver bravery of the altars, and the waxen flowers made by the deft fingers of the nuns. Much of the glory of these churches has evaporated, but there is still a wealth of woodwork, gilding, discomforting pictures, and grotesque figures of saints, to satisfy the craving after antiquities. In the Dominican church, we got as near to the inmates of the adjoining nunnery as unregenerate man may get. There are only four and twenty maidens in the establishment now; but their isolation is as emphatic as when there were three score. A stout iron trellis barricades the west end of the church. Behind it the nuns hear the echo of the mass and the sermons. This trellis is pierced at either end by a little hole. The one hole serves as station for the Dominican confessor, within the church, who thus listens to the invisible nun on the other side, while she disburthens herself of her trivial sins. The other orifice is large enough for the passage of a small cup. Hence, daily, the nuns receive the Eucharist. Man gets no nearer to them through the tiresome pilgrimage of their lives, than this priest pushing the holy wine from the church to the convent precincts.

There is something in the Spanish temperament that, at least as much as her education, impels a girl to sigh for the seclusion of the convent. Were the number of nunneries in the island as great now as it was two hundred years ago, it is probable they would all soon have their full complement of inmates. Not long ago, indeed, a young girl, notwithstanding the protests of her parents, expressed her determination to enter this Dominican nunnery of Laguna; and, after other vain attempts to gain her purpose, stole to the church one day, and climbed the twenty feet of iron bars which separated the outer from the inner conventual life. Once within the nunnery, she stayed, and there she is to this day.

To us, of England, it seems that the women of Spain are hardly used. They may not grow up, untrammelled by irksome etiquette, like our own girls. They are pruned by that stupid blunt old knife of propriety until it is a wonder if, as maidens, they have any measure of self-confidence left to them, and no wonder at all if, as married women, they resolve to indemnify themselves for the many restraints which were formerly, with so much injustice, put upon them. The unmarried woman, so long as she is under the paternal roof, may be said to have no character. She bends, unresistingly, whichever way the string pulls. Until she is emancipated in spirit, therefore, it were imprudent to set her face to face on even terms with the outside world. And when the maiden becomes a wife, bred up as she has been bred, she is at the best but an indifferent companion for her husband. He therefore goes his way largely, and she, forsooth, may look abroad for her entertainment, if entertainment she needs. At the club he finds congenial souls; and she may without difficulty gather to her other wives, who, like herself, pine for society, whether conjugal or otherwise. He loses his money at monté, or wagering in the cock-pits; and she, willing to follow in his steps, according to her promise at the altar, finds she may just as easily empty the domestic purse at the feminine card-parties, which are the only dissipation at her command. Is it a marvel, then, that married life here is not as a rule very satisfying? Or that maidens still crave, for lack of other chance of escape from the certain woes of the world, the cold retreat of the convent walls?

Here are some suggestions for the amendment of society in the Canaries, taken from a recent novelette published in Tenerife "with a purpose." It is a gentleman who dares thus to champion the weaker sex; and did not these propositions so forcibly indicate a manner of existence that must be grievous indeed to the sufferers, one could be amused at them :—

"First. The duenna must be suppressed.

"Second. From sunrise to sunset, let it be permissible for a lady to go out-of-doors in our towns *whenever* she pleases.

"Third. Outside the town and in the country, let it be permissible for *two* ladies to go about unattended —from sunrise to sunset only, of course.

"Fourth. That when a young man pays a visit, it be not obligatory for the mamma to stay in the drawing-room the whole time, but that her daughters may safely be left to entertain the callers.

"Fifth. That in the hours of darkness a lady may go out in the company of a gentleman who is either a friend or a relation.

"Sixth. That unnecessary or absurd regulations be no longer protected simply and solely because they were in vogue in times past."

Of course it is not difficult to understand why these severe rules of life have been instituted in a southern country like the Canaries. But here the end does not justify the means employed for its attainment. Neither priests nor people can aver that the morality of a people who have foundling hospitals in every town has touched the bounds of perfection. Common sense, not coercion! this is the cry among the more chivalrous men of the islands; and they stand justified with their motives by their unswerving fidelity to the Church, although it is the Church which has to be thanked for the initiation and perpetuity of this social slavery.

But if Laguna bears witness to its past in its two or three surviving monastic establishments, it can boast of an effort of concession to the march of modern enlightenment. The most splendid of its old palaces, that of the Marquis de Salazar, is now a working men's club. The builder of this superb piece of decorated work was one of the descendants from that stalwart old grandee of Castille, Lope Garcia de Salazar, who, in the time of Alonso the Wise (*circ.* 1284), is said to have had a hundred and twenty sons, who went to the wars escorted by a troop of forty of his sons, and who died in harness at the age of a hundred, fighting in siege of Algeciras. In connection with this house, a tale is told also of a certain native Tenerifan, one Botazo, who from his name may have had Guanche blood in him. Botazo, while engaged with others in its construction, killed a man in a brawl, and fled to Spain for safety. Here he had the luck to meddle in another brawl, whereby he saved the life of a courtier in so creditable a manner that the king summoned him to the palace. "What can I do for you?" asked his Majesty. Botazo could think of nothing more congenial to his tastes than a skin of wine. The monarch straightway, without a thought of the consequences, awarded him a skin of wine daily for the term of his life. It is not recorded how long Botazo lived to enjoy this benefaction.

This palace, then, is now a club house, and we walked through the long high chambers, transformed into library, theatre, billiard-room, &c.; saw the Laguna working man playing at chess, practising on the violin, and reading the daily paper: and descended the broad cool staircase of lava into the dishevelled *patio*. My friend, one of the organizers of the innovation, was proud, with reason, of the success of the movement, but I would fain have had his marquiship back in his palace, silken hangings covering the bare walls as of yore, and the gentle faces of young high-born women brightening the rooms, instead of the squeak of violins, the rustle of journals, and the loud political arguments of a knot of contented cobblers.

The churches of Laguna, though rich in traditional interest, are not in themselves remarkable. The Cathedral is the Church "de los Remedios," in spite of the struggles of the Church of the Concepcion. The white marble pulpit, supported by the figure of an angel, is beautiful, and, added to the influence of the Four Evangelists who are sculptured on its panels, ought to help in inspiring those who mount it. Here also lie the bones of Alonso de Lugo, the *conquistador*, whose image is reproduced, cap-à-pie, as a finial to the decorated reredos of most of the churches of Tenerife. In the Church of the Concepcion one may see the wonderful picture of St. John, which has now exhausted its ability to work miracles like the miracle of 1648. I was better pleased with a dainty little bronze bell, brought forward by the *cura* of one of the older churches. An inscription in old German, and the date, 1551, seemed to link it with the Netherland States, then on the eve of their disruption from the Spanish Empire. The *cura* himself, however, thought lightly of the relic, and would have sold it for a dollar. To him, a rude and horrifying wooden Christ, life size, blotched with blood and wounds, and eloquent of painful dying, was a treasure indeed. This grotesque horror, which ought to have been condemned under Bishop's Murga's rubric, was centuries of age, and had movable limbs. I daresay the sight of it, cunningly manipulated, has scared many a conscience, and moved hearts that a royal mandate would nowadays leave wholly unaffected.

The library of Laguna, incorporated with the educational institute, would gladden a bibliomaniac. It holds about 20,000 volumes; but such volumes! Hardly a duodecimo among them! For the most part they are portly quartos in parchment or vellum, first editions, issued from the more famous printing offices of Europe. They fill one large room from floor to ceiling, and stay on their shelves from the beginning to the end of the year, pleading in vain for patrons. The classics, and patristic, and Canarian literature seem to predominate. But lighter reading also has its niche, for during two or three hours of the day I spent within it, a chubby boy, one of the members of the deposed university, sat opposite to me enthralled in a big Robinson Crusoe, such as a book-loving cleptomaniac would have thought it his duty to lay hands upon. In Canarian literature—that Stygian pool!—the library is of course particularly strong. A man might read for a year, and not exhaust this one subject. Perez de el Christo's reason in 1619 for putting forth his book served but too well as a precedent, so that later it seemed as if no one had a right to esteem himself a patriot unless he could point to a volume or a pamphlet about the islands from his own pen. " It is my own country," says Perez in his pathetic preface, " I was born and baptized in it, and that suffices to make me undertake this work."

From the public library, we went to the private study of a modern savant, the Professor of Natural History to the Institute. This gentleman had recently made a discovery. Digging in a cave upon a seaside property, he had found a spear-head, in material like a stalagmite. This, to his joy, upon inspection, proved to bear certain marks, which were at once assumed to be relics of the Guanche language—in fact, the only existing relic of the kind. The good Professor was now, therefore, composing a pamphlet, to be published with the records of a Madrid learned society, and containing a full description of the innocent spear-head, with I know not what bulk of conjectures as an appendix. The age of the stone was put at B.C. 300: the scratches were to be read from right to left. Thus weighted with honourable responsibilities, it will be criminal ingratitude if the thing do not, in fact, turn out to be, as it is conjectured to be, veritable testimony of the Berber or Phœnician origin of the Guanches; and so, with the best intentions, led by his own amiable enthusiasm, this worthy man is adding his mite to the hillock of Canarian bibliography.

I learn that in the Laguna district, as well as in

other parts of the island, belief in the *mal d'ojo* (the evil eye) is common. An old woman with an ugly expression gets exalted into a witch, no doubt much to her delight and profit, as it is then considered advisable to propitiate her. Again, when I meet a yoke of oxen in a wood, I must instantly look away, lest by inadvertence evil goes from out of me and enters into the beast, to the detriment of its owner. Laguna is full of broad-hatted priests, who can have nothing to do for most of their time. It would be a good work if they were to try to free their flock from some of their superstitions. But they no doubt would find it hard to discriminate equitably between one superstition and another.

Had I arrived at Laguna in Holy Week instead of later, I might have had a surfeit of vestments, processions, and grievous singing. Religion here then puts forth all the pomp at its disposal. I am disappointed of another spectacle. In olden times, and even of late years, it was the custom to concoct a figure kin to our Guy Faux, dress him in smug respectable clothes and Hessian boots, embroider him with crackers and squibs, and, after subjecting him to much abuse, set him on fire. The dummy was of course Judas Iscariot, and the excitement of Holy Week never failed to bring the people, by Easter, to such a pitch of hatred for the traitor, that they vented their malice and revenge against it in a most realistic manner. Sometimes, indeed, the figure was gigantic, with a large hollow stomach, into which certain hapless cats were put. When, on Easter Day, the match was set to Judas, the cats naturally began to scream, and with the advance of the flames, and the tumult of abuse from the spectators, their screams waxed diabolical. The poor creatures were fortunate if, when the fire burnt an opening in the dummy, they could leap forth ere they were roasted.

In Orotava, the holocaust used to end with a noisy lugging of the remains towards the sea-shore. The people whipped the body with all their might while it was within reach; but eventually what was left of it was tied to a boat, taken into deep water, and there finally sunk out of sight.

This year, alas! there is no such spectacle. Funds are wanting, it is said. Perhaps, however, it may be due to the fact that the islands are temporarily without a religious head, and therefore suppositiously in a state of spiritual anarchy. The bishop died recently, and though a successor has been appointed, this gentleman declines the honour. I ask if the nominee holds the bishopric in contempt; and learn that it is quite otherwise. It is etiquette to demur to promotion in the Church. Only when the higher authorities have convinced the bishop-designate that he is a better man than he thinks he is, and have argued him out of the last shreds of his humility—only then will he consent to take the dignity. In the meantime, however, he is as surely the bishop as if he had already been consecrated.

CHAPTER XIII.

The Anaga Hills—The woods of Mercedes—A dainty greensward—The Anaga edges and abysses—The "Cruz del Carmen"—The "Cruz de Afur"—Taganana woods and village—The Cura—A rustic beauty—A Guanche idyl—" El Roque de las Animas "—The monk and the nuns—Bencomo and Zebensin—Tenerifan economics—Return up the " Vuelta"

EARLY one hot April day, my good friend of Laguna and I started for the romantic village of Taganana. This village nestles in a mountain hollow, facing the Atlantic to the north, and is only accessible by a track which winds along the *summits* of the central peaks of the Anaga Mountains. These mountains rise to the height of 3,000 feet, and are as fantastic as a crazy imagination can make them. Their steep sides and ravines are clothed with brushwood, ferns, and flowers, and forests of laurel and heaths; but the peaks themselves are stern trachytic humps and pinnacles, grey and red, round which the cloud masses of one aerial current love to clash and struggle with those of another and contrary current. Our path was often therefore sublime, as well as dizzy and beautiful.

My friend gave me his own horse, a white pink-nosed Andalusian, more than twenty years old, with an original sort of movement, but much vigour. The animal was sick in the lungs, I think, for it wheezed like an asthmatical subject, and sweated so that it soon soaked a coat I had laid athwart it. But the poor beast worked well. We were also accompanied by a man for each of our horses, and to carry the dinner which we proposed to eat sooner or later in Taganana.

Though we were in the saddle by eight o'clock, the heat was oppressive, even in Laguna. A south wind was blowing, which in summer brings Santa Cruz to a purgatorial condition, and is at all times very warm. But it served our purpose, as in all other winds the Anaga hills begin to cloud over soon after dawn, whereas a south wind often leaves them wholly free for the day.

Nothing could be more lovely than the country through which we rode from the grassy streets of the old city in the fresh morning air. The orchards were in heavy blossom, and as full of song as of perfume. Geraniums, aloes, wild roses, and the homely bramble, made a thick hedge by the track side. And we tripped between the big stones of the path, summoned every minute to return the hearty greeting of a peasant with an axe on his shoulder, a troop of bare-legged lasses bound for the city, singing at full pitch while they walked, or older women taking their eggs to the Easter market. Thus we rode into the woods of Mercedes, which form a *cul de sac* to the plateau of Laguna in the north-east; and from the burning sun we stepped into a close cool shade as absolute as that of a pyramid of Cheops. From under our green canopy, we looked back at the glittering city, its fringe of scarlet hills, and the prodigious Pico de Teide, which swelled behind it towards a blue sky without a cloud.

These woods of Mercedes are in every way charming. Miniature cascades trickle down miniature defiles, and no drop of their precious liquid is wasted. In the valley below, the sum of the waters is collected in a conduit, and carried to Laguna and Santa Cruz. Here, the ilex, laurels, and other trees show their gratitude for the moisture by sheathing themselves in a verdure of moss and ferns that even Devonshire might be proud of. And the narrow red ruts in the soil, along which we stumbled uneasily, showed that in this part of Tenerife rain is an institution, and at times abundant enough to be embarrassing.

From these cool natural grots and mossy glens, we ascended to the summit of the woods, and suddenly broke upon a stretch of turf, whence the hills fell boldly towards Santa Cruz and the south. There lay the city, like an irregular patch of snow by the blue sea. Over the water, too, the island of Grand Canary was very clear. But though beauty lay all around us, it was fairest under our very feet. The green turf was the brighter for countless bugloss and white iris.

Leaving this heavenly spot, we made for the mountains and the mountain air. What indescribable vistas to the right and left of us, as we rode on the watershed of the acclivities! In this part of Tenerife, the island forms a peninsula about ten miles long by five or six in width. Imagine, then, with how delicate and reserved a hand Nature has had to work to bring within this small compass mountains and valleys as high and as deep, and, I might almost say, as numerous as those comprised in the two or three hundred square miles of area of our own precious Lake District! Giddy spurs sprang from our narrow path, and plunged down by a series of barbed pinnacles, until their course was hid by their perpendicularity, or veiled by the light haze which lay at the bottom of the abysses. Here were dozens of extensions of the Crib Goch which has given old Snowdon its one element of awe. And contorted into the weirdest shapes, as if a sudden chill had come upon them in the midst of agonized writhings, and thus perpetuated their woes!

With an instinct of worship common to Orientals and Southerners, the Spaniards of Tenerife have built a chapel on the crest of this path to Taganana. The cross which precedes it, and still stands amid the herbs and wild flowers of the restricted plateau, is called "La Cruz del Carmen;" and here the peasants keep periodic festivals, dancing and singing among the clouds, and on the edges of the precipices. There is but little level space around the chapel. This little, however, is bisected by two paths, each equally trodden. Men follow the path to the left; women that to the right. This is an explicit survival of Guanche times, when it was a law that men and women when they met should go on their way by different roads, without interchange of speech—infraction of which law was punishable with death.

A little further along the ridge, and we came to another cross, the "Cruz de Afur," set against a grey precipitous wall of lichened rock, tufted with heath. A third cross, the "Cruz de Taganana," marked the turning point on the very steep mountain which, concavely, guards the village to the south, east, and west.

Between Mercedes and Taganana we passed only two or three habitations on these breezy heights, wooden châlets perched on precarious green slopes, that seemed apt to slide down to the depths with but slight stimulus from the winds and the rains. The tinkling of goat bells, and the horned heads of the goats among the bushes, told us that these were the mountain dairy farms of Tenerife. We saw also, in a dark glen, that seemed as unattainable by the mere aid of legs as the bottom of a coal mine, the small village of Tavorna, with a sugar-loaf hill brooding narrowly over its white houses.

The wood of Taganana, through which we descended with difficulty to the village, takes first rank with the very few sylvan spots in this hot Atlantic island. It is as dense as a tropical forest. Its laurels grow to timber, and, with the heaths, all moss-clad and fern-becovered as to their trunks, are fifty and sixty feet high. Springs burst from the summit of this mountain about 3,000 feet above the sea, and perenially tumble their waters, by cascades and pellucid pools, into the village below. Northern vegetation follows the descent of the rivulets, the ferns and grasses attaining a gigantic size: and when, after two hours' work, we get clear of the decaying trunks and stones, and are on the hem of the village, we find bananas and palm trees as eager to profit by the water as, 2,500 feet higher, were the brackens and ivies of England and Scandinavia.

The path down to Taganana is a severe task for a horse. La Vuelta de Taganana (the turning or zigzag of Taganana), as it is called, is a spiral with sixty-four twists in it, some of which are at so small an angle that a horse slides down them, whether he likes it or not.

Once again we rode at length from the shade of the forest into the full blaze of a southern sun. The heat in the red-roofed little village was indeed quite suffocating. The very sea in front of us shone with a quiet but intense glare that made one gasp to look at it. And so by the time we had stumbled into the Plaza, and to the door of the white church, we felt completely unstrung, and demoralized in body. We sat on a low wall sheltered by some pepper trees, gave up the horses, and left to the men the work of finding a hospitable citizen who would lend us a cellar, as the most desirable of dining-rooms on such a day.

Then came the priest of the village, a white-haired old man, and a friend of my friend's. He had lived in this quiet little nook for thirty or forty years, hardly ever leaving it for a day or two in the large towns so near and yet so hard to reach. Inn there was none in the place; but his own house, a square ochre building, with a clump of dragon trees and palms at its eastern corner, was at our disposal. It was on a ledge of rock two hundred feet above us: a climb out of the question on such a day! And so we ate our eggs and bread, and drunk our wine where we were, under the curious gaze of the women of the house.

Taganana claims to rear the finest women in Tenerife. Even the priest acquiesced when my friend quoted a saying about the virtue and the beauty of the ladies of his flock. "But," he added, "they are neither so good nor so beautiful as they ought to be. Like others, they are getting to have their own way too much, and it does not become them." However, we had the fortune to see one swarthy, blue-eyed woman with long black hair, who might well have moved a misanthrope. She had the bold, almost impudent, expression of a gipsy, and suckled a child in public. Her mother was reputed to have been even handsomer than herself; and for many years an object of interest to visitors as "the beauty of Taganana." These two women may be representatives of the Northmen, who, according to a legend, set foot in the place before the Spaniards came. They may, on the other hand, be descendants of royal Guanches; for it was in these overhanging woods, to the music of doves and falling water, that the Princess Guacimara, daughter of the king of Anaga, and the love-stricken Ruyman, carried on their sweet unconscious courtships, disguised from each other, what time their sires and friends were straining nerve and sinew against the Spanish invaders. Viana tells the story in his epic.

But the mildest sketch of Taganana would be imperfect if no mention were made of the extraordinary rocks on the east of the village, and the no less eccentric mountain pinnacles to the west. The former are two in number, the one conical, and the other abrupt, precipitous, and unscalable. The bolder of the two is indeed a fair diminutive of the Matterhorn, though its red scar knows nothing of snow. Where it falls into the sea it may be fifteen hundred feet perpendicular, and it offers a tempting climb of many hundred feet, nearly "as steep as a house," from the level of the village. The priest called it, "El Roque de las Animas" (the Rock of Purgatory); and the name is a good one. The two mountains are commonly called "the Men."

As for the serrated pinnacles in the west, wrought by rude Titanic gashes in the ridge of a mountain, the insulated rocks shapen fantastically by wind and weather, they are known as "the Monks and the Nuns." The good priest had no difficulty in distinguishing the ladies from the gentlemen; but the story itself was too scandalous to be communicated. Seen from the north-western extremity of the Taganana hollow, they are very striking, with bushes of golden gorse where they break from the mountain mass.

In spite of the heat, we suffered the *cura* to lead us to the seaward boundary of his parish. Else, he said, we should miss a grand scene of shore cliffs and surf; and he was right. From the edge of the valley of Taganana, where the land slopes steeply into the sea, we looked east at the pointed islets of Anaga, basaltic rocks not unlike our home "Needles"; and west to the Punta del Hidalgo, another astounding agglomeration of mountain-tops, like the fretwork of a huge saw running out into the sea.

Where we stood among the aloes and dusty fig-trees on the boundary of the village, we were also, unconsciously, on the limits of the old principalities of Anaga and Hidalgo. For into such petty realms was Tenerife subdivided after Tinerfe's decease. Of the master of this Cape of Hidalgo, a story survives which is but another tribute to the sterling worth of Bencomo, the King of Taoro. Zebensin, the Achimencey of the district, was son of a bastard of Tinerfe, and as such was of less esteem than the legitimate princes of the nine greater divisions of the island. The appellation Achimencey (poor knight —Hidalgo—or ruler) was given to him in contrast with that of Mencey, borne by the other sons. And he seems to have exemplified the hard condemnation whereby the sins of the fathers (if among the Guanches bastardy could have been regarded as a sin in the sire) are visited upon the children. His principality was only a seabound promontory, and so he stole what he needed from his neighbours.

The aggrieved shepherds bore their losses for a time, but eventually complained to Bencomo. This sturdy king at once set forth from his palace, alone, and *incognito*. When he reached the cave of Zebensin, he found that princeling about to dine on a kid which he had cooked with his own hands. Without preface, and using the roast meat as a text for his upbraidings, Bencomo dilated to his half-cousin on the iniquity of his conduct, in living upon the hard-acquired possessions of others. The Hidalgo (Achimencey) stammered excuses, and, on the pretext of seeking food fit to be set before the King of Taoro, tried to leave the cave. But Bencomo, taking him by the arm, detained him, and, with angry eyes, bade him take no trouble about preparing meat and drink for him. "Be warned," he said, "and know that a prince must not live upon the blood of his unfortunate vassals, whom he ought always to regard with the loving care of a father. Give me *gofio* and water, and that will be for me a banquet delicious beyond anything."

Bencomo, with his own fingers, mixed the flour and water, and then ate the dough, unseasoned even with salt. "Ah, cousin Zebensin," he continued, "if only you knew how savoursome this is, when compounded by clean hands, and eaten at the expense of no tears from the poor! Tender kids and fat lambkins, cooked in milk, but cruelly reft from their dams, and from the bosoms of the helpless shepherds, will, so far from making you rich, only make you detestable and deserving of all my wrath."

One is glad to know that the scapegrace prince took this lesson to heart. He professed repentance and determination to amend his life; and, confiding in him, Bencomo recommended the convert to his cousin the Prince of Tegueste, who gave him the control of a hundred shepherds.

The poor knight of the Punta no doubt rejoiced in his reclamation to the paths of virtue. For Tegueste is now, as it was then, one of the most smiling provinces in Tenerife. A carriage road runs down to it, between the mountains, bordered by blue gum trees, cork trees, and geraniums, and its rich lands are devoted to vines and country estates for the prosperous merchants and officials of Laguna and Santa Cruz. The Punta, on the other hand, is a hard sterile rock, projecting into the sea.

Taganana, from its situation at the base of a great amphitheatrical mountain, boasts of good soil, and abundant harvests of everything except barley, which seems choked by the heat. But elsewhere in the neighbourhood, and indeed all over the island, the inevitable results of reckless denudation are being felt. No sooner were the Spaniards in Tenerife than they began to cut down and even to fire the forests, without a thought of posterity. Two centuries of this work changed the character of the island largely; water grew scarcer every year; and then the Government interfered. But even now the charcoal burners give the high pines little rest; and though the Government nominally preserves the forests, it seems to be indifferent to the wisdom of replantation. Thus, when phenomenal rains come, the more precarious vineyards and grainfields, deprived of the shelter they got from the patches of woodland behind or above them, yield before the downrush of the quick waters, and, like the swine of Gadarene, slide headlong into the sea or the subjacent valleys. Every score of years many score of careful acres disappear wholly from the bare rocks upon which they were either laboriously raised, or had been brought into cultivation, when laurels, chestnuts, or pines, offered them some protection and encouragement.

Under these circumstances, and considering the fabulous fertility of the best kind of it, land in Tenerife is very costly. Everything, however, depends on its vicinity to water, without which it were but dust and ashes, save in certain parts of the Laguna district, and in the cloud zones. In the Vale of Orotava, £300 an acre is paid; but, as a set off, it must be remembered that the returns are there almost mathematically sure. The fields are irrigated by strong canals of cement, and by due payment of the water rate for so many hours' flow per week, this, the only incentive to full crops that is needed, is assured. In the Laguna district, however, where irrigation is not thought to be essential, because of the frequent rains, occasional years of ruin diversify the life of the agriculturist, as with us in England.

Farming implements are primitive in Tenerife. An improved exhibition plough serves as a spectacle of wonder; but no one thinks of substituting such an invention for the simple cross-sticks, like the old Highland caschroms or cascheedas. These have served generations, and are likely to serve as many more generations. The other day someone introduced washballs among the peasantry in a certain part of Tenerife. They were tried for a brief time, then universally discarded. Clear spring water, a couple of pebbles, and some native soap, were much preferred.

The principles of economics seem to be but feebly

understood here. A man wishing to buy an estate or a house would be asked to pay a preposterous sum. He could get the same property, however, by advancing upon it in mortgage half, or even a quarter, of its market worth. A man does not borrow money upon his land until he has brought his mind to the wrench of parting with it. When he borrows, therefore, he assumes that he is selling. He does not think of repaying the loan or mortgage, but chuckles if he can coax the mortgagee, in a friendly way, to advance him a little more money upon the title deeds. Thus the chain tightens, and in time he quite acquiesces in the legal conveyance to which he was from the first thoroughly resigned. In this way, property worth twenty thousand dollars passes into other hands for five thousand dollars.

But I am wandering indeed from sunny Taganana. When the *cura* had shown us his landscapes and the more beautiful of his parishioners, and the little church, odorous with rose-leaves, and curious for an emblematic picture where Death is portrayed hewing his victims limb from limb with a madman's ferocity—then, he said, we had exhausted Taganana.

Besides, we had the terrible ascent of the Vuelta before us. In truth, this was a most formidable business. One of our men had drunk all the wine we had left, which was much; and he was therefore incapable. My horse sweated and stumbled and gasped till the still woods echoed with its groans and efforts. Of course I did not ride the poor animal. But I could not prevent the drunken man hanging on to her long white tail, though at the peril of his life. The other day, in the course of this climb, a horse had fallen over into the stream, where it purled eighty to a hundred feet below; but neither that nor any humanitarian notions would prevent a tipsy Spaniard from working his beast to the uttermost.

After an absence of ten or eleven hours, we reached Laguna in the short gloaming, when the Peak in the distance was capping itself for the night.

CHAPTER XIV.

Traditions about the Peak—First Account of an Ascent—Preparations for the Climb—Our Start—Glorious Day—In the Clouds—Above the Clouds—El Pico de Teide—Stages of the Ascent—The Retama Plain—Obsolete Hardships—At the Foot of the Pyramid—The Estancia—Bedmaking and Eating—Sunset—A Restless Night—On by Moonlight—An Unexpected Meeting—The Rambleta—Sunrise—On the Summit—In the Crater—Hot and Cold—Sulphur Men—The Ice Cave—The Descent.

"SINCE experience proves that a man cannot breathe on the top of the Peak of Tenerife . . ." From this unsound predicate, Jacob la Pereyre, an ancient author, writing about the Universal Deluge, makes the terrible deduction that, if the Flood had risen a few yards higher, no one would have been able to breathe in the Ark.

Before mountain climbing came into fashion, others besides this old writer had exaggerated ideas of the Peak. Gregorio Leti, a biographer of Philip II., says of it, " There is in Tenerife a mountain so immeasurably high, that it is impossible to climb it without great difficulty, and in less than three days. Hence it is believed to be the highest in the world. Nevertheless, it is said that from its base to its very summit are to be found the dwelling-places of a number of people, absolutely wild and cruel, and that they are more like ferocious beasts than reasonable beings." Even so late as the beginning of this century, certain geographers held to the opinion that the Peak was nowhere surpassed in height. But the *ipse dixit* of Leti's about natives residing on its summit is very odd, when we remember that for centuries this has been a crater of hot sulphur. A man might as reasonably be said to reside in a half-quiescent lime-kiln.

Neither the Guanches nor the early Spaniards felt much affection for the Peak itself. Its very name was hurtful to polite ears—*Echeyde* (Hell); from which, of course, the more modern Teide is a simple transition. So long ago as 1402, in a navigation treaty between England and France, reference is made to the piracies of a certain Norman, Béthencourt, the original conqueror of Lanzarote and Fuerteventura, and to Tenerife as the "Ile d'Enfer!" And certainly, if, in the middle ages, the cone rising from the sea more than 12,000 feet was then (as it is said to have been) in a state of constant eruption, the sight of it, visible, according to Humboldt, for a circuit of 260 leagues, must have been very impressive to generations of men prone to see diabolical agency in all uncomfortable phenomena of nature. Hence, too, the Spanish peasantry called it "the devil's cauldron, in which all the food of hell is cooked."

Perhaps the first detailed account of an ascent of the Peak is that by Sprat, Bishop of Rochester, in the infantine days of the Royal Society. It narrates the trials of certain English merchants in 1650. These gentlemen were probably the local agents for the sale in England of the wine of the Canaries, which was then in full fame. But their loyalty was soon to be shrewishly requited by the marriage of Charles II. with a Portuguese princess, and the consequent patronage of Portuguese, and notably Madeira wines, to the detriment of the Canarian trade. They got to the top, having felt many portentous tremblings of the earth on the way. But, when they came to open the luncheon-basket, they found their wine so congealed that it had to be thawed, the brandy debilitated, and the wind so strong that they could scarcely drink the health of the King of England, or fire a volley in honour of His Majesty. These good royalists were doubtless made much of when they safely returned to the lowlands; and their performance has gained them immortal fame in the Transactions of the Royal Society.

But let the truth be told. Among all the mountains of the globe, there can be few of the same height as the Peak to compare with it for the ease with which it may be ascended. Though its final 3,500 feet are steep, with an inclination of from 35° to 42°, the average slope is not more than 12·30°. From first to last, life is never endangered. It is not even necessary to pass a night on it. By leaving Orotava in the evening, and travelling through the darkness by the aid of the moon or torches, it is possible to be on Teide before sunrise. Nor is the night that is conventionally spent between the big boulders, known as the English halting-place

(Estancia de los Ingleses), by any means so arduous an experience as one expects to find it. A camp in the open air at an elevation of 10,000 feet ought to be a little trying; and that is all that it is. But when the deed is done, and duly subjected to quiet analysis in retrospect, one is forced to admit that the toil is trivial, and amply compensated by the scenic and other rewards attendant upon it.

We made our ascent on May 11 and 12. By the Spaniards, it was thought to be rather soon in the year: to their warm imaginations the least snow seems a very formidable obstacle to mountain climbing. What, then, were they likely to think of the two Englishmen who, so early as March 12, together with two or three ladies, had dared to make the trip? Indeed, events seemed to prove that these brave compatriots of ours were somewhat harebrained. For, though they safely reached the top, over the sheets of ice which masked the Piton, as the cone is called, it was at no little risk, seeing that they were unprovided with ice-axes. Moreover, they fell out with their guides, who stayed below, leaving them to their own bold wills. And as for the ladies, they gave it up after a while, reserving what little strength and breath remained to them for the congratulation of their lords when these descended with the glow of victory upon them. But for many weeks after this exploit the Spaniards of Tenerife used the word *loco* (fool, or madman, according to your humour) and Englishman almost as if they were synonymous. Nor dare I repeat for English readers what a stalwart old hidalgo said to me in free comment upon the part played by our countrywomen in the excursion.

We started from Puerto at seven o'clock in the morning, under the care of Diego Zamorra, a guide. Zamorra is not the best guide of the place, but his betters happened, on this occasion, to be out of the way. We were a party of three *caballeros*, and, to look after our horses, and attend the two mules that accompanied us, laden with overcoats and wraps to keep us warm in the night, Diego took with him a brace of stout boys; so that in all we mustered six human beings and five brute beasts. As provisions, we carried good store of roast chickens, soup, eggs, bread, butter, and cheese, and some bottles of wine, all provided by our hotel; a sack of potatoes and *gofio* for the boys' supper; and, lastly, a barrel of water. The water was a very important article of freight, for we had to traverse a parching desert of pumice sand, quite innocent of springs, and for more than twenty-four hours, to be wholly dependent for our supply upon what we carried.

Our cavalcade made a stir as we rode through the streets of the red-roofed little town. Diego and the boys knew everyone we met—from the big, brown, bare-chested driver of the span of oxen going out into the fields, to the withered little old crone hurrying her one goat from door to door, with a tin cup in her hand to measure the milk she sold as she went along. It is not every day that Teide is assailed, and therefore people of all ages, and many different professions, came to their doors when they heard our men's proud babble to their friends about the Englishmen and El Pico.

A GOATHERD OF TENERIFE.

Nor was I less elated than the men. It was a glorious day. The sea below us did but ripple under the blue sky, save where it throbbed into white foam on the rough black lava shore. The country was in summer beauty. The geraniums were still in flower, as pertinaciously as if they bloomed but for one month instead of twelve months in the year. Oleanders sweetened the air. The vines had leafed and begun to blossom. The fig-trees and mulberries were darkening with ripe fruit. Myriads of poppies, red and yellow, twinkled in the grain fields, though many a bronze patch showed where barley had already been cut and carried. Stately palms, broad, ragged bananas, glossy eucalypti, and great aloes were on all sides of us, cheek by jowl with our own humble daisies. The villas of this happy country were as gay as its vegetation. They stood forth from a bower of foliage—red, blue, buff, green, yellow, white, or brown, sometimes stencilled in pretty patterns; they and their surroundings alike reflected in the still pools of the water tanks, which are a necessary appurtenance of every garden. Of the Vale of Taoro or Orotava as a whole, I have already said something. But on this particular day, to its other constituent parts must be added a straight bank of motionless black cloud, which hangs down the mountain-side to within about 3,000 feet of the sea. We cannot see through or above the cloud. But our climb through and above the cloud is to be one of the stages of our work towards the Peak. The Peak itself is invisible: the bank of cloud over the valley had not lifted for nearly a fortnight. Out at sea, fifty miles away, it could be seen; but to us, close at hand, it was a mere matter of faith.

We climb through the valley, past the two remarkable volcanic humps which are so bold a feature of it to the village of Palo Blanco, almost on the hem of the overhanging vapour. Tropical vegetation is now below us; we are among budding chestnut trees, potato fields two months later than those on the sea level, meagre barley, and pear and cherry trees instead of figs, bananas, and oranges. Close at hand, to the right, is the precipitous wall of Tigayga (so named after a brave Guanche warrior), about 7,000 feet above the sea. It is in the profoundest shadow, thanks to the clouds. Not even the profuse fresh verdure of its steep ravines can do much to modify the gloom of its great precipices. And here we leave behind us the two famous villages of the Upper and Lower Realejo, so closely associated with the history of the conquest.

As Palo Blanco offers us our last chance of fresh water, we halt by its fountain. One by one, the animals are allowed to take a long and a strong pull. Poor beasts! they seem to understand that they have an unpleasant prospect before them. They drink and drink, until Diego wrenches them violently from the trough; and then they stand aside, and watch the next animal having its turn, with eager eyes and nervous ears, ready to make a rush the moment the man's attention is relaxed.

Hitherto, the track has been a thoroughfare of some importance. We have had rocks and stones to clamber over which we would have avoided if we

A BEGGAR OF TENERIFE.

could; but we have never been out of touch with human beings. Country people descending to sell their market stuffs were constantly, to their surprise, coming upon us. In the fields, too, were men and boys, weeding or hoeing their potatoes. And children of all ages, bright-eyed and alert, seemed ever on the look-out for such objects of interest as strangers. "Mariquita!" screams a beldame from her hovel porch to a well-grown lass at work in the fields a few hundred yards ahead of us, "make haste, and be ready to ask the gentlemen for a *quartile* when they pass you." A *quartile* is rather less than a halfpenny, but it is enough to stir the desire of Mariquita; and so, when we reach the boundary of her field, there she stands, with her large dark eyes full of appeal, and her brown little palms outstretched as she beseeches for a "*quartile, señor, quartile!*"

This unabashed begging is quite a strong feature in Tenerife, since the English have acquired the habit of visiting the island. The children beg, whether they want anything or not. Their parents turn them all loose upon a stranger whenever the chance offers. They plead laughingly, but with a perseverance that does not incite their victims to laugh. However, this time we sent Mariquita back to her potatoes with a smile of real contentment on her face; and, ere we were in the clouds, we could hear her singing away like the larks above her, while she broke the red earth with her old-fashioned hoe.

For the next half-hour or more, we ascend through a sparse wood of heaths, with the fog grey and persistent all around us. We naturally button our coats as we enter this zone of vapour. But it is only for a minute or two; as we soon realise that the cloud is a dry cloud, and that we are rising through it to approach a region of heat instead of cold. We have gone but a little way, in fact, ere it is apparent that the sun is shining brilliantly above us. And so, at an altitude of 4,030 feet, we emerge from the shadows, and look around to discover that we are in the clear upper air, with a sky of the purest blue over our heads, and a powerful sun in the heavens. The summits of the lower slopes of the Peak, and the long back of Tigayga, seem close to us in this refined atmosphere. They are suffused with a lovely coral-pink and blue haze, through which the scant bushes of retama, which alone diversify them, gleam like spots of silver. Towards the head of the Guimar valley, on the south side of the island, the rocks are a dazzling crimson, due to the ferruginous nature of their volcanic earth. But the oddest impression of all is that of the very clouds just left beneath us. They stretch from the one great mountain flank of the valley to the other—the dark masses looming from them like islets in a sea. The vapour hangs immobile in mid-air, with a broad, undulated surface, in the most singular of contrasts with the distant fringe of blue sea, which forms our horizon, I know not how many miles away. The cloud was tenuous enough when we were enfolded in it; but, viewing it at our feet, and from the untroubled upper air, we pity our friends in Orotava, that they are cloaked from the sun by a nebulous stratum

THE PEAK FROM PUERTO: SHOWING THE TIGAYGA RIDGE.

of such apparent weight, opacity, and obstinate determination. It is a distinct migration from northern to southern climes. Swallows are soaring about our heads, happy in the sunlight, and quite careless of the serious fact that they are nearly a vertical mile above the sea.

But with this change in our surroundings begins the real heat and toil of the day. Of course, there is no more shade to be expected. The only vegetation hence to the other side of the Peak, ten miles away, is the retama, a shrub in close affinity with the

> Odorata ginestra,
> Contenta dei deserti . . . . ;

and though on the pumice plains the retama broadens so that its branches attain a total girth of forty or fifty feet, it is never tall enough to cast a shadow of service to man. The track winds upwards by tiny defiles in the grey rock *débris*, until it brings us to a land of absolute desolation. From slopes of yellow pumice dust, hard to climb, and suffocating alike to man and beast, we clamber towards masses of reddish lava, sharp and irregular, and to the eye as fresh and capable of annoyance as if it had flown forth from the side of the Peak only the other year. The brilliant lichens which fasten upon the lower lava, and hasten its decomposition, are lacking here. Everything, in short, is lacking, save the burning sun above us, which radiates from the fused iron under our feet to a degree that makes us gasp.

This being so, it is hard to condemn our guides for the want of self-control that is proverbial with them in an ascent of Teide. They are for ever falling into the wake of the mule that carries the water-barrel, and one after another seizes a moment when he thinks he is unobserved, to pull out the plug, and tilt some liquor down his parched throat. *Muy bonito* (very pretty!), remarks Diego, with an indefinite wave of his hand over these hideous mounds of red and russet lava; and, under this pretence of devotion to the interests of his employers, whom he hopes he has thereby adequately diverted from himself, he goes in the rear to the barrel. After a time, however, we decide to keep our water mule in front. A little of such larceny is permissible, whereas much might be disastrous.

We are more than 5,000 feet up before we round the mountain shoulders sufficiently to get our first view of the Peak from high ground. It peeps over a near heap of scoriæ with an affectation of littleness that might have deceived us. But the guides were of course on terms of acquaintance with it, and hailed the diminutive pink-purple cone with a convincing shout of, "El Pico de Teide! El Pico! El Pico!" By and by, we saw more of it. The ethereal beauty of its summit was modified by the stern black lava pyramid upon which it appeared to stand, even though the lava, in its turn, was made somewhat less depressingly gloomy by the white veins of snow which scored it. It continued to swell upwards as, little by little, we rose to the level of the great crater-bed of the Cañadas, in one part of the circumference of which it is set with the completest symmetry; so that, by one o'clock, when we were on the skirts of the crater, and 6,000 feet above the sea, we saw it before us from base to summit. It was then a superb spectacle, but its angle of elevation seemed so very steep that I fancy we viewed it with feelings of alarmed respect as much as admiration. But we were tired and scorched, and not in a fit state for judicious appraisal of the old volcano's difficulties. And long ere we had finished our lunch—sprawled on the hot sand, in the middle of a Titanic coil of scoriæ, and under an improvised screen of wraps and retama bushes — we voted the Peak a hill of infinite assumption, and ourselves able to manage a mountain twice its height, with guides or without them.

The ascent of Teide, from Orotava, may be conveniently divided into a certain number of stages. Of these the first must end with the Monte Verde, or Green Mountain, where we were in the clouds and among the heaths. The second is the Portillo, or entrance to the Cañadas. We were close to it when we lunched at mid-day. It is an imaginary gate to the third stage, on the Plano de Retamo, or Plain of the Retama, a wearisome plateau of yellow pumice, varied with blocks and small fragments of obsidian, and studded with the welcome shrub that gives it its name. This plain is the ancient crater of Tenerife, from which the Pico proper soars upwards. It is about eight miles in diameter, from 7,000 to 8,000 feet above the sea, and girdled by the angular rocks of the Cañadas, striking contortions of superb reds and browns, and in places rising nearly 2,000 feet above the plateau itself. Where we enter the plain by the Portillo, the Cañadas' rocks seem to have been carried away by a ponderous stream of old lava. The gate is, in fact, forced: the toilsome climb across the scoriæ antecedent to our lunch time was over the molten mass which, ages ago, had wrought their ruin on the circle of the Cañadas. The fourth stage of the ascent is the passage of the Montaña Blanca, a rounded hump at the foot of the Peak, and of a pumice material rather whiter than that in the plain. The fifth stage includes the first thousand feet of the climb of the pyramid—a tedious course, amid lava and obsidian in immense blocks, and terminating at the Estancia de los Ingleses. Here is a level space upon which are poised two or three great boulders of rock about twenty feet high. It has acquired so recommendatory a name from the fact that our countrymen have been content to try and sleep between these stones on their way up to the final crater. I do not know when the place was so christened. Early in the eighteenth century it had the name. Possibly, therefore, it memorialises the halt of the party of scientists who paid the Peak a visit in the reign of Charles II. These gentlemen obtained special ambassadorial permission to make experiments upon Teide. The Spanish envoy at the Court of St. James's thought they were joking when they declared their purpose of crossing the sea to weigh the air on the summit of the Peak of Tenerife. He repeated the joke to Charles II. himself, with much added laughter of his own, and was then rather disturbed to find that the King of England chanced to be one of the promoters of the Royal

Society, under whose auspices the expedition was being arranged. Accordingly, one may assume that these valorous servants of science have given us this creditable mark of fame in a distant island of Spain. From the Estancia, one ascends another thousand feet, over sliding pumice of a vexatious kind, to the site called Alta Vista. Here is a white wooden house in a sheltered recess. It is a solid erection that would soon be provided with a refreshment contractor, and two or three beds for travellers interested in the sunrise, if the Peak of Tenerife were in England. As it is, the house belongs to a sulphur company, still engaged in exploiting the sulphur of the Peak. Its door is kept locked, and only by its window is it possible to enter, in acrobatic fashion, among the pickaxes and mattocks. It was close to this house, 10,700 feet above the sea, that Piazzi Smythe, in his laborious surveyal of the characteristics of the Peak, set up his tent some years ago, and lived for a while in extreme cold and extreme heat. Here also, a few years later, Dr. Marcet followed Piazzi Smythe's example, and wondered with professional wonder how a constitution merely human could bear the test to which it was subjected by a temperature of the sun's rays during the daytime of about 212°, and a temperature at night of but 35° or 40°, a variation in twenty-four hours of 175°! The ledge of Alta Vista is the sixth stage of the ascent. The seventh is a slight semi-circuit of the final cone of the Peak, known as the Rambleta; about another thousand feet higher than the sulphur house. This is a dreadful pile of obsidian blocks of lava, thrown into confused association by a pre-historic eruption. Between the masses there are innumerable fissures into which it would be awkward to slip. And yet, for all this thousand feet of vertical rise, the ascent has to be made by a series of careful skippings from lava point to obsidian edge, and from obsidian edge to lava point. One is fortunate to reach the Rambleta with no worse wounds than barked shins and frayed hands. At the Rambleta, the work seems done. The rosy Peak is just above, at the head of a fine straight slope, only some five hundred feet high. But this slope is at an angle of from $40°$ to $42°$. Moreover, it is little else than a cone of fine ash and dust. Humboldt has averred that an angle of $42°$ is the steepest that can be climbed over ground covered with volcanic ash. We may, therefore, take it for granted that this final pull up the cone of the Peak to the crater rim, which is the eighth and last stage of the climb, is all but impossible. It is certainly an insufferable flounder. But it may be avoided or mitigated by bearing to the left, and scaling a lava flow which dives from the actual crater.

After luncheon amid the lava, we were ready for the third stage of our travel—the Retama Plain. In the records of those ancient explorers who published their narratives in quartos, or among the pages of learned periodicals, the trials to be endured from this pumice are said to be severe. I expected to be blinded by the glare of the sun reflected from it, and choked by the dust eddied by the wind and stirred by the feet of our horses. No such thing, however.

The sun was hot, but was so far from depriving the landscape of interest by the torture it inflicted that I recall this pale yellow plain, broken with purpled pinnacles of molten rocks, and bestrewn with the silver-grey retama bushes, as one of the most picturesque tracts of country in my experience. Here and there the retama had been burnt, and the long whitened trunks and roots, where they had been pulled from the soil, lay along it like the bleached bones of an extinct race of mammoths. But little imagination was necessary to make us fancy ourselves in a section of the Sahara, untrodden by man, and invaded by beasts only at the peril of their lives.

Again, according to the old voyagers, who ought to have been tough enough, the cold on this plain is as acute as the heat of the sun is prodigious. Their finger-nails became discoloured, they lost the use of their hands, and the skin of their lips roughened to such a degree that these bled when they talked.

Well, I would not discredit such records; but none of these incidents came to relieve the monotony of our tramp across the desert. After the Peak, with which by this time we were thoroughly at home, nothing took our attention like the water-barrel. Of course the dust irritated our eyes; but this was only a trivial novelty in the midst of a scene which, with its various parts, was wholly novel and absorbing. Two or three patches of snow in the sheltered side of the Montaña Blanca informed us of our slow but certain progress upwards. Two or three hawks skimming in this clear blue air were the only objects to remind us that we had other living beings in our vicinity. The almost inaudible thud of our animals' hoofs in the hot sand, their quickened breathing, and that of the men, were the only sounds to be heard in this still, soundless plain. The clouds, now far below us, yet fenced the lower world from us like the broad brim of a hat. We seemed in another zone of life, with a bluer sky and an intenser sun dominant over us.

With occasional brief halts to rest the animals, and allow the men to wipe their streaming faces and begin a fresh cigarette, we continued thus to the foot of the actual pyramid. The view upwards is here instructive and extraordinary. All of the steep slope that we can see at one glance is seamed with black lava rivers. These are of lengths as various as their courses. Some have run down to the plain, and mixed with the pumice. For the most part, however, they do not overstep the slope. Here they have cooled, and here, under ordinary atmospheric influences, they ought long ago to have decomposed, and formed a soil more or less cultivable. But the atmosphere at this altitude is extraordinary, and so these rivers are preserved in all their freshness. The pumice beneath them is also littered with a number of vast red-brown spherical boulders, natural bombshells spewed from the Peak in the course of centuries, and sent rolling down the slopes until they have come to rest about 4,000 feet from their starting point. Orotava lies north-east of the Peak ; but we have to make a detour ere beginning to climb the pyramid. So sharp is the rise from the sea to the north and north-west that, with a good impetus, a stone might bound from the crater mouth, and never cease moving until it fell into the sea, several miles distant.

Our day's work is almost over at this point. It is already four o'clock—time we were making our beds, building a house, and laying the supper table. With this cheerful prospect before us, therefore, we worm our way up the shoulder, breasting current after current of lava, and grinding the pumice into a powder that soon paints us all a bilious ochre colour from head to toe. The men do not dissemble their groans. Even the water cannot give them much satisfaction now; for the heat and the shaking have made it look and taste like a puddle in a clay-pit. In fact, we all hail the rocks of the Estancia; and even the bits of beer-bottles, the rigid crusts, and the relics of tins that once held potted lobster, are welcomed as genial indications that we are, in a measure, at home, rather than as nauseating proofs that nothing is sacred from the invasion of civilised beings. The horses are soon tethered. They know the Estancia, and instinctively go to the spot where they lingered through a restless night the last time they were up the Peak, may be a month ago. As for the men, their first impulse is to indulge in *dolce far niente*. We have, therefore, to brisken them a little, point to the mellow glow creeping over the mountains and plains beneath us, as signs of the coming night; mark out our bedrooms, and send our chamberlains in quest of retama for our couches, for the big fire we propose keeping up through the night to warm us, and for the little fire that is the first step towards supper. We take upon ourselves the more artistic task of building a wall on the weather side of the opening between the rocks, of laying the tablecloth, and drawing corks. And when all these agreeable preliminaries are ended, there is time to walk to and fro in the pumice alongside the Estancia, and watch the death of the day. Our thermometer, set in a niche of our bed-chamber wall, is at 45°, while the sun is yet above the horizon. But the sun's heat is by this time quite withdrawn from us, as we are on the south-east side of the mountain. Nor do we expect a much greater accession of cold than we already feel at this bracing height of 9,770 feet above the sea.

The sunset pageant was very odd, and entrancingly beautiful. The stratum of cloud which we had traversed some six or seven thousand feet lower than the Estancia, still hung thick and unmoved below us. In fact, it girdled what of the island was visible to us, and the sea also to the horizon line. But, seventy miles away, the mountains of the island of Grand Canary pierced this dull grey corrugated cloud plain, and were dyed with rosy light. It was the same with the nearer island of Gomera, between Grand Canary and the west. As for the reddish rocks over Guimar, which we had already noticed earlier in the day, they were all of the colour of fresh blood. Again, the plateau beneath us and the Cañadas cliffs put on the tenderest of tints. The pumice grew to a pale primrose and saffron, and the mountain pinnacles were of crimson, and brown, and red, merging into purple.

But how rapidly the scenes changed! The shadows

pursued the lights at a measurable speed. The air seemed to chill as the intenser colours faded. We thought it was all over, and were turning towards our camp, when suddenly another great beam of crimson light broke upon the land, the clouds, and the sea, this time from the western side of our slope. In the midst of the sunset splendour there was now a triangular shadow, clearly defined, the apex over the mountains of Grand Canary. As the sun sank, this shadow rose. It rose fast, so that soon it seemed to hang in the heavens, isolated, with the blanching hues of sunset on all sides of it. A few minutes later, and the stars were out. This shadow was the outline of the Peak, traced by the sun, and projected scores of miles seaward.

We were reminded of our altitude by a singular contrast during this sunset spectacle. About thirty miles from the Peak, in the north-east extremity of Tenerife, we could see the infantine mountains of Anaga, peeping grey and subdued from under the clouds, while our upper air was still transfigured with sunlight. For them there had long been no sun. It was only for such monarchs as Teide that the sun continued to shine.

Of the night bivouac that followed, I cannot speak with enthusiasm. We made a roaring fire of retama logs, the thick smoke of which periodically drove into our faces. The men lay down in a concentric circle, wrapped in their blanket cloaks, with their heads towards the fire. They snored contentedly, and were as indifferent to the renewal of the fire as to the excitement of my horse: the beast had some good blood in him, and neighed and tossed up the dust whenever he saw anything he could not account for. However, the sparks now and then fell on a soft part of their skins, and made them jump up in despite of their wishes.

Although the thermometer went no lower than 42°, it was bitter cold. The rarity of the air had something to do with this, no doubt. I could not sleep at all, and found more pleasure in keeping patrol, tending the fire, and watching the ascent toward the zenith of the half moon that was to guide us to the summit, than in trying to sleep. Moreover, one of my comrades had succumbed to the situation. The air and the exertion had made him sick. We mixed him some grog in a saucepan, using a lump of hard snow instead of water; but even the grog did not do everything. He admitted his disinclination to go on when the time came; and so there was nothing for it but to arrange a division of the party. They would not consent to my return, unsatisfied, with them; it was decided, therefore, that Diego should take me to the top, and one of the other men should accompany them back to Orotava. We were to start simultaneously at about two o'clock. The boy who was nominated to guide my friends homewards at first said he would do no such thing. He pleaded timidity; he wanted more sleep; he wished to proceed to the top, &c. "I will not go," he said, flatly. But a bribe made him revert from this lofty strain of obstinacy, and, at the appointed time, my friends and I separated with an interchange of good wishes.

It was full night when we started upwards in the

teeth of a gentle wind that pinched me like an Arctic zephyr. The moon was bright above us ; too small to illumine our path completely, but sufficiently lustrous to cast a bewitching glamour over all the scene that was visible to us. The clouds lay below, still as ever, silvered like mother-o'-pearl. Irregular patches of snow, frozen hard, now and again loomed to the right and left of us, from the stern, almost palpable blackness of the lava. Had I had any superfluous energy to put at the disposal of my imagination, these phantom forms might have played pretty pranks with my head. But of this there was not the least chance. The climb was so severe that it monopolised every faculty. We slipped and slid on the pumice, stumbled over scoriæ half in shadow, and sent blocks of obsidian speeding down to our friends at the Estancia, in our attempts to move upwards. It is *possible* to make this stage of the ascent on horseback. Some people have the hardihood to accomplish it. But to the animals it is a terrible effort, and their riders at times have to pay for it by a fall backwards that might end disagreeably.

Humboldt said it took him two hours to reach Alta Vista from the Estancia. Diego and I did the work in less than an hour and a half, including the time spent in a humiliating number of rests. These were unavoidable ; so great was the call upon our muscles, so persistently did I pant in this high atmosphere. But it was sweet encouragement at last to see the wooden sides of the sulphur house close to us, and to realize that we were now only about 1,500 feet from the summit. Though doubtful if our friends could hear us, we signalled to them with loud whoops, which echoed with weird emphasis from the "enormous masses of sublimity," as James Montgomery might have called the dark shapes in our vicinity.

But a surprise was in store for us. If ever a man may assure himself that he is unlikely to meet any of his fellow beings, and most unlikely to come across an acquaintance, might he not do so on a small island in the Atlantic, 11,000 feet above the level of that island, and at three o'clock in the morning! One would suppose so. At the moment, however, when I had given the word to Diego to move forward, the figure of a man appeared from below. At first this gentleman did not perceive us, though our shouts must have forewarned him of our proximity; and no sooner was he on the smooth ground than he thrust his fists into his sides, and began to dance a hornpipe under the vague light of the moon. But I soon arrested this uncanny exhibition of vitality by asking him who and what he was; and then we found that we were acquaintances. He was a Frenchman, the Count de la Moussaye, with only a few days' holiday at his disposal; and he had come direct from Orotava, resting not at all on the way. Here, at Alta Vista, he purposed supping at the fine Parisian hour of three a.m. His guide followed him with the supper, and, after a short survey of the house, which was only to be entered by a heavy wooden window-flap, high up, one after the other, we climbed to this vent, and vanished like harlequins within. A couple of candles were produced, a bottle of Madeira was uncorked, and the temptation to devote an hour to my new friend was so irresistible that I suspended work with Diego. The two guides forthwith rolled themselves up in their blankets, and slept outside until our pleasure was over. It was really colder within than without the house: we discovered afterwards that a slab of ice several inches thick lay between the boards and the ground, adapting the building for a refrigerator with complete success.

At four o'clock, we renewed the climb. It was that most cold of hours—the hour before the dawn. We were gradually narrowing the area of mountain shoulder which shielded us from the gusts that now whistled about us. And we had for a task the clamber over as pitiless a wreck of rocks and molten substances as the world can show. The least pressure of a finger upon the sharp points and edges of these scoriæ resulted in a scratch or an abrasion. Between the masses were crevices and fissures of uncertain depth. The snow lay hard as iron in some of them. Others were caked with ice, where the internal heat of the mountain had melted the snow. Over this unpleasant tract we stepped daintily from pinnacle to pinnacle, in clear profile against the sky. Of little use was my alpenstock here. Rather, it became a snare, for the smooth obsidian boulders gave it no secure purchase, and more than once it earned me a fall that made me groan. After a while I turned it to account as a balancing-pole; and as such it was not amiss. Thus, going in a very leisurely manner, we attained the Rambleta, or last stage but one of our work.

This is really another ancient crater of the Peak, from out of which, on an awful day or succession of days, centuries or even millenniums ago, the sugar cone, or Piton of ash and lava, was suddenly ejected, raising the height of the volcano by some five or six hundred new feet, and carrying the active crater upwards for the same distance. The Piton, or actual summit, is therefore the representative or survival of two old and expunged craters—the Rambleta and the Cañadas. Just as the Rambleta superseded the Cañadas, so the Piton has superseded the Rambleta. Before the last eruption from the centre of the mountain, the Peak of Tenerife was a truncated cone, like so many of the South American volcanos. In fact, it is still so; but the area of the terminal crater now bears so very small a proportion to the great bulk of the mountain, that one almost forgets that it is not absolutely pyramidal in shape—an isosceles triangle moulded by the hands of nature.

From the Rambleta we saw the sun rise. It was as memorable a show as the sunset of the previous evening. The clouds below were at first almost terrifying in their vastness and immobility, but they took glow after glow of brilliant hues that soon changed their character. Before the sun touched them they were like a limitless prairie of opaline billows, materialized by superhuman alchemy. But the long, crimson line in the east, many minutes before the appearance of the sun, coloured them divinely, and prepared them for the saturating flood of golden light which streamed upon them when the sun did appear. The shifting scene of splendour that ensued is quite indescribable. At the outset, only the cone of the Peak was touched by the dawnlight. The lower slopes, the hills, the valleys, and the sea, were all in grey shadow when this early flush came over us. It seemed to pause for a few moments on the dimpled crest of Teide, and then it moved downwards with smooth continuous speed as the sun rose high. We were soon absorbed in it. Then the mountains of Grand Canary came within its radius; and the island of Gomera, close to the left of us. The Cañadas next caught the glory, and in one rapturous instant the Plain of the Retama was spread with cloth of gold. Thus, for long minutes of time, we watched the gradual illumination of the lower world, until at length we knew that the sun had risen for the ships at sea as well as for us, 12,000 feet above them. The Peak sees the sun nearly twelve minutes before it is visible from its base. Of course the day is similarly protracted in the evening. Hence the Peak's day is about twenty-four minutes longer than the common day in latitude 28°.

The curious phenomenon of the shadow of Teide was now repeated. The enormous pyramidal phantom was thrown from east to west. At its origin, it fell over Gomera, only fifteen miles from Tenerife, and was distinctly of an isosceles shape. But the advance of the sun broadened its base and changed its direction, so that when, half-an-hour later, we saw it from the summit of the mountain, it was a burly equilateral, with the apex resting on the rosy tops of the Caldera of Palma, an island sixty miles to the west of Tenerife.

In the meantime, we had to scale the Piton of ash and pumice. The first hundred feet were trying in the extreme : so abrupt is the slope, and so insecure the foothold. But, afterwards, the going is firmer, though very steep. We were here in an atmosphere markedly sulphureous. Jets of vapour oozed from holes in the rock to the right and left of us, and the temperature of the vapour was insupportable to the hand. Sulphur in various forms took the place of pumice. We sank deep in the soft, adhesive crust, which burnt my boots so that they yawned conspicuously. It was really hard to breathe at all, what with the asphyxiating smell of the sulphur, the extreme rarity of the air, the nipping winds from all points, and the labour of the final climb. Dr. P—— of Puerto, had suggested that I should feel my pulse on the top of Teide : it was 140°. But what did it matter ? We had climbed the Peak, and here we were at six o'clock in the morning, with the world at our feet, and a blue sky above us that put all other blues to shame.

Certainly nothing could be more expressive than the name "Caldera," or cauldron, applied to the crater of volcanoes like Teide. It is but one step from the outer rim of the cone to the inner sheathing of the crater. A rugged wall of fused rock skirts the basin; there is an opening in the wall ; one passes through this opening ; and, immediately, the foot sinks in the blanched, burning sulphur, where it slopes to the bottom of the crater. The rocks of this outer wall are a few feet higher in one part than elsewhere. This is the highest point of the Pico de Teide ; and here, for two or three mortally cold minutes, I perched myself, half persuaded that the feeling of vertigo which has thrilled several respectable travellers in the same position was a sensation not to be doubted. This rock point is scarcely a yard in diameter. A mountain 12,000 feet high could not culminate in a pinnacle much more satisfying to the imagination.

Had not the impermeable barrier of cloud, nearly two miles down, hung between us and the greater part of Tenerife, our view from the summit would no doubt have been prodigious. Even with the clouds, it is not to be forgotten. Of the seven large islands of the Canarian archipelago, the mountains of Palma and Grand Canary, and the greater part of Gomera, were alone visible. It was easier to-day to see the coast of Africa than the coast line of Tenerife; but we saw neither. The whole circuit of the Cañadas was distinct in every detail, and the scarlet swellings on the south-west flank of the Peak. These are the result of Teide's more recent lateral eruptions. Probably none of them are two centuries old. Their brilliant colouring, and that of the forest of vivid yellow pines, diving to the cloud-zone, refreshed the eye. But, in the same direction, between the Peak and these hills, is one conspicuous volcanic boil that must not escape notice. It is the mountain of Chahora, only about 2,300 feet lower than Teide, and with a crater of beautiful formation nearly a league in girth. From our standpoint, we looked into this crater, and could mark the passage of the lava that streamed from it in 1798, when it was active for several weeks in succession. The rugged areas of desolation over which it broods tell their own story. But, however one might try to be judiciously sympathetic in one's survey, it was easier to admire the sombre bronzed and jetty colours of this lava, under the unclouded sun, than to think of the ruin it indicated.

The descent into Teide's crater is a matter of no difficulty. It is but fifty or sixty feet deep, with a diameter of perhaps three hundred feet. True, with pressure, my alpenstock went to the handle into the soft sulphur; but there was no danger of my sinking to the same extent. The heat was oppressive; the warm fumes stirred by our every displacement of the soil were very strong, and the white banks tried the eyes. Nevertheless, the crystals of sulphur, of many shades between pale yellow and dark orange, were quite irresistible, and I had soon given Diego as many specimens as he cared to carry. Humboldt dwells upon the iniquity of his guides in this particular. When his back was turned, they threw away the blocks of obsidian and pumice with which he burdened them. In praise of Diego, therefore, I must say that he did no such thing. But perhaps it was rather because he had no vigour for revolt left in him. For he was by this time a piteously frozen object : the red and blue handkerchief which he had tied from his pate to his chin, to put warmth into his cheeks, harmonized only too well with their wintry hue; and all the while we were on the summit he was enthusiastic but once—in his hearty " Si, señor," of assent to my proposition that we should leave it.

No doubt it will be supposed that when we departed, these sublime solitudes were left to themselves, to be untroubled by humanity for weeks and months. It were natural to think so. But ere we left it, the romance of the Peak was totally destroyed by the arrival of ten stout countrymen, with mattocks on their shoulders. We watched them climbing the ash cone, not a little amazed at the sight of them. They were merely beginning their day's work, however. No sooner had they accosted us with ten affable good mornings, than each man plunged into the crater, and began to dig up the sulphur. Conceive a person going nearly two miles and a half skywards ere he enters upon his daily labour! As for the risks attendant upon such labour, they are as nothing compared to the hideous desecration it implies. There is even a hut in the bottom of the crater, for the convenience of the Sulphur Company, and these brawny-legged workers of it!

In our descent, we visited the famous ice-cavern of Teide. It has the appearance of a chamber or big bubble in the lava, going far within the bowels of the mountain; but investigation is difficult. Within was a pool of lustrous green ice, large enough to skate on; and the huge contorted icicles, uniting the pool to the roof of the chamber, were beautiful beyond the dreams of a manufacturer of chandeliers. Hither in summer come the confectioners of Santa Cruz, to fetch ice for the compound of sweet cooling drinks. Alas! how Teide's majesty seems lessened when one knows that it serves such various useful purposes!

Anon, we are once more at the Estancia. The

sun is broiling, and we cling to the shadow of the rocks of our bedchamber. Breakfast is spread, and we have fresh snow to cool our wine. M. le Comte protests that he is not tired, and indeed he talks like a man refreshed. But, as for me, I am dead beat, so that when later we cross the terrible desert of pumice, with 120° of heat in the air around us, I sleep fast in my saddle. At four o'clock in the afternoon, we are again in Orotava, after an absence of thirty-six hours.

OUTLINE OF CHAHORA, AS SEEN FROM THE SUMMIT OF THE PEAK.

CHAPTER XV.

Palma from Tenerife—The weekly *correo*—The misery of it—A fair night at sea—Topography of Palma—Origin of its name—Guayanfanta—Conquest of Palma—The brave king of the Caldera—Alonso de Lugo's mean shift—Later history of Palma—Tenerife named by the people of Palma—The Bishop and the convent cake—Independence of Palma—The Vandewalle family, past and present.

THE island of Palma is hardly more than a plausible myth to the stranger who spends a few days at Orotava, and then goes away. He is told, may be, that it is about fifty-five miles west of Tenerife: and that if he looks steadily towards the golden glamour of the clouds at sundown he may distinguish four or five purple paps rising with an air of substantiality in the midst of the glory; and that these paps are the mountain tops of Palma. But much determination must second him in his attempt to see mountains where, to the common eye, clouds only are to be seen.

Once a week, in the evening, a battered, frittered, and ineffably dirty little smack of about fifty tons' burden sails from Puerto, at a venture, for Palma. This barque carries the royal mails and merchandise. As an after-thought, passengers also are carried, rather as ballast than as a source of profit. They pay a trifle (about 6s.) for the convenience; and it is understood on both sides that nothing whatever will be done for their comfort on board the barque. They may lie where they can, and must accept the consequences if they get in the way of the crew, or if a storm comes on, and it is found that the ship goes heavily, to the imperilment of the mails.

With only a dim presentiment of the nature of the boat, the English chaplain at Orotava (Mr. Goddard) and myself agreed to cross to Palma, view the island, and return in a few days. Alas! man proposes, and God disposes!

To get on board was easy, speaking comparatively. True, the day was lowering, and the sea ran high on the coast. But the bulwarks of the *correo*, or mail boat, were so low that we had only to wait until a wave lifted the shore boat to their level, and then leap to the deck. Here we found ourselves among a medley of chains, ropes, sacks of potatoes, and boxes, some two score swarthy men and boys, and several restless cats; and at every roll of the ship her miscellaneous live and dead cargo was mixed in a most confusing manner. With such favourable conditions for sea-sickness, no wonder some of us were ill long ere the barque lifted her anchor; and the gracious panorama of olive slopes, dark headlands, and billows of cloud, touched by the setting sun, where they swayed round the base of the Peak—this was nothing to us, in spite of its beauty.

Then the stars shone forth, and meteors shot by hundreds across the bright heavens. There was a paltry moon; but this was put to shame by the glowing cone of the Peak, which, when we got from under the lee of its clouds, shone down upon us, with a silver track in the phosphorescent waters, like a divine beacon. The coppery crew now left the ship to sail unaided, trusting in the land wind. They smoked and spat, and sang shrill songs, and lurched to and fro in the wake of a big pot over the galley fire, and caught the red beams of the fire on their faces and their bare skins, and tripped over the passengers who lay groaning, prone upon the boards, among the chains. It was a diabolical night, not without a charm through all its agony. But, eventually, the dawn came to cheer us, and the bold, jagged peaks of Palma's higher *cordillera*—all crimson and clear under the first beams of the sun— brooded over us with a kindly affectation of nearness while yet we were a dozen miles off. And so we landed on this strange shore as we had got on the boat, with a timely jump, heedful of the brisk recession of the long wave which gave us our opportunity.

Palma is the third of the Canaries in size. It is, roughly speaking, twenty-five miles long by fifteen broad, with a configuration similar to that of Tenerife. Tenerife has for its nucleus the Peak: the *barrancos* and slopes which trend thence to the coast-line are, with the exception of the appendix of Anaga, the material of the island. And Palma, in like manner, centres upon the Caldera, that prodigious old extinct volcano, the very measurement of which must be conjectural, but with a crater said to be six miles in diameter, and girt by mountains 7,000 feet high. Save the tract on the west of Palma known as Los Llanos (the Plains), all the island is mountain or plateau; and the *barrancos* which radiate from the Caldera are tremendous ravines, as formidable to the traveller as the worst of those of Tenerife. Viera compared Palma to a palm tree. Its gorges stand for the fronds of the palm, and the *cordillera* running from the Caldera to the south is the stem of the palm. The similitude is ingenious, and may explain the name of the island. But, since we once more touch the etymological puzzle, it may be remarked that the Mallorquinos, cruising in these seas in the fourteenth century, reached the island and landed. It is not improbable, therefore, that these mariners, with their thoughts veering to Palma, the capital of their own island of Mallorca, are responsible for the true christening of the Canarian Palma. Of course there are other conjectures, but we will not concern ourselves with them.

This island has less claim on the historian than any of the other six islands of the archipelago. I have mentioned the melancholy character of its robust aborigines, their singular religious ritual, and their stoical manner of leaving the world when life grew burdensome. Their women seem to have had the nobler souls, as well as muscular bodies. Of their strength, the sad story of Guayanfanta may give an example. Guayanfanta was a beautiful and majestic native woman, who aroused the admiration of certain marauders from Hierro. These men saw and pursued her. Fearing to fall into their hands, Guayanfanta turned, seized the nearest of her assailants, put him under her arm, and hurried to a near ravine, where she purposed holding him over an abyss until she had arranged for her own safety with the others. Unfortunately, the poor woman was overtaken; and the ruffians, angry at being so treated by a woman, broke both her legs, and left her to die.

Alonso de Lugo, the *conquistador* of Tenerife, had subjugated Palma before attacking the Guanches. He landed at Tazacorte, on the west coast of the island, on St. Michael's Day, 1491, and on May 3, 1493, he achieved what he called "a glorious victory" over Tanaúsu, the King of the Caldera, the last monarch of the twelve in Palma to hold out against the invaders. As usual, the particulars of the conquest vary with the chronicler. According to Nuñez de la Peña, all the force of Palma mustered near the shore, to oppose the nine hundred men whom the Spaniard disembarked. The two armies sat inactive, each doubtful of the prudence of attacking the other. De Lugo, in this extremity, fell on his knees, and with fervour invoked the Virgin and his own patron saint, Michael, to help him, promising Saint Michael that the land should be dedicated to him if the Spanish arms were victorious. Simultaneously, a panic seized the natives. "It is better to obey than to die," they cried; and thus they all accepted the sovereignty of Spain, without striking one blow for their independence. Nuñez de la Peña's version of the conquest may accord with what one would expect from a nation of men in subjection to their wives, but it is on the whole incredible.

The likelier narrative tells us that Alonso had no difficulty with eleven of the kings or princes of Palma: they dubbed themselves vassals, were baptized, and subscribed to the Christian religion as soon as they understood the alternative course ; but that he was for a time seriously defied by the King of the Caldera. Tanaúsu lived in the vast crater of Palma, a retreat easily made impregnable ; and he, with his subjects, broke the necks and backs of the Spaniards by showering pine trunks and rocks upon them when they attempted to enter the defile leading to the royal residence. Marking these failures, Alonso tried treachery. He invited Tanaúsu to a conference in the plains outside the Caldera, pledging his word that no harm should be done to him. The poor barbarian was not rogue enough readily to scent the roguery of others. He left his fortress, and this was at once possessed by the Spaniards. A captive, he bitterly refused the Christianity offered to him by his lying foes, who then tried to transport him, uninjured, to Spain, to be exhibited at court as a king in chains. But Tanaúsu had the spirit of a Roman patriot. No sooner did he understand what his lot was to be, than he leaped from the ship into the sea, and was drowned.

This was in 1493. During the intervening four hundred years, Palma's history has been of a parochial character. The conquest ended, the land was divided among the conquerors, and the natives were shipped to Cadiz to be sold as merchandise, not the less attractive, commercially, for the rude garments of skins which they wore in Spain as they had worn in their own hot valleys. Alonso then prepared for war with the Guanches. From Palma the Peak of Tenerife is a magnificent spectacle, and the *conquistador* would be encouraged in his plans by the constant sight of the mountain, apparently suspended between the waters and the heavens.[1] Certain of the new proprietors of the land cared less for their estates than for the chance of more war, and they therefore left the peopling of Palma to deputies. Convents, churches, and monasteries sprang up in different parts of the island. Later, some noble emigrants from Spain and Flanders brought hither a wholesome leaven of good blood. Everything, in short, seemed done that was needful to incite Palma to become a distinguished addition to the Empire.

But the island has, in fact, lived ever since in a state of happy obscurity. It has been spared the cares and hazards of greatness or conspicuousness. The other islands of the Canaries duly gained laurels in self-defence against Drake, Blake, Jennings, Nelson, and other sea captains; but Palma achieved no victories. In 1553, the capital, Santa Cruz de la Palma, was sacked by a body of seven hundred Frenchmen; the town's archives and several houses fell to the flames. In 1570, again, a community of Palma Jesuits, forty in number, were attacked at sea, and all murdered by the French. These are the

---

[1] Tenerife is said to owe its name to the people of Palma, who, being able to view it as a whole, had better right to the christening than the Guanches themselves: Tenerife "Tener," white snow; and "Ife," a high mountain.

chief sorrows of the island during the last four centuries.

Palma was also largely left to itself both by the civil and ecclesiastical rulers of the Canarian province. It was not quite so oblivious of the passage of time as its neighbour, Hierro, the people of which island were for long wont to despatch a ship annually to Palma to ask when Lent ought to begin. But its distance from Tenerife kept the authorities aloof from it. During a hundred and seventeen years, it was traversed but twice by the bishop of the diocese. On one of these two occasions, an event occurred indeed which may have frightened subsequent bishops. The nuns of a convent in the capital, in congratulating their spiritual lord on his presence among them, sent him a superb cake, home-made, and elaborately decorated with sugar and almond excrescences. But, in their nervousness, the girls seem to have put poison into the cake as an ingredient. Luckily, they discovered their mistake ere the prelate tasted the cake. As it was, the prelate's pages, who had picked at its ornaments, were the only sufferers.

But this very isolation and abandonment, which would tend to degrade most communities, has been of some service to Palma. The merchants of its capital have established a trade, quite their own, with Havana and the West Indies. Their ships go backwards and forwards, independently of the other islands and the peninsula, and thus the foundation of a robust individuality has been laid in this small island.

In spite of this mercantile energy, however

Palma is bound by a long series of unfractured links to its calm past history. In 1555, a certain native of Bruges named Vandewalle, who, with his father, a burgomaster of Bruges, and thirteen brothers, had fought through various wars in the Netherlands, sailed from Cadiz, of which city he had been the governor, for this Atlantic island. Here the Vandewalles soon acquired fame as civic administrators and religious benefactors. This fame has gained fresh increment with each century, and now, in 1887, it is still, as in 1587, the Vandewalles who are looked upon as the prime notables of Palma. The family has in the meantime been ennobled. I was fortunate enough to have a letter of introduction to the Marquis de Guisla, the present head of the house, a gentleman who bears his official responsibilities lightly, though he fulfils them none the less effectually therefore. He and the friends who frequented his house devoted their leisure to stamp-collecting. Whenever I paid the Marquis a visit, I found his stamp album open on the table, and himself, with his friends, busily engaged in pasting or preparing his stamps with the earnest assiduity of a schoolboy. Our talk was of duplicates and " provisionals," rather than of local commerce, politics, and the other subjects of current use for casual acquaintances; and to these gentlemen in the prime of life the impending exhibition in Antwerp of collections of foreign stamps was a more serious matter than the movements of all the European Powers put together.

CHAPTER XVI.

Santa Cruz of Palma—A warm town—The mole—Steep streets—Palma women—Don Pedro and his wife—Palma fashions—Morning routine—The craterette of Santa Cruz—Architecture and industries of Santa Cruz—The Church of San Salvador—Altar machinery—Our Lady of the Snows—The cockpit—A series of fights—Palma's dependence on England—Local wines and tobacco—Weevils—Locusts—Legend of the Peak of Tenerife, and the Caldera of Palma.

SANTA CRUZ DE LA PALMA, the capital of the Island of Palma, is a hot, but markedly picturesque town. It is built, in fact, on the extremity of a section of a crater, which faces the sea on its southern side, with a remarkable brown precipice terminating in the water. North, the city is pent by long bare promontories, falling from the buttresses of the great Caldera, three and four thousand feet above the sea level. South, this crater cliff, a thousand feet high, with a broad plateau of rich cultivated country proceeding from it in a south-westerly direction inland, shields the city from breezes in that quarter. While, lastly, tier after tier of high, wooded mountains rise steeply behind the city, to form the backbone or *cordillera* of Palma; so that the ascent west, in little more than a mile from the main street of Santa Cruz, is between

A WARM CITY.

a thousand and fifteen thousand feet. The city gets a breeze from the sea, east and south-east. But as

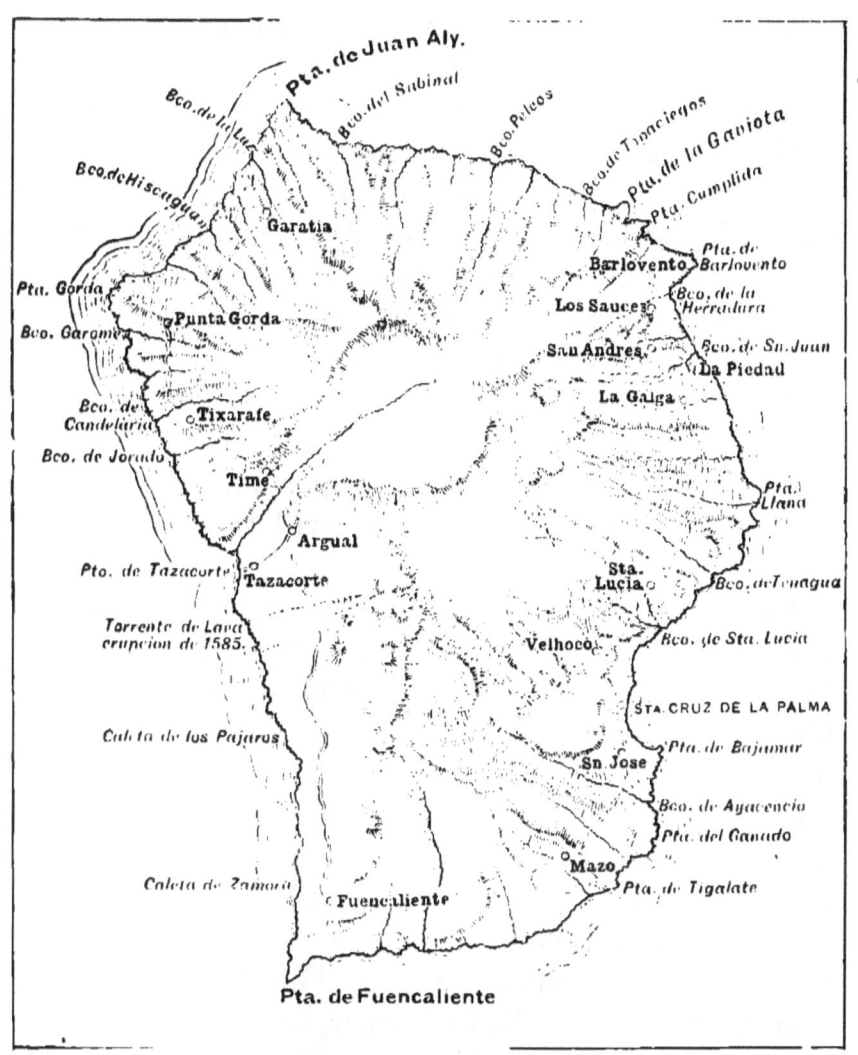

PALMA: Extreme dimensions 26 miles by 16.

these quarters are notorious for their heat, the breeze is not so refreshing as it might be.

Already, in mid-April, we found it very warm here. In the shade of the roof of our hotel, the thermometer registered 84°, and our bed-room seldom marked less than 70°, night and day. Notwithstanding this, the people of Palma are curiously loyal in defending their climate. They learn that the English have made Tenerife a health resort, and they also are determined to build a sanatorium or a big hotel on a cliff a thousand feet over the city. To question the wisdom of this step is to touch a native gentleman on his most sensitive part: to point to the thermometer, and to ridicule the *correo* as a means whereby delicate people are to get to their haven of rest, is to risk a quarrel. Thermometers are not to be believed: the *correo* will be superseded by a fine steamer! If we ask when this will take place, the reply is, *Paciencia!*

In the meantime, the city is working hard at its mole, in readiness for the visitors who are to come to it. Scores of men are employed making huge blocks of concrete, thirty to thirty-five tons in weight. These are one by one lugged to the end of the mole, and foisted into the sea, where they make a rough but ponderous foundation for the pier itself. I know not how many hundred of the blocks are required, but if five in a week are tumbled over the edge, it is thought a good week's work. The director of the undertaking is a skilled engineer, with a medal from the Philadelphia Exhibition of 1876, and under his green umbrella he defies the sun for the good of his country.

In other respects, there is more energy here than

one looks for. The chief streets, O'Daly Street (evidently of Irish origin), and Santiago Street, are flanked with large shops and warehouses of astonishing importance. They would not be out of place in Regent Street; and yet they and their crowd of genteel shopmen all have an air of prosperity that it is hard to deduce from a population of but ten or twelve thousand people. There is not much traffic. The streets, save those parallel with the shore, are abominably steep. Their cobbles, too, seem made for the fracture of limbs. Thus, in all the town there seems but one span of oxen, used for the concrete blocks already mentioned, and a single shrewd, flat mule cart, which the mule drags about with oscillations suggestive of the sea. Pack-mules and asses do the hard work. Of good horses there is a distinct dearth, and when a rich proprietor comes clattering into the city, with the tail of his steed distended behind him, all the shopmen hurry to the doors, and the ladies in a hundred houses appear at the windows to see the curiosity.

Methinks the women of Palma in a measure maintain their old supremacy over the men. Some of them are tall and stalwart enough for grenadiers, but their beauty seems to be rather coarse, and of the masculine order. The landlady of our hotel is a fine example of a Palma woman. She is large and dark, with strong features, and a deep, melodious bass voice. Her husband, on the other hand, is small, dapper, and hysterical in his movements and manners. He is, moreover, so completely in thrall to his own excitable feminine temperament, that it brings him to serious humiliation ten times a day. He and his wife quarrel across the banisters or the *patio* of the building; but the bass voice always has the best of it, and Don Pedro, the small man, goes away wiping his moist face with his silk handkerchief, and muttering something about women and the weather.

There is more character in the dress of the Palma women than in Tenerife, or rather in the head dress only. Some of them wear ridiculously little white straw hats, a few inches in diameter, and set, with a forward inclination, upon the silk handkerchief which first covers their hair. Others, in common with some men, adopt the *montera*, a unique thing. This is a cylinder of dark blue cloth, with a head-piece attached at right angles. When put on, the two open extremities hang one on each side as if for ventilation. Neither of these fashions is becoming, but then it is probable that these stern women would laugh to scorn the notion that they decked themselves to ensnare the affection of such nonentities as the men.

The fashions and physiognomies of Palma are best to be seen early in the morning. Soon after dawn, the tinkle of goat-bells sounds in the streets, and countrymen with calves and vegetables and eggs collect on the two sides of a dry river-bed which bisects the street of Santiago, near the old church and the stately post-office of the city. Here the hum of gossip and chaffering continues until the sun is high. Men of the north of the island, in goats-hair caps, with a peak and a tailpiece like a coal-heaver's bonnet, in short cotton drawers, and leathern aprons, meet the more ordinary costumes of the rest of the island. The congregation by the iron bridge, with the dry stones of the river, the flutter of palms higher up the bed of the stream, the towering mountains, clear of cloud for a few hours after sunrise, the nearer architecture : the decorated portico of the parish church ; the sumptuous chiselling of the sixteenth century post-office ; and the tall houses, with green and scarlet balconies—all make a pretty and lively picture.

Indeed, one must live early here. Every sensible man, woman, and child gets out of bed when the goats give the signal. Then is the time to bathe in the Atlantic rollers, from the black volcanic sands of the shore, upon which nothing but a tamarisk bush or two obtain a footing. One may then see many a pretty face taking the air, innocent of the powder which later covers its beauties without mercy. The citizen and his wife then take their constitutional ; and the gay youth who may have lost a year's pocket-money at the card table last night, forgets everything in dutiful attention to his mother, whom he now escorts up and down the sands with amiable ingenuousness. For the aged and infirm, there is the roof of the house. They take their morning cup of chocolate among the geraniums and roses, with an unimpeded view of the mountains on one side, and the pale blue tranquil sea, with the divine white cone of the Peak far away on the other side. So still is the air in this brief interregnum, when there is wind neither from the land nor the sea, that it is easy to talk from a roof in one street to a roof in another.

And it is also easy in the clear atmosphere to mark Donna Isabella's smiling acknowledgment of the various glances of admiration which proceed through as many telescopes, cavalierly levelled at her from roofs far and near. But all too soon the heat is fit to crack the cement of the *azoteas*; and the ladies who were so graceful when seen watering their flowers, or pacing the roof arm-in-arm, retire indoors : nor do they re-appear until the sun is down.

The crater, or craterette, seeing that it is only half a crater, close to the south of Palma, offers a pretty piece of exploration for the morning hours. It seems very near indeed ; but it is a long hour's climb to the top of it. The bare basaltic and gritty masses, which lie from it in sharply-inclined planes towards its base, are soon heated ; and while yet Santa Cruz is cool, thousands of bronze and purple butterflies and locusts are here disporting themselves in congenial temperature. The shape is boldly amphitheatrical, with an upper edge from twelve to fifteen hundred feet above the sea. This is tufted in two or three places with palm trees; a white convent crowns the bracing height at its loftiest ; and a crucifix looks down from a perpendicular crag at the city and the Atlantic. We clambered along its edge, amid clusters of bugloss and white iris, conjecturing about the origin of the volcano, and the singular offshoot from its summit of the inland plateau of Buenavista, with its rich *fincas* and groves of palms. A man proceeding from the country to the coast, in ignorance of local geography, might well be surprised suddenly to find himself on the top of so gigantic a concavity as this. But towards the city, the crater gets somewhat isolated: a well-defined moat, with abrupt outer sides, marking the ancient Piton of the dead and mutilated volcano.

As we were the only English who had visited Palma that year, our acquaintances in Santa Cruz civilly made much of us. None of the treasures and antiquities of the city were hid from us. There was the flag which Alonso de Lugo, in 1492, led through the island, at the head of his 900 filibusters! Its crimson silk and silver thread bore the arms of Spain and De Lugo on different sides. It is kept in the town hall: the stately colonnaded building which is also the post-office. The city also boasts a museum, spick and span, meagre, but in careful hands. A few Guanche skulls, as they are called, may be seen; but the people of Palma were not Guanches, and the heads are local heads. The geological collection is neat, if not extensive. It is much surpassed by the private collection of a friend of the Marquis de Guisla's. But the good people of Palma were proudest of all to show us their industries. There was a silk factory, for instance, which we entered through the circular arch of an old convent; the bell tower, with its red balconies, looking down at us from above. Here the history of a silk dress was unfolded, from the green cocoons, purchasable at three shillings per pound, to the soft fabric which in the machine-room came forth from the loom, crimson and delicate, ready for the milliner. The worms were on large trays, from those at a day old, of the size of ants, and as lively; to those at twelve days, respectable in size, sobered with age, and full of staid energy for the due fulfilment of the business of life. Their surroundings were charming. From their trays they might look forth at a cool little garden of palm and orange trees, geraniums and china roses, all centring upon a marble fountain. On the other hand was the disused refectory of the convent, with a rough defaced fresco of Christ on the cross at one extremity, and a knot of swarthy men stitching the white sails of their ships, seated on the steps of the building. The industry is under the control of a skilled Frenchman from Lyons, and much is expected from it. Aniline dyes are not admitted to the laboratory: the local cochineal is, with good reason, preferred.

The parochial church of San Salvador is, within and without, one of the most tasteful in the archipelago. The chiselling of its portico is minute and elegant, and the dark woodwork of its interior is cleanly carven. Inside, it feels and looks like the church of an opulent people, though its pavements may be crowded by barelegged peasants bearing every mark of poverty. Among its curios is a painting by Esquibel, in 1841, of the Transfiguration, at a cost of £150. The fine colouring of this picture gladdens the eyes after the rubbish that generally fills the Canarian churches. But San Salvador is richest in its actual bullion and its vestments. We were dazzled by the glint and value of the gold and silver of its monstrances and chalices, and patens—some antique, and curious in shape and design; by the number of the silver candlesticks and silver-cased staves which are part of the formulæ of the church's processions. There were sets of silver sheathing for the altar; and some careful relievo work on silver book-rests and book-covers. As for the vestments, their gorgeousness holds the tongue mute. We looked upon embroidered copes and chasubles, heavy with gold and silver lace woven upon silks and velvets and satins, purple, crimson, green, and blue, until we wearied of the magnificence. One of these robes, made at Toledo, represented in gold and silver upon silk and satin, all the native flowers of Palma. They told us a curious tale about a certain cope of gold and silver and damask, and the broad marble font, thickly decorated with figures and landscapes. Both were said to be from our Cathedral of St. Paul's, of the time of Henry VIII., and presentations to Palma. Elsewhere in the Canaries, one hears the same story. It may be, however, that they are wrong about the date. For it is possible enough that when Philip II. of Spain was also king consort of England, certain of our church properties got distributed to aliens.

Here in San Salvador an uncommon mechanical apparatus is used to relieve the officiating priest at the altar. At a word of command, the sanctuary opens and shuts, contracts or expands, by invisible agency. Another signal educes a short flight of wooden steps from the body of the altar; and when the priest has used these steps for reaching the Host within the sanctuary, they vanish as mysteriously as they appear, the breach closes, and no sign of the magic remains. Few theatres have their stage machinery so well in hand.

But though the parochial church of San Salvador

is the most ornate in the island, it does not hold the affections of the people like the lesser building dedicated to our Lady of the Snows. This stands on a green knoll of volcanic tufa at the head of a deep *barranco* near the capital, and with the wooded peaks of Palma's *cordillera* soaring almost from the church walls. Since 1646 the islanders have loved this little church with an intensity we Northern Protestants can but dimly understand. In that year Palma was terrified by one of the worst volcanic eruptions in its modern history. Four streams of lava were running at the same time. All the south-west of the island was menaced with destruction. Then, in their distress, the people besought our Lady of the Snows, and a procession carried her image from the chapel in the *barranco* to the capital. On the following morning, snow was seen on the summits of the mountains, and the eruption had ceased. As this happened to be the festival of our Lady of the Snows, and the time of summer (August 5), the miracle and the mediation were both equally definite. And thus, in grateful memory of the past, Santa Cruz continues to honour the chapel in the *barranco*, and every five years carries her image into the town, with a pomp and thunder of cannons, and general festivities, that draw the other islanders hither by hundreds.

It is in this famous little chapel, moreover, that the seamen plying between Havana and Palma still make their vows. Its walls are hung with grotesque old pictures, signifying the miracles wrought at sea by this gracious Virgin. In 1704, for instance, the captain of a Canarian barque, in conflict with a

Turkish pirate, invoked the Virgin of the Snows, with such success, that during a three hours' fight not one Spaniard was killed, but many Turks. Here again is another simple story: "The barque of Nicolas Marques, having gone from this port for the isle of St. Michael, the 25th February, on the 26th day of the voyage, in the night, there came on a fierce storm, and having in the strife seen a star, they invoked Our Lady of the Snows, and the trouble was soon at an end—the year 1702." The ship figures as a little boat tossed in the white water, while a star like a sun is shining in a blue sky over a bank of purpled vanishing cloud. Elsewhere in the church, a heap of old sails, and innumerable waxen legs, heads, and arms testify, as thank-offerings, to the thaumaturgic worth of the shrine.

With such a reputation, the chapel is likely to be rich. Two hundred pounds a year is gathered from its alms-boxes alone: no small sum in an island where it is hard to exchange money's worth for money. It is, indeed, the wealthiest establishment in Palma, and the happy priest who has it in charge lives in a sequestered house hard by, in a garden of many fruit trees, and sheltered from all rude winds by the verdant slopes and cliffs of the mountains, cloud-capped as to their heads.

In enumerating the chief buildings of Palma's capital, I have omitted one—the cock-pit. This is a white octagonal, with a cupola of crimson glass, and a gilt vane. From the sea, nothing in the town is more conspicuous; and one is prone to assume that it is the residence of the Lieutenant-Governor.

During the earlier centuries of the Spanish occupation, bulls were brought into the island arenas, as in Spain still. Subsequently, for some unknown reason, the bulls were discarded; and game-cocks, of English extraction, now supply the populace with that surfeit of blood and death which seems to be a need of the Spanish temperament. Don Pedro, our landlord, at first fancied we were drawn to Palma by a certain cock-fight in which a famous veteran was to take part. He appealed to us, as authorities, on several technical points in the frays, and was amazed to learn that in England it was illegal to practise the sport which he conceived to be one of the most brilliant features of English life.

The series of duels I witnessed in this white arena one Sunday morning differed but little from the duels that take place daily in every lusty farmyard, save that they were to the death. Five or six hundred townspeople crowded the building, the brown legs of the boys hanging down from the gallery towards the more aristocratic vicinity of the cockpit. Not Epsom paddock five minutes before the Derby start ever presented such a scene of tumult as this small place when the birds were rubbed beak to beak as a preliminary to each main. The lads roared their wagers in cents; the richer citizens and the nobility offered dollars and tens of dollars. A marquis, with his own hands, untied the blue or crimson ribbons which attached the sheath to the maiden spurs of the birds. Another estimable gentleman held the scales while the combatants were weighed, and plucked feathers from the tailpieces, where this was necessary to equalize their bulk. Then the poor proud pugilists were set at each other, amid a yell of encouraging shouts, which dazed the novices and made them an easy prey to the older birds, who had already tasted blood, and been often caressed by their happy owners.

What mean pitiful pastime this cock-fighting is! Only the more brutalized of the birds have their heart in it, beyond a certain point. When one stately warrior, having lost an eye, and got half choked with its own gore, lowers its head, quails, groans, and flies in pain and terror before its antagonist, the latter, left to its own instincts, is disposed to throw down the sword, and sign a truce. At least, I hope the common barnyard bantam, undebauched by human applause, has so much of chivalry in its nature. But here such conduct was unacceptable. The bedraggled, bleeding victim had to be pursued, overtaken, wounded again and again, bereft of its other eye, stabbed in the throat, and worried slowly into insensibility. Even this did not suffice. When at length the poor creature had rolled on to its back, and lay with its feet in the air, laboriously sobbing in its death agony, the conqueror must needs perch on the dying body, peck it finally and completely to death, and hoarsely crow forth its conceit.

Only one of the five mains on the programme gave me any pleasure. The birds in this case were superb fellows. They carried their heads high, swaggered like Alsatians, shook their gay plumage, and were no sooner introduced than they crowed in each other's faces with a loud bluster of challenge that brought roars of applause upon them. A rare tussle! prophesied every one, from the marquis downwards. In fact, however, when the warriors were released from their owners' warm hands, and set on their own legs, they viewed their responsibilities in another light. Instead of leaping straight at each other's throats, each went smartly to the right about face, and began to run round the arena in flight. When, in their scamper, they met, simultaneously they turned again, and continued their flight. Their running was beyond praise: they had such long, strong legs! But fight they would not, for all the maledictions of their backers, or the insidious cajolements of their masters. So that, after a while, all Santa Cruz joined in a shout of contumely, and the cocks that were willing to race but not to fight were caught by the tails, and thrown out of the ring, as cravens unworthy of further notice. Don Pedro, among others, went red in the face over this humiliating scene. Nor would he believe that I did not mock him and the national pastime when I vowed it was the best fight of all, and the only one fit to be seen by a man of humane impulses and sensibility.

Don Pedro vaunted the English origin of the gamecocks of the town. He also flouted in the faces of his Spanish guests at the dinner-table that his cutlery, rum, plates, tumblers, and much of the tinned meats he gave us hailed equally from England. Moreover, every little *venta* in Palma, as in Tenerife, has its row of beer bottles from Burton or Edinburgh. But this anomalous dependence upon our island was complete when we came to be offered

English cigars in a country that has close and constant intercourse with Havana. Palma herself, indeed, grows fair tobacco. It is the one absorbing desire of certain of her planters to get their produce tried in London. Yet I do not think they would profit by the fulfilment of their wish in this respect. Their prices are certainly cheap; but strong cigars with an aroma that brings tears into the eyes are dear even at but three to four shillings per hundred. We tested several growths of local excellence, and dissatisfaction generally ensued.

It is the same with the wines of the country. There are as many different qualities as parishes. In one village we were discomfited by a juice as sweet as the wine of Samos; in the next by a strong liquor that stopped the breath; and in the next by a wine that even the famous "resinata" of Greece cannot match for nastiness. Perhaps improved processes will change both wine and tobacco for the better.

It is much to the credit of Palma that it rears no noxious animals. To be sure, fleas abound wherever there are human beings, the lower classes are infested with lice, and in summer there is no lack of mosquitoes. Moreover, the prickly pear and euphorbia bushes which mass the rocky slopes are linked together by the tough intricate webbing of large spotted brown or black spiders. But these feeble vermin are of small account.

The island is reputed to contain an indigenous bat, but naturalists are not, I believe, quite sure about this. Thanks to the abundant pasture of the euphorbia, there is also an extraordinary number of weevils here. We found them now and then in the very hard bread of the hotel; but as Don Pedro only laughed pleasantly while taking them between his finger and thumb, and the other guests were not aghast, the weevil in Palma is no doubt a dainty feeder, and by his presence stamps the food he favours with the hallmark of quality.

But the locust claims mention, if only for the suggestion of doom that accompanies him as he hops, chirping, in the sunlight. About once in a century, these insects come in desolating hordes. In 1812, for instance, they lay in parts of Fuerteventura to a depth of four feet. Then the Canarians take prompt measures. The military are ordered out to dig trenches all over the land; to shovel the locusts into these pits, and cover them up for their extinction. But such trivial opposition seldom saves the islands from total ravagement for the year. If, by burning and burying the bodies, they may avert the pestilence that is apt to ensue upon a dearth of food, and the stench of the decaying layers of insects upon the sea shore, this is as much as can be expected. Happily for Palma, however, it is somewhat protected from this scourge by the intermediate islands of Grand Canary and Tenerife.

Indeed, the shadow of Tenerife is, and always has been, a potent factor in the routine of life in Palma. According to a legend, the Caldera of the one island and the Peak of the other are as closely related as a sword to its scabbard. For, long ago, it is said, a diabolical storm raged in Palma, and, in the course of it, a mass of rock five thousand feet deep was torn from the mountains, and whisked over the waters to Tenerife. Here it righted itself upon some high ground; and it is now known as the Peak. The fable gives an idea of the stupendous hole of the Caldera. To the people of Palma, the Peak acts in some sort as a weather guide. Like the ancients, who supposed that it linked the heavens to the earth, perhaps they are wont to think of it with an exaggerated respect. To climb it was to be heroic indeed, in their esteem. In fact, from Palma it has a look of profound majesty —whether at dawn or sunset, with a lingering ruddy light upon its cone; or at noon, when the clouds lie thick along its flanks, and only its head caresses the blue. But, day by day, during our sojourn in Palma, the hot April sun melted the snow from " inimitable Teide," as Viana calls it, so that when, after long delay, we once more went aboard the detested schooner, the mountain was changed from white to black, with only a delicate pencilling where the snow still lay in the ravines of inky lava down its sides.

CHAPTER XVII.

Preparations for a tour round Palma—*Barranco* de Galga—A red land—San Andrés—Los Sauces—Its merry mill—*Barrancos* de Herradura, Gallegos, and Peleos—Awful roads—A beautiful country—We lose our way—The timid shepherd boys—A fairy fog—The kindly proprietress and her hospitality—Tricias—Its elevation—Primitive quarters—A mill by cow-power—More *barrancos*—Bad water—Candelaria—Its ancient church—A gracious noonday rest—On the Caldera edge—Indescribable panorama—The Caldera—Its colours and immensity—The Pico de Bejanao—Volcanoes and lava flows.

WE stewed for a week in the town of Santa Cruz of Palma, getting daily more limp and indisposed for exertion of any kind. Then, with an effort, we decided to throw off the inertia that gained so fast upon us, by a methodical tour in and round the island. Forgetting where we were, we proposed at first to walk; but Don Pedro's impertinent laughter at such a notion changed our pedestrian into an equestrian tour. During two days we discussed the essential preparations; studied maps with the Marquis de Guisla, cross-examined men with horses, asses, or mules to let; and wondered whether the country fleas and smells could rival those of our town hotel. Don Pedro confessed to the smells, and to relieve us he periodically burnt certain herbs and messes in our room, which exhaled a brief fragrance, but were no match for their antagonists. But he said the fleas were trivial, and that we should meet with more in the villages than we had an idea of.

A mule and a lean white mare were therefore brought to the portico one bright morning late in April; and, having provisioned ourselves with eggs and bread, cheese and wine, we clattered away to the north for the first of the many *barrancos* we were to cross in the next four days. I need not again describe the glorious outlook from the capital on a sunny morning. The scene seldom varied. The Peak over the blue water was but more or less distinct; the wooded escarpments behind the town were always green against the pale blue sky, that seemed already veiled by a foreboding of the thick clouds which in an hour or two were sure to blow up round the mountain peaks, and slowly descend until they hung about two thousand feet from the sea level. Such were the routine scenic effects of Santa Cruz soon after dawn.

Our day's march was not destined to be extensive in direct mileage. We were to sleep at Los Sauces, fifteen miles distant. But direct distance in these islands gives no idea of the actual toil. We crossed nine *barrancos* of size on the way—one, the *barranco* de Galga, about eight miles from Santa Cruz, being really a compound or involution of *barrancos*: the main rift broken into pinnacles and ridges which had to be passed independently. The magnitude of this typical cleft may perhaps be better understood when I say that it proceeds from the summits of some of the highest of Palma's mountains, where they are not more than seven or eight miles from the sea. Before beginning our descent into the *barranco* de Galga, we stood on its turfy edge in the zone of heaths, and almost on the fringe of the pines; but we descended to the Atlantic level, and in the hot contracted channels sweated amid new surroundings of darting lizards, prickly pear, and euphorbia.

The road throughout our tour was on the whole bad. In places, it was indescribably bad. This is in part due to the hard lava surface, and in part to the neglect of the authorities, who spend thousands of pounds on two or three miles of first-class road on the skirts of the capital, but are reckless of the maintenance, still less improvement, of the remote tracks which are locally known as highroads. For use on the high roads between one village and another, the peasant always carries his *lanza*, a long wooden pole, spiked at the end ; and, indeed, he needs it.

We breakfasted at a miserable little wine-shop set on a nude hill slope. Here they used stones for weights, in selling the men their *gofio*. I ought to say that in Palma a man has to be hired with his beast. We therefore had two guides, because two animals. The men ate figs, sugar with their *gofio*, biscuits, and any small indiscriminate luxury among the wine-shop store which chanced to please them. They hoped we would pay for it all. We did so on this occasion, but not until we had made them blanch through their brownness by assuring the wine-shop keeper that their indulgences were their own affair.

Then, for three melting hours, we climbed and descended among some picturesque red hills, with a soil good for lupins, but otherwise uninteresting. We got up to the chestnuts, then fell quickly to aloes and palms. Shade there was none, and the men a-foot streamed with moisture. Even the animals lagged, and had to be baited forward with bunches of young barley, unceremoniously plucked from the adjacent fields. The lizards ran about underneath us by scores. Once my mule bit at a fine thistle, and almost swallowed the large bee that was upon it. This sensation made the poor fellow go smartly for several minutes.

At noon we halted by the village of S. Juan, which does not appear on Berthelot's map. The fountain here was notable for its abundance, and the beautiful drapery of red geraniums, nasturtiums, cacti, and a red-berried shrub which hung down from the wall of rock above it. We ate by it, in the cool of its waters, with the villagers looking down upon us. The dress of the people was simple, home-spun being the basis of the women's clothes, while the men wore as little of anything as they could. Some prolific orange trees near tempted us to try and negotiate a purchase; but when the proprietor heard of our needs, he generously sent us provision as a present. One curiosity of S. Juan must not be forgotten. On our way out of the village, we saw an old lady holding a hen by a string tied to its leg. This hen was attended by thirty-six chickens, all her own ; and she still had energy enough left in her to struggle mightily with the string that kept her aloof from her children.

At five o'clock we entered the village of San Andrés, between Los Sauces and the coast. This place, with its ancient church, was founded in 1614 by Captain Don Juan de Guisla Vandewalle, an ancestor of the Marquis de Guisla. The church stands in its dishevelled little Plaza. It is remarkable for nothing except its melodramatic paintings, its altar, dated 1694, and an antique wooden ceiling. The sacristan showed us everything, even to the *cura's* mildewed boots and socks, which he kept in the vestry, alongside the holy vessels.

San Andrés and Los Sauces are now a single town, of which the former is the lower part. The district is famous for its waters, its fertility, and its sweet bracing air. If Palma must have a sanatorium, it may be built at Los Sauces, the upper part of which is over a thousand feet above the sea. Sundry large handsome houses, and *fincas*, with gardens attached, give a degree of splendour to the outskirts of the town, which is belied by its rough bare interior. One extensive old monastic establishment, as solid as a citadel, has a superb perch; and the Plaza boasts an Italian garden of palms, orange trees, and a multitude of shrubs and flowers interspersed with statuary. But this garden has for long known no gardener, and its graces struggle with and strangle each other.

There is no inn at Los Sauces, but we carried a letter to a certain proprietor, who made us comfortable. I know not how many local tatterdemalions followed us, in wonder, to this gentleman's door; and while we stayed with him we had no privacy: the Alcalde, or this or that friend of our host, or the muleteers came to see us eat, and strolled about in the drawing-room which had been turned into our bedchamber, quite careless of the chairs which, in the latter case, had to be pushed from the door ere we allowed our cage to be forced. Our host, good man, could not understand how we longed for rest after our fatigue in the sun. Before dinner, he led us a-foot nearly two miles into the mountains, that we might see ere sunset the best thing in Los Sauces. This treasure was only a watermill; but so strong a stream straight from the Caldera, is, to a native, worth seeing. The mill was merrily grinding *gofio* for the housewives, who no sooner got their measures than they hurried home to eat it ere the aroma fled. Potatoes and barley were abundant in the Los Sauces district; but our host bewailed the scarcity of money. Everyone had enough to eat; this he acknowledged: but, since the decay of the cochineal industry, save a little wine to Cuba and England, there was no lucrative export left to them.

Punctually at five o'clock the next morning, our chief muleteer awoke us. From our windows the Caldera summits, only four or five miles distant, were then a clear crimson. But we had a very long day's work before us, and could give no time to the exclusive enjoyment of natural beauties. Everyone, except ourselves, said it was preposterous to think of trying to reach Garafia between sunrise and sunset. Trusting to our maps, however, we said it must be done ; and then, with shrugs of the shoulder, Ave Marias! and Carambas! the Alcade agreed with our host that the thing was certainly possible, though difficult.

Thus, half an hour after dawn, we plunged into the first of the twelve *barrancos* which were to give individuality to the day—the *barranco* de Herradura (Horse-shoe), a yawning abyss that began almost at the door of our friend's house. On the other side of it, we trotted cheerfully through many acres of rich arable land, grain, jewelled with red and yellow poppies, and fields of lupins. We then rose to a plateau of crimsoned soil, equally fertile, past the village of Barlovento, studded with eccentric windmills, and famous in Palma for the lighthouse which guards this, its north-eastern extremity. We ascended until we were among the heaths, with the pines of the mountains, cloud-swept by this time, close to us on the left. Then, as the northern country of the island appeared below us in broad slopes towards a rocky surf-beaten shore, we were able to guess at the obstacles before us. *Barranco* after *barranco* to the horizon! From the edge of these superb gullies, we looked down precipitous sides eight hundred and a thousand feet deep, and wondered how they were to be passed. In fact, the paths were not free from danger. They were cut in sharp zigzags down the face of the brown cliffs, and, where it seemed easier to do so, pine trunks had been bored into the rock, set parallel to each other, loosely covered with furze and dirt, thus composing a hanging road, three or four feet wide, to fall through or over which were a method of dying as certain as it were simple! Even the mule did not think highly of such engineering. He had to be lugged carefully by the man ahead, and pushed and coaxed behind. The trunks of the road were in places rotten, and once the animal put his foot through the track.

But though so laborious, these *barrancos* (and especially the *barrancos* de Gallegos and Peleos) were so grand that they stilled our groaning. In their upper parts, the woods were thick; we could see and hear thin cascades falling into their deep beds through brakes of creepers: and, now and again, the clouds which hurtled about their heads lifted to show us huge peaks and pinnacles, startlingly near, with blotches and heaps of snow in the crannies of their sides.

Our two places of bivouac this day were both, though differently, engaging. We breakfasted on some greensward by the blue stones of a *barranco* bed, with walls of rock hung with brambly withes of great length up the ravine, and a contracting outlet seawards. About eight hundred feet above us was a little black house, the last we should see for hours, said the men. Hither, after breakfast, we toiled, to buy raw eggs at two for three halfpence, and eat curds and whey, with a few grains of sugar, carefully weighed by the housewife like a precious drug. This was at 9 a.m. At 2 p.m. we thought we were justified in again calling a halt. What lovely country we had traversed in the meantime! Wholly uncultivated, if not wholly uncultivable! From ridges of turf set with asphodels and Canarian buttercups, we had climbed to pinnacles of rock crowned by gigantic pine trees, with trunks a yard in diameter, straight and unbranched for eighty to a hundred feet. Now we were winding through a thicket of laurels and gum-cistus, and now treading softly on a carpet of pine-droppings, with an interminable vista of tree trunks on both sides of us, and in an air as balmy as it was bracing. Thus we got to a small glen, arched by intermingled laurels and pines, and full of the song of blackbirds. Here was a spring, and by the side of the water we gave ourselves half an hour's rest in the cool shade.

For seven or eight hours we moved briskly forward through this broken upland country. Then, when the light began to mellow across the bright tops of the pines, the men admitted that they had lost their way. It was no wonder, but somewhat annoying. They shouted, one after the other, as we went dubiously along, up hills and down hills, hoping some stray shepherd might hear us. In this we were fortunate; for after a time we heard the tinkling of goatbells, and on a grassy pine-topped conical hill, we saw the horned flock and a couple of boys in long white cloaks. The boys were so frightened that they said "Yes, sir," to our every inquiry. Only when we had left them, did the bolder of them volunteer in stentorian voice some sort of advice.

This direction led us up into the mountains again. On our way we stepped into a local fog, dry and innocuous, through which the sun partly pierced, so as to play strange tricks of beauty with our surroundings. The gold of the lateral branches of the pines was tipped with purple, the rocks flushed crimson, and the house-leeks, which here covered them thickly, were like so many amethysts in a gorgeous setting. The very moss under our feet was dyed prismatically, and thus, for a few brief minutes, we and everything suffered a transfiguration as romantic as it was exquisite.

But help came to us through this fairy glamour, in the form of a rich lady, travelling home from a distant town, in company with her maid. She was a tall graceful woman about thirty, and wore her black glossy hair in two thick tails which reached to her hips. What objects of interest we were to her! And how she invoked the Virgin when she heard the tale of our day's proceedings! We had wandered miles from the right track, and, instead of being on the skirts of Garafia, we were within half an hour of Tricias, a village much farther towards the west of the island. To Tricias, therefore, we turned, glad if the light would hold until we were within view of its houses. Our lady friend, however, would not let us part with her so abruptly. We were to pause in the woods, while she and her maid sped to her house behind an acclivity; and then accept what she sent us. This came duly: a decanter of wine, plates and napkins, figs, walnuts, and almonds; and while we ate and drank, the two kindly souls stood on the hilltop, and waved their handkerchiefs. The transition from despair to mental tranquillity, and such sensual enjoyment as nuts and wine, was too much for our guides. They emptied the decanter, and, after inciting the animals into a mad-cap gallop, brought us among the red roofs and squab-shaped cottages of Tricias with disgraceful hullabaloo. We had covered about twenty-four miles of country, equal in its configuration to at least forty-five of but common irregularity.

Tricias is only a small village between the more important townlets of Garafia and Puntagorda. It stands high, at least 3,000 feet above the sea, and overlooks the broken plain of Puntagorda, with a forest of magnificent pines in the south-west, and one bold volcanic hill by the coast, over Puntagorda town. While the men reconnoitred for a lodging, the last glory of the sunset seemed to burn this volcano top: its indented crest glowed like fire, while the sea beyond, and the lower country, was a pale saffron. But a rush of cold clouds from the Pico de los Muchachos made us shiver in spite of this warm panorama. Tricias is the nearest place in Palma to this Pico, 7,234 feet high, and the chief mountain of the Caldera. On this, its western side, it falls to the coast in graduated ridges, pinnacles of variegated volcanic rocks, and slopes of shaly *débris* clumped with pines. It ought to be scalable either from Garafia or Tricias. But, save for the view down its precipices into the Caldera, it has little preeminence over the other edges and needles which form the rim of Palma's supreme natural curiosity.

We had rough but hospitable quarters in Tricias. The miller of the place received us into his house; and a small adjacent building, of untrimmed stones inside and out, provided us with a bedroom. Two trestle beds in this airy chamber gave us the content of kings, and, having guided the trembling hands of our nervous hostess in the preparation of supper, we ate it among the boxes, linen chests, sheepskins, knives, axes, and miscellaneous odds and ends of the family living-room. Splints of pitch pine were stuck in the kitchen walls for lights, and the only water obtainable was brown and stagnant, from a big elaborate tank outside. Notwithstanding the fleas, a thermometer at 42°, a room stifling with smoke from the kitchen fire, and the wails of our host's baby, we slept soundly in Tricias.

Before starting at 5.30 the next morning, we were taken to see the mill of Tricias, worked by a couple of cows. It did not interest me hugely; but our guide's enthusiasm was extreme. With him the mill was always the measure of the village, and his first question to a peasant in an outlying part of the country was about the nearest mill and its characteristics.

We left Tricias in a driving fog, cold and wet. All the household were coughing or clearing their throats, while the land three miles below us was bright and verdant under a southern sun. "There is some phthisis up here," said our host; "but down there, oh, no." Very soon, however, we in the uplands had also as much sun as we wanted, and the vineyards in the purpled loam, the fields of poppies and barley, and the pines and heaths round about us put on their full beauty.

This day's journey along the western side of Palma was monotonous compared to its predecessor. The *barrancos* were less formidable than those to the north; the pines disappeared; and, as we got nearer to the mouth of the Caldera, the soil thinned, and we found ourselves gradually ascending obliquely to the summit of a long broad back of a mountain which fell smoothly below us to the sea. But among the dozen *barrancos* which we traversed, two or three deserve notice. In the *barranco* de Garome, near Puntagorda, there is a precipitous volcanic rock, the natural cells of which have been appropriated as residences and storehouses. How these various flats were to be attained by their occupiers we could but surmise; for the doors let immediately upon a serious abyss. The *barranco* de Tinizara, the next of importance, boasts of a spring; its waters trickle down a rock clad with ferns, lichens, and bramble; but the supply is not abundant, and it is soon absorbed by the dry thirsty land below it. This was in fact the only fountain we passed in fifteen miles. Tanks are essential appurtenances to a dwelling between Tricias and Timé on the Caldera; but the tank water is often fetid. The *barranco* de la Cueva gets its name from a spacious cave in its upper part. The cave is utilised as a house, with a stout wooden door, and geranium bushes at its postern. The *barranco* de Jorado is bridged by some serrated rocks; the arch below is devoted to a crucifix, and by the crucifix is an old shrine, now inhabited by commonplace mortals, who climb to their eyric by a ladder. From the blue and brown stones of this *barranco* bed, the cross and the shrine in this natural tunnel, prominent against the farther sky, strike the fancy.

About halfway between Tricias and Los Llanos,

our destination, we reached the townlet of Candelaria, a place of disappointment. We had postponed breakfast four hours that we might eat it here. But all the town clubbed together could with difficulty, and after a weary hour of tarrying, give us nothing but a bowl of eggs, some bread, and insufferable wine. The sacristan of the church, the mayor, and a knot of others made a pother about us that was brutally vexing in our hungry and heated state: and uncertain whether we were to fast or be fed, we moved backwards and forwards between the church and a dull room that had been offered us. Luckily, we had nuts and figs in our saddle bags; for the men had not scrupled to take and store all the fruit the good Samaritan lady had sent to us the evening before in the forest.

The church of Candelaria is reputed the oldest in the island, after S. Andrés. It was certainly built for a larger congregation than the dismal little town which now surrounds it can muster for its broken pavements and rickety chairs. The reredos, too, has not its equal in Palma for ornateness. The Apostles are set in niches upon it, bearing marks of their identity. St. Peter of course carries his keys; St. Simon, a long iron saw, in memory of his martyrdom, &c. Above these images are paintings, coarse indeed, but suggestive. But the cruellest picture of all is a great black representation of a window, daubed on the northern chancel wall, to match a real window on the opposite wall. The exterior of the northern porch of this uncouth old church is decorated in fresco with a beamed sun;

and the artist has given the planet nose, eyes, and a mouth. The west porch is similarly frescoed with a rude tower. It was not to be expected that the sacristan could explain these insignia. They had been there a long time, he said; and that threw the burden of explanation upon his ancestors.

Candelaria's population is 2,308. I am glad to state it exactly, out of gratitude to the Mayor, who, after a long consultation with his fellow-citizens, and some sort of an impromptu census, thus gave us the figures. The district claims to be very poor; but our friends, lay and ecclesiastical, were able to bring twenty-five eggs, hard-boiled, to satisfy the appetite of a couple of men. A sixpence "for the good of the Church" almost brought tears of gratitude into the eyes of the burly sacristan who accepted it. Though hens were plentiful, minted money was no doubt very scarce in Candelaria.

Hence we rode over some grilling rocks in the heat of the day, with a fellow-traveller. He was a landed proprietor in the district, and civilly went out of his way to take us for an hour's rest to one of his farms. The tenant was a cobbler, who was anxious to mend our boots when he saw the sorry plight to which they were reduced. He admired the magnificence of the ruins, as you or I might admire the Parthenon. But though the rest was grateful to us, we did not stay long among the leather of our friend's tenant's workshop. "Allow me to catch a flea for you!" said our entertainer, in the midst of conversation. His quick eyes detected the insect on my coat. It needed no inordinate amount of sensibility to realize that many others were about us, though invisible.

An ascent of another hour's duration brought us at last in sight of the great goal for all travellers in this small Atlantic island. The smooth greyish slope, the summit of which had for long been our horizon, suddenly ended. We stood upon the crest of the ridge. Below us was the *barranco* de las Augustias, which puts all other *barrancos* to the blush. To the left, through a clear purple light, was the wonderful Caldera. Beyond the *barranco* the laughing country of Los Llanos sloped to the sea, in a profusion of greenery. And beyond this fertile village-dotted plateau was Palma's *cordillera*, or mountain backbone, detaching towards the south of the island into isolated volcanic peaks of brilliant colours and exquisite symmetry. We had stepped from the uninforming conventional soil of the outer slope, upon the inner section of the great cliff, torn asunder by the *barranco*, upon masses of red-brown scoria, and cellular crags still eloquent of the torture which once held them molten and plastile. Words cannot describe this extraordinary prospect, which, as a landscape, can have few rivals throughout the length and breadth of the globe.

To compare the Titanic with the infinitesimal, imagine the Caldera as a pear divested of its pulp, and laid longitudinally on a table. Remove the upper part of the skin of the pear, and then we have in miniature a model of this long-extinct volcano, with its portly nucleus and narrowing elongated stem, where a river flows out by the *barranco* de las Augustias into the sea. But the sides of the pear must be six and seven thousand feet high, soaring into peaks and edges of every conceivable shape; and, precipitous though these environing mountains are, they do not now, like the walls of the pear, bend concavely towards their base. The pear, too, must be twelve or thirteen miles from head to stem, and more than six miles across in its broadest part.

In truth, however, the Caldera baffles pen or pencil. Its immensity defies the artist, and a pen must here be inspired, indeed, to reproduce for others the effect it strives at. One may tell of its length and breadth, enumerate the mountains that hem it so zealously from the outer world, or even analyze the rocks and pebbles that cumber its terrific bed, and guess at the millenniums which have sped since its deep fires illumined the precipices that sink into it, thousands of feet, almost perpendicular, from its circuitous lip. But what, after all, will such dry records represent? The colours of this great basin cannot be caught. It is impossible to do more than merely suggest the vivid contrasts between the tremendous walls of rock where they stand in shadow, and where, again, the sun brings forth their beauty by tracing the crimson, purple, and white crystalline lines which score them irregularly from peak to base; between the sombre trunks of the firs that have died from old age, untroubled by the woodman's axe, and the fresh young pines glowing under the noonday sky with a vigorous intensity of life; between the size of this gap, isolated from the world, and the stillness of it, broken but rarely by the echoing crash of an avalanche into its tumultuous depths.

Long ages ago, the Caldera was probably inaccessible from above. The mountains then did actually frame it concavely; and from the Pico de los Muchachos, now about 7,500 feet above the sea, one might have looked fearfully over into this crater, at that time maybe 10,000 feet below, from an edge that positively impended. But, since the extinction of the Caldera, its inner configuration has undergone a vast change. The mountains have fallen in: every avalanche that still echoes through the chasm helps to prove it. Their own elevation has been reduced, and the bed of the crater raised to its present level, about 2,000 feet above the sea. Thus the Caldera has become what it is, little more than the meeting place of the long slopes of *débris* that shoot down into it. Pines and firs clothe the slopes; goats browse on them; and in the heart of the pit a farmer has set up his dwelling. In short, but for the history told by the rocks in the Caldera bed, and the unmistakable marks of fusion in the rifts of the mountain side, one might well doubt its volcanic origin.[1]

The southern side of the Caldera, unlike the northern, swells into a single shapely mountain, that

---

[1] Leopold von Buch well terms the Caldera "the great chimney or vent for the energy which raised the island above the sea-level." Looking down into it from the edge of one of its precipices, four thousand feet high, he, like the rest of us, exclaims: "Where can anything so prodigious be found to rival this?"

of Bejanao, crag upon crag, until a castellated turret crowns the pile. The outer bulk of Bejanao falls smoothly towards Los Llanos (the plains), just as the western slopes of Candelaria, Tigarafe, &c., rest upon the axis of the Pico de los Muchachos.

From this Olympian standpoint, we were able to draw a precise line between the old and the modern volcanoes of Palma. The Caldera and all the north of the island have suffered volcanic ravages, but they are now at rest. On the southern side of Los Llanos, however, the faint yellow and purpled cones of two or three mountains show the symmetry of volcanoes recently in action. More than this. From depressions in their sides, we can trace broad gray-purple lines of lava trending seawards down the incline of the land. One stream is that of 1585, which is said to have cooked the fish in the sea for a distance of two miles from the coast. Another, of a lighter colour, makes a bold curved score upon the land, due to the diversion of older outflows, and then meanders past the red-roofed town of Los Llanos, stopping a little way from the shore. In the midst of these rivers of ruin are two or three islets, fertile and green with fig-trees and grain. Nor are the stereotyped cinder hills wanting to Los Llanos. One is a rich maroon colour; another green with tobacco-plants; a third yellow to its base; and a fourth is carefully terraced into vineyards. Around and beyond them are the towns of Los Llanos, Argual, El Paso, and Tazacorte, while countless gay villas nestle in the thick foliage of this sunny, prolific land.

All this wealth is due to the Caldera: the thin white lines which run along the *barranco* edge, and dive into the plateau, are aqueducts, carrying its never-ceasing waters into the fields and gardens.

CHAPTER XVIII.

Los Llanos—Its *fonda*—Curious visitors and fellow guests—Argual—Paso and the Mayor—Paso's school—The Caldera, by the *barranco*—Under the Pico de los Muchachos—The Caldera bed—The Cumbrecita Pass—Steep crags—Clouds brewing in the Caldera—The old and the new road over the *cordillera*—The volcano of Tocade—We desert Don Pedro—A cruel voyage from Palma.

WE descended the walls of the *barranco* de las Augustias by a series of precipitous zigzags cut in the loose and consolidated volcanic ash, white and black, of which its lower parts are composed. The river crossed, a tiresome corresponding ascent brought us, in about two hours from the rim of Timé (as our vantage point is called) to the town of Los Llanos.

Here we stayed awhile. Los Llanos is the second town in Palma. With its adjacent townlets of Paso, Tazacorte, and Argual, it has a population of about 7,000, who seem to live merrily upon the fruits and *gofio* which abound on this happy plateau. At a distance, Los Llanos is a gay town: the red roofs contrast brightly with the tufts of palms in their midst, and the flat, black bell-tower of the church is not displeasing. But, within, it is dead and still. The streets are grassy, and the houses are mean.

Our beasts brought us to the door of the inn with a clatter that put the place in a tremor of excitement. Even the *cura*, who was cannily estimating the merits of a number of game cocks in crates outside a dealer's house, lifted his spectacled nose to see what it meant.

Los Llanos has a *fonda*. That is to say, an enterprising merchant of the town keeps an empty house, into which a visitor may be inveigled, and wherein he may be forced to wonder whether he is to feed upon the furniture. The arrangements were in fact eccentric. We had good beds and few fleas; but it was difficult to get anything to eat. Dinner was nominally at six, yet we did not see the soup until half-past seven. Then, indeed, when we had disturbed the whole neighbourhood with our objurgations, a fat cook-maid would come flying into the house, obscured by savoury steam; and the signal having gone down the street that the Englishmen were about to be fed, citizen after citizen dropped in, to watch us, and enjoy themselves. The owner of the inn, who aspired to sell his wines in London, made us taste them all; and what grievous colics did we not suffer in our attempts to oblige him! Men and women were all anxious to know whether the methods of life in London agreed in any way with those of Los Llanos; and the young chemist from over the way civilly strangled a fowl under our noses, that we might see how cleverly such feats were done in his country. The cobblers who visited us gaped at our boots. The very domestics of the place asked to see our arms, to satisfy themselves that we had blue blood in our veins. For, in our impatience, we had condescended to empty wash-basins, and search the larder with our own hands and eyes.

Nevertheless, I recall Los Llanos pleasurably. When we were not hungry, or anxious to be off somewhere, the stillness of the inn was soothing. One night, however, a waggon-load of peasants and others was shot into the house for a share of the accommodation. They played cards, with beans for counters, in the broad ante-room adjoining our bedchamber; and when they were tired of cards all the score of them lay down on the boards, and serenaded us with snores till break of day. A certain tall red-nosed lady, of questionable habits, also associates herself with this inn. She assumed mediæval attitudes in our presence, and in her wilder moments could, by stratagem only, be kept out of our bedroom, though we were washing or lay in bed. To this day it is a problem unsolved whether she was ripe for Colney Hatch, or systematically inebriate. It was one or the other. And yet she had in her the raw material of a typical Palma woman. She might have been handsome and imperious, under the control of a reasonable mind.

Of course, the Caldera is the chief loadstone of Los Llanos. But in the rich estate of Don Miguel Sotomayor, of Argual (a relation of the Marquis de Guisla), we had attractions of another kind, and a surfeit of agriculture of the highest class. This gentleman (who owns the Caldera) showed us his plantation with pardonable self-satisfaction. Here was a veritable garden of acclimatization. Enormous chestnut trees were side by side with superb royal palms, their unfoliaged boughs stretching over fields of sugar-cane ripe for the sickle. An ilex stood between a banana and an orange-tree. Potatoes and tobacco were in parallel fields. Don Miguel also, though with the kindest intentions, helped us to new stomach-aches by pressing upon us certain alcoholic distillations from his various crops. The secret of the exuberant fertility of this estate lies in the water. Tanks, with a fresh strong current through them, abounded; and Don Miguel had also erected a luxurious bath-house, which nature had adorned with a wreathing of maidenhair ferns, geraniums, and China roses. Sotomayor's estate is indeed a byeword in Palma for all that is perfect. It is administered in patriarchal fashion. The house precincts are approached by a spacious quadrangular courtyard, the entrance being shaded by some enormous eucalypti. And on three sides of this enclosure are five or six distinct mansions for different members of the family, with marble heraldic bearings surmounting them. The name of Sotomayor appears in the list of Spanish conquerors in 1495; it may be, therefore, that for four centuries the chief inheritors of the name have lived together in this amiable clannishness.

At another time we rode about a thousand feet higher up the plateau to the town of Paso, to whose Mayor we had a letter. His worship received us with the usual Spanish hospitality. But he had his business to achieve at the same time. Old crones and boisterous younger people bothered him with all sorts of pleas, while we chatted with him in his unpretentious office. Nor could he get his petitioners to leave him, when they found such uncommon subjects of interest with their municipal father. But he had private as well as public annoyances. His orange trees were a prey to rats, who were wont to trot up the trunks, and clear out the pulp of as many fine fruit as they had time for. To remedy this, the mayor had clad the stems in sheets of tin, which he hoped would trick the dapper feet of his foes.

The churches of Los Llanos and Paso are not interesting. In Paso there is an eccentric pulpit of painted wood, and this was hung with common penny engravings of the Holy Family, such as our own Roman image-shops abound with. Paso's school was more to our taste. The mayor was proud of it, and so was the spruce young schoolmaster who presided, under a painting of Alphonso XII., over the seventy-five or eighty scholars of the school. Education is improving in the Canaries. In 1860, out of a population of 237,036, no fewer than 206,214 could neither read nor write. Now schoolhouses are broadly sown over the land, and the schoolmaster talks glibly of the number of pupils who have matriculated during his time. And, as in Paso, the pine-boarded walls of the schoolroom are hung with placards of moral maxims, in large type, for the incidental profit of the scholars:—

"Be true children of the Church, and it will lead you along the road of temporal and eternal happiness."

"After the Church, nothing deserves so much

respect as your school—in which the child is matured and the man is completed."

We visited the Caldera twice from Los Llanos— once by the conventional entrance, following the bed of the river; and by the Cumbrecita, a pass on the south-eastern side of it. I know not which route is the more amazing. But the view obtained from the heights over Timé, between Candelaria and the *barranco* is the most comprehensive and thrilling of the three.

From Los Llanos, it is but an hour's ride to the gorge of the Caldera. The scene comes unexpectedly. The barley and rye fields north of Los Llanos suddenly cease; we turn a rock-shoulder; and the prodigious gap is seen in the distance, with its spherical boundary of mountains. The track falls rapidly from the hill-side towards the river— too rapidly, indeed, for the precipice dropping to the gorge is about fifteen hundred feet. And, on the other side, the northern wall of the *barranco*, where it soars towards the Pico de los Muchachos, towers from a base of gray matrix about a thousand feet perpendicular.

This entrance cannot be made too soon in the day. At daybreak, and for the three or four succeeding hours, every purple pinnacle of the Muchachos' mountain, every yellow pine on the Caldera spurs, and the rainbow-hues of the gorgeous rocks of the cavity are all preternaturally clear to the eye. The Caldera then seems to be bathed in an atmosphere peculiar to itself. But between nine and ten o'clock snowy wisps of vapour begin to form *in* the basin.

They do not sail over the island from the sea, get transfixed on the mountain points, and thus descend within. The clouds actually generate under our eyes, and ascend until they attain an exterior current of air, which either rends them to shreds against the encircling rocks, or carries them away from the Caldera. But once the clouds have formed, view of the phenomenon as a whole is impossible. With the drifting of the vapour, the mountain tops may be temporarily uncovered or concealed; but, save on exceptional days, it is said to be rare for the Caldera to clear again until the evening.

From the southern side, we fell to the river bed and, crossing the water, climbed a steep slope of ash and slag and granitic rocks. By a multitude of deviations, we at length got to a fountain under the final precipice of the Pico de los Muchachos, where it rose sheer above us into the clouds. Here we lunched sublimely, to the music of falling water, and the occasional boom of an avalanche. In front of us, across the basin, the Pico de Bejanao fought with the clouds—was now obscured; later, uncloaked; and again hid, save as to its purpled head, which kissed the blue high above all things terrestrial.

With difficulty, I clambered to a remote cavity in the Muchachos' mountain. Here, deep in a fissure, the matrix was seen rugged and congested as only fused rocks can be. Hence the view into the depths of the Caldera was weird and beautiful. From all sides, save the south-west, verdant spurs thick with pines, plunged abruptly down to a common centre, some three thousand feet below us. This deepest depth if I may so call it, though small in area, was in sublime disorder. Pillars and blocks, hundreds of feet in vertical height, jostled each other in the contracted space of a few acres. The wreck of the avalanche of an hour ago had to accommodate itself among this ruin of the ten thousand avalanches that had preceded it. But, thanks to the many rills of water streaming from the mountain sides upon the chaos, and thanks to the fierce sun, which, when vertical, seems able to shine through the clouds of the Caldera, fallen rocks, crevices, and the new shadowed soil under the rocks, were all mantled with greenery.

A few hundred feet below my perch was the house of the farmer of the Caldera, set on a knoll of turf fit for an English park. Enormous pines were above and below it; wild fig-trees, bracken, and many a flower helped to deck the surroundings of this lonely house. And the tinkle of goat-bells contrasted with the noise of the tumbling rocks. Yet it is not too much to say that at any moment a mountain crest may topple over from the Muchachos' ridge, and crush house and outbuildings as a steam-hammer cracks a common nut.

Our third view of the Caldera was by the high pass called the Cumbrecita. To revert to my analogy of the hollow pear skin. We had first crossed the pear at its stem: this was going from Timé to Los Llanos by the *barranco* de las Augustias. Secondly, we had entered the pear by its stem, proceeded along it, and climbed to the northern side of it where it is broadest: this was marked by our rest under the cliff of the Muchachos. Now, by the Cumbrecita, we ascended the plateau east of Los Llanos, and turned sharply to the north between the buttress of Bejanao and the terminal cliffs of the *cordillera* of Palma, so as to strike the Caldera, or the pear, on the southern side. Speaking roughly, the Cumbrecita is about 3,000 feet above the sea level. We were therefore nearly half-way between the pit bottom and the mountain edges of the Caldera lip.

The day was again serene and clear at the outset. The volcano de Tocade, south of the plain, enchained attention by its delicate coral and saffron colouring, in contrast with the black river of lava which had poured from a depression in it. The pines fairly dazzled us with the glow of their gold; and the stern ravines of the *cordillera*, as we neared them, ennobled the scene as a whole.

But all too soon the clouds brewed around us: we had barely time to groan over the glorious sunny heat of the crater, and, in a series of apostrophes, express our rapturous admiration of the Muchachos' rocks in front of us, when everything was obliterated, and we were in the heart of a mass of seething vapour. The *arête* of the Cumbrecita is grand in the extreme. The Pico de Bejanao soars from one side of it, and on the other the Pico del Capitan stands sentinel with a perpendicular cliff of at least 1,000 feet, and an isolated pinnacle of about 400 feet, called the Rock " de la Paira," adjoining it. Of this last, our guide said that it was too steep even for goats—" but shepherds have ascended it, two or three in company, tied with ropes, for the sake of the good herbage upon it."

Before the clouds were upon us, we had time to scramble for about a mile along the eastern curve of the Caldera, following an aqueduct, dated 1858, which taps a fountain in the side of the Pico del Capitan. Our course was rugged enough, and the dive of the mountain spurs beneath us so abrupt that the stones we dislodged soon rolled out of sight, with a noisy rumble that told of their inevitable trail. But, with the generation of the clouds, the Caldera was blotted out, and we had to recur to memory for an idea of it, though we were in its midst. And here, swathed in the dry fog, while we sat with our backs against the pine trunks, our guide would have slept till nightfall if we had permitted it.

There are two direct roads between Los Llanos and the capital of Palma. Both have to surmount the *cordillera* which bisects the island. The older road, known now as such, bends to the south, winds between Palma's modern volcanoes, and finally strikes through the mountains by a pass that is tedious but not very steep. The "new road," as it is called, elects to follow a bee-line between the two towns. On each side of the *cordillera*, it concedes but little to the sharp rise of the country. The zigzags to the watershed are nearly as severe as those of Taganana in Tenerife. From the summit, one looks down the western incline, through a noble forest of firs and pines, at the plateau of Los Llanos and Paso, spread with the precision of a map; and east, by heaths grown to trees, laurels and chestnuts (each in their respective zone), to the high ground over Santa Cruz, and the Peak of Tenerife beyond the sea. It is curious that the line of demarcation between the pines and heaths should here be so emphatic. At the same altitude of about 5,000 feet, pines alone grow on the western side of the watershed, and heaths alone on the eastern.

Of these two roads, the longer is the more attractive. Twice did we traverse the shorter and steeper road. Once a loose tongue whispered in Los Llanos that the mail boat was on the eve of sailing for Tenerife. In hot haste, therefore (for our time had run out), we sped towards Santa Cruz, only to find, upon arrival, that the report was false. For its ferns and huge laurels, moss-clad as to their trunks, and for the sweet transition from chestnut woods to groves of palms, and lanes of tropical flowers perfumed with tropical odours, this route is worthy of praise.

But the other is much the more varied. By it we wind, at a gentle elevation, through some dainty pine forests, bestrewn with lichened rocks, and balmy with their own breath and that of the gum cistus bushes which also abound in it. As we ascend to the volcano of Tocade, the outline of the Caldera behind gradually defines itself against the sky. We trace the elongated pear-shape as we had not before traced it. And, with disinterested feelings, we can admire hence the pictorial effect of the eddies of white cloud which chance to be driving from the sea into the crater, by the *barranco* mouth.

But the exceeding beauty of the tints of the volcanic ash-slopes round about us draw off attention even from the vanishing Caldera. This district is only a few square miles in area; and yet it provides all the choicest features of a great land burnt and torn by subterranean fires and forces. At one time we are struggling up an ascent of the finest pumice, a trial to the eyes, and passing an ochre hillock with sparse yellow pines upon it. Ten minutes later, we have done with the hillock. Before us is a miniature desert of black ash, from which an isolated cliff of gaunt reddish scoriæ is protruded, and with natural bombshells scattered over it. The heat of this dark ash is such that, though riding, we sweat hardly less than the men on their feet. But a moment's pause, and our faces are dry, so absorptive is the warm, invigorating air!

By this road, we pass close to the crater of 1585. The volcano of Tocade itself is so smooth in its modelling that it seems nothing but a gigantic sand-hill. Its reddish-yellow slopes support hardly a handful of vegetation: some wisps of feeble grass, some thyme, and mean retama; nothing else. A few red-beaked choughs fly screaming over our heads, as if in disgust with this unproductive desert.

Thus gradually we reach the water-shed in this part of the island, about one thousand feet lower than that by the new road. Several narrow ruts in the bright red matrix mark the dividing point. The descent briskens, and here we are confronted by magnificent aërial effects. We are level with the clouds, and close to them, yet separated from them by a strip of unclouded space. They hang like a colossal fleece, with a menace of suffocation, thick and ponderous. Nevertheless, over the crest of them (which proves that they are lower than they seem) the Peak of Tenerife is visible, sunny and divine, framed between its own blue sky and the extraordinary white cumulus, in an incomparable vignette of Nature.

Hence the descent is more and more rapid, as we enter the laurel woods; but three tedious hours have to pass ere Santa Cruz is within hail.

We were no sooner again settled in the stuffy capital than the local lethargy overcame us anew. So that our six last days in the island were devoted to little save eating and drinking, bathing and conjuring a ship to appear. On our return from Los Llanos, we had been compelled, out of respect for our health, to separate from Don Pedro and his large wife. The smells of his hotel were really, as we told him, too paralysing. Besides, the bedroom he gave us was too public for our English tastes. It had a couple of windows, opening not upon the air of heaven, but upon an inner passage, which was a thoroughfare. Thus we were not even to be asphyxiated in comfort. Rude ragamuffins lounged perennially outside these windows from the first cock-crow; and the mysteries of our toilet, from the tub in a patent indiarubber bath, to the washing of our teeth, were bared to them, to be discussed later by all their ragged companions.

This flitting was a cruel blow to Don Pedro, but it could not be avoided. In his conceit at lodging us, he had opened his mind at odd times, and declared his loftiest ambitions. There was no English vice-consul in Palma; or at best a superannuated one. What would not he (Don Pedro) give if he could have the honour of unfurling our flag upon his house-top? In short, he nudged us to speak a good word for him in London. This sly intriguing, however, did not deter him from the impolitic step of presenting us with a bill conceived on purpose for us. And so we parted, not friends.

Of the other hotel in Santa Cruz, but few words need be told. The proprietor was overjoyed at our preference for him. We were the guests of honour at his table d'hôte. Such extra luxuries as new milk and sponge cakes before breakfast, and chocolate late in the evening were genially provided for us. All our reasonable wishes were laws. And in his elation of heart and gratitude, the good man let us into the secret recesses of his establishment, where he made soap with blue veins in it, and of no ill-smelling ingredients. Here we paid 3s. 4d. a day, and gained flesh every hour. And here, after three long weeks in Palma, we met the *padron* or master, of a smack, who purposed sailing for Tenerife, as soon as he had had his breakfast. His boat was small but clean; and we were welcome to a passage.

I will say nothing about an abortive excursion, one hot afternoon, in search of the cave of Mazo, the inscription upon which I have already mentioned. We had a guide who was drunk, and who felt such astonishment that my friend should object to his tipsy embraces, that he left us in a huff. He was a gentleman, he said, and he expected to be treated as a gentleman. We wandered for a few hours over the lava-beds of the south-east of Palma, and returned defeated. This was an apt prologue to our new night at sea.

The smack sailed gracefully while the day lasted. The *padron* even promised to land us that same evening. But the wind lulled; dark clouds congregated ahead of us; when the sun set we were only half-way between the islands, and all the portents were bad. Then up sprang a gale; and throughout a wild night we had nothing to mitigate our miseries except the hope of day. The dawn broke, and showed us the land—all black and awesome, and deep in cloud, save where the surf swelled into gothic shapes as the sea rushed upon the shore. "Impossible!" said the master, when we urged him to run in and drown us, rather than prolong the elephantine oscillations with which his ship indulged us, while he lay off in hesitation. There was no help for it. In the storm we could not land at Orotava; and so the order was given "On to Santa Cruz." For seven hours more, therefore, we took our buffetings, while the vessel slowly fought her way round the island, and laboriously tacked into the harbour of the capital.

CHAPTER XIX.

Historical summary—Béthencourt and his successors—Disputes about the Canaries between Spain and Portugal—Generous native princes—Rejon, and the conquest of Grand Canary—Las Palmas—Ascension Day in the cathedral—Bones and copes—Paintings—The hospital—The English sailor among the Spaniards—Theatre and markets—Spanish justice—The harbour—Cloudy weather—The evening promenade—A funeral and burial.

"GRAND Canary is so called because Almighty God created it to be the head of the other six Fortunate Islands." This is the opinion of the Jesuit Sosa; and for the last two centuries, Las Palmas, the capital of Grand Canary, has never ceased to urge its superior claims to be the capital of the archipelago. Even now, in 1887,[1] the contest between Santa Cruz and Las Palmas is very keen; the merchants of the two cities are in unequivocal rivalry. "We have the shipping trade—there can be no doubt about that," says Santa Cruz. "And we shall have it"—with no less assurance, says Las Palmas—"when our grand new harbour is com-

[1] And now, in 1888, I daresay the deplorable collision and loss of life in the harbour of Las Palmas will be pressed into service as a fresh proof of the superiority of the Grand Canary capital, in drama no less than in prospective commerce.

pleted." Las Palmas is more energetic than Santa Cruz; and I fancy it will in the end crush the present capital even as that superseded Laguna.

The history of Grand Canary, before Spain annexed it, is very creditable to its aboriginal inhabitants. It is, in fact, so much involved with the European adventurers previous to De Lugo, the conqueror of Tenerife and Palma, that a few words of general Canarian history may be given to help forward its elucidation.

Until the year 1402, the various European mariners who touched in Canarian waters did so with no definite idea of conquest. Contrary winds, the need of water, curiosity, and a thirst for slaves, led the first Mallorquins, Genoese, French, and Spanish vessels into the island harbours; and, their purposes satisfied, they sailed away. But in 1402 a certain Norman gentleman, Juan de Béthencourt, sold his lands, fitted out a ship, and expatriated himself, with serious designs in his head. He had heard vague reports about the Canaries, and, with but slight attempts to substantiate these rumours, he started on his romantic expedition—

> "Con gallardos Franceses y Españoles,
> De sojuzgar naciones codiciosos. . . ."

At Corunna, the ship narrowly escaped destruction by the Earl of Crawford, and sundry other Scotch and English adventurers. But Béthencourt eluded these enemies, surmounted the hesitation of certain of his comrades, whose courage failed them at Cadiz, paid his respects to the King of Spain, under whose patronage he promptly put himself, and in due time reached Lanzarote, the most north-easterly of the islands. Here he was pacifically received by the king, Guadarfrà, who met him attired in a cloak of skins, and wearing a diadem of seashells; and Béthencourt at once took possession, when the native potentate had accepted the proferred friendship and protection of the King of Spain. "I cannot be vassal to anyone, because I was born a lord," said Guadarfrà; but this incidental demur did not prevent the Europeans from portioning out his territory, and domesticating themselves.

The conquest thus achieved (and indeed nothing could have been simpler than the acquisition of Lanzarote and Fuerteventura), Béthencourt returned provisionally to Spain. Henry III. gave him audience at Seville, and willingly allowed him to do homage for the island that was already his, and for the other six islands which, he doubted not, were no less easy to acquire.

"The good disposition of your mind is proclaimed by your acknowledgment of the rights of my crown, and I am much gratified that you have come to render homage for these certain islands which I am told are about two hundred leagues distant, and of which my own subjects have scarcely heard so much as a word."

Thus spake the King, and he gave Béthencourt money and men to aid him in the conquest that was yet before him.

But, in the meantime, the gentle-blooded colonists

of Lanzarote had begun to slight the innocent natives who had welcomed them with such extraordinary benignity. The chaplains who had accompanied the expedition made converts, and baptized all who consented to be baptized. But, to the despoiled Guadarfrà, this new religion could not justify or atone for the deportation of his own kith and kin to be sold as slaves. "What a people are these Europeans!" wailed the hapless ex-monarch. "And what kind of a religion is theirs, which, while they praise its sanctity, allows them to behave traitrously towards us, and like tricksters among themselves? They tell us we have an immortal soul, and all proceed from one Father; but at the same time they despise us as if we were the vilest of beings; they sell us for slaves; they treat us as barbarians and infidels, and forget how greatly we have honoured them, and that we have never failed in the fulfilment of our agreements with them." Is it not pitiful that such plaints as these have been the eternal outcome of what we are pleased to call the march of civilization?

In justice to Béthencourt, it must be said that he did not sanction the malpractices of his friends. When he returned to Lanzarote, he composed matters, and inaugurated a rule of benevolence and strength conjoined. Guadarfrà was baptized under the name of Louis; and many of the natives were enrolled with the Europeans to help in the subjection of the other islands.

Fuerteventura, which adjoins Lanzarote, soon fell Thence, Béthencourt sailed west to Palma, but, meeting with a repulse, he moved towards Gomera instead, where the natives were at first as gentle and unsuspicious as the Lanzarotes. From Gomera he passed to Hierro, then famous for its fabulous tree (the " Tilo," or *Laurus fœtens*), which supplied all the land with the water distilled from its leaves; water, moreover, which had the power of giving fresh hunger to a sated man. Here the king, with a hundred and eleven of his chief subjects, offered hospitality to Béthencourt, who requited it by selling the entire hundred and twelve into slavery.

This ended Béthencourt's work in the Canaries. He withdrew to Lanzarote to arrange the government of his principality. Finally, he again returned to the Continent, to plead in Spain, and before the Pope himself, for a bishop to take over the spiritual control of this new fold of Christendom. In this endeavour also he attained his end; and then he died, in 1425, in his own country of Normandy.

The complications and troubles which confuse the history of Europe in the Canaries during the ensuing three quarters of a century would demand a volume for their narration and analysis. But to us they are not worth such tedious elaboration. Suffice to say, that neither Hierro nor Gomera was conquered without much loss of blood; and that, as time passed, and new warriors came to the archipelago, ousting or inheriting from the earlier conquerors, the puzzle of proprietorship grew as complex as the history of the islands. Portugal claimed the Canaries by right of purchase from Maciot de Béthencourt, the first Béthencourt's degenerate nephew and heir. Spain held to its original suzerainty, and moreover had fresh claim through a Spaniard, De Campos, to whom, no less than to the Infanta of Portugal, Maciot had disposed of his rights. The Pope, Eugene IV., in 1431, adjudicated this difficulty in favour of Spain; though Portugal continued to vex the islands with expeditions and new claims.

During these initial land-grabbing forays, Tenerife and Grand Canary were treated with the respect that proceeds from fear. While Béthencourt was swearing fealty to Henry III., Gadifer, one of his captains in Lanzarote, made an attempt upon Grand Canary. This was repulsed. Again, in 1405, Béthencourt himself was driven back to his boats by the king, Artemi, when he tried to possess the island *de facto* as well as *de verbo*. It was then, according to some historians, that he gave Canary its prenomen of Grand; though, according to others, this pre-eminence was only due to the surpassing size of its dogs.

In 1420, Prince Henry of Portugal sent an expedition against Grand Canary. This the Canarians, "whose vigilance and energy were unceasing," easily discomfited. For the next forty years, they received the reward for their bravery by being left generally untroubled. Lanzarote and Fuerteventura, but a few hours' sail distant, were, in the interval, being thoroughly Europeanized. But, in 1461, the epidemic of invasion again seized the original conquerors and their descendants. Diego de Herrara, the inheritor of the Canaries, in 1461, got a footing on Grand Canary, by promising not to commit the least act of hostility, and to establish a perpetual peace with the islanders. He then formally took possession, decamped to his boats, and had the fact of his ownership notified in Europe. Five years later, another Diego, Diego de Silva, sails to Grand Canary on behalf of his master of Portugal. He is not permitted to make any definite conquest; but nevertheless he enrolls the island among the possessions of the Prince of Portugal. Thus the old dilemma recurs. Spain and Portugal are in new conflict, and a private person, De Herrara, profers his claim in the teeth of them both, though as a suzerain indeed of Spain.

An arbitration at Lisbon, in 1470, seems to settle this dispute in favour of Spain; and, immediately afterwards, the Portuguese of De Silva are amalgamated with the Spaniards of De Herrara for a definite and complete conquest of the island. But such unions seldom last longer than the echo of the words which express them. And so we find the Portuguese fighting independently, and getting into trouble from which they are free to escape as best they may, unaided. De Silva let himself and his men be cooped up in a circular walled space, used by the Canarians as a place of punishment; and here, but for the interposition of Guanarteme, the king, they would assuredly have died at the hands of the outraged and angry natives. This monarch visited the prisoners privately, and when De Silva pleaded to be let out, and allowed to leave the country, he thus addressed him: "European, you and your men have of your own free will imprisoned yourselves in this corral, the place of evil-doers. None of you can elude the consequences of your temerity. You have done me grievous wrong, and yet I am willing to forgive you, in the face too of this multitude, who demand vengeance for your insolence. If you were Canarians, I should have confidence in you, and would propose a stratagem to save yourselves from this danger. I would advise you at once to lay hands on me, to secure me, and even to make as if you would kill me unless my subjects allow you to withdraw. . . ."

Before such nobility of soul, no wonder De Silva fell on his knees, with sobs of gratitude. To this ruse, he owed his deliverance. But Guanarteme the king had sacrificed his country to his own generous instincts. His subjects suspected him; he became a Christian: and joined his voice with that of the Europeans in trying to evangelize his fellow-countrymen. At this conjuncture, Spain determined to make the most strenuous efforts, once and for all, to occupy Grand Canary. De Herrara was by special grant recognized as king over the four islands of Lanzarote, Fuerteventura, Hierro, and Gomera. His claim to Grand Canary he surrendered absolutely. Tenerife and Palma were still unconquered.

Thus it happened that, on Ascension Day of the year 1478, a troop of between six and seven hundred Spanish soldiery, under a brave captain named Rejon, landed on the narrow strip of yellow sands which separates Las Palmas from the Isleta at the northern extremity of Grand Canary. They were accompanied by an ecclesiastic named Bermudez, who said mass as soon as the men had made a camp on the sands ; and, weapons in hand, all the men joined their priest in a loud prayer to God to help them to exterminate the miserable barbarians they

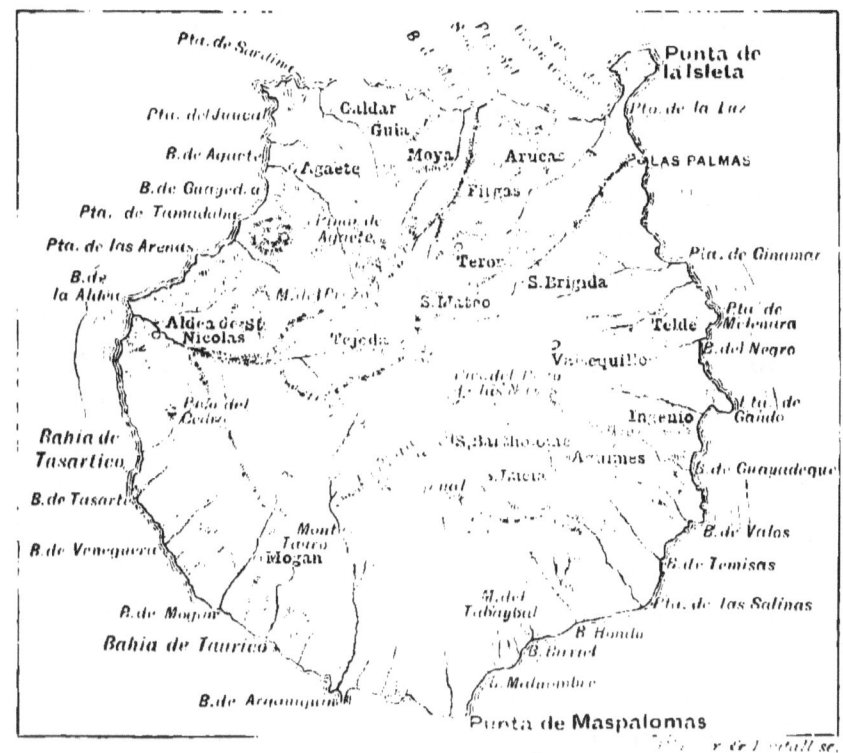

GRAND CANARY : 72 miles in circumference.

were about to attack. However, six years of incessant fighting had to elapse before Spain could sing Te Deum in Canary. In the meantime, Rejon had been transfixed by a spear (while fighting in Gomera) ; Bermudez had been banished for his presumption by a later leader of the assailants ; and thousands of men-at-arms who had done well in the wars of Granada died bruised to death by the stones and big clubs of these "miserable people." The Canarians showed more valour, more martial strategy, and very much more of the generosity that ought to appertain to Christian men than these doughty, braggart Castillians. Nor were they so completely crushed when the Te Deum was sung that thereafter they gave their conquerors no anxiety and no care other than that of separating them into bands, for sale as slaves in the Eastern markets.

This was four hundred years ago, and now, in A.D. 1887, we find by the site of Rejon's first camp a city of some 20,000 inhabitants, with tall business blocks shading the chief streets, public gardens, clubs, hotels, and a stately cathedral of lava-stone facing the municipal building across a broad pavement which the citizens and their wives adapt for their promenade in the cool of the evening. The early Spaniards christened the embryo capital from the number of palm trees in the neighbourhood. The palms still grow among the houses of the town, and clumps of them, fifty and sixty feet high, cap the hillocks and cliffs of the broken upland country which lies beyond Las Palmas. Moreover, the cathedral is dedicated to Saint Anna, because, soon after landing from his ships, Rejon saw the figure of a woman, whom he identified as the mother of the Virgin. The vision was an omen of good ; hence a vow which is now ratified in the Cathedral of Santa Anna. Rejon himself is memoralized in the street Rejon. Thus, here, as elsewhere, one may read history in stones, and find profitable diversion in marking how the past and the present are indissolubly blended.

Like Rejon and his troop, I landed at Las Palmas on Ascension morning, after a quiet passage in the night from Santa Cruz of Tenerife. A drive of three miles along the sandy peninsula which separates the harbour from the town, brought me into the capital of Grand Canary. When the wind is cross, this loose sand must be as troublesome as that of Pesth.

Las Palmas was in a joyous mood on this 19th of May. The daily papers were able to report "the happy intelligence that His Majesty the infant King of Spain has successfully cut his first tooth." Added to this, was the very grand religious function at the cathedral in an hour or two : an epoch in the year. The citizens questioned each other about it, and were as much interested in its success as a ring of Chicago merchants in the contrivance of a "corner" in pork. Which of the reverend fathers would lead the service ? Were the boys with the sweetest voices to take the solos, or were these to be given to careless little urchins, who no more heeded the tone of their throats than the state of their scarlet cassocks ? Would his illustriousness the Bishop attend ? or was he still confined by a cold to his stately palace of black and white stone, so luxuriously sequestered among groves of palms, orange trees, and oleanders, but a bullet's cast from the cathedral porch ? How would the fair Concepcion look on this bright day, while trooping with the other maidens of her convent school into the cool aisle of the church ? Would she be promoted into a bonnet, in honour of the festival? Alas! it was also but too probable that, under this sunny sky, she had bloomed so rapidly since the festival of the Invention (May 3rd), that her smooth cheeks would now be hid by their first coat of powder, permitted by the sisters as an early mark of young womanhood.

Ascension Day was as much to the children of the city as to the adults and the young men and maidens. Was not the cathedral floor, from the west portal to the foot of the high altar, where the paschal candle lifted its six yards of wax towards the clerestory windows—was not it all thick with rose-leaves which, when the function was over, might be gathered by any that pleased, and taken home ere the episcopal blessing and the smell of the incense had evaporated from them?

It is by such bonds as these, tender as well as strong, that the Catholic Church keeps her worshippers in affectionate union with herself. It is a great relief, and undoubtedly bracing to the spirit, to be purged from sin, and the thought of sin, once a week or once a month. But by these gracious and cheerful religious galas, the church proves that she is as genial as she is vigorous and benevolent.

The cathedral was early crowded with a motley congregation: majestic matrons, who fanned themselves, while they gossipped upon their knees; troops of school-girls, those of poor degree in black dresses and quaint bonnets of the " poke " style, and others in short blue dresses, white sashes, white stockings, high-heeled boots, and tall hats of yellow straw, from which their hair hung tailwise upon their backs; young men, interested in the maidens, stood against the pillars of the church, with the handles of their canes in their mouths; and here and there a wonder-struck countryman, whose bare legs and sheepskin cloak made the acolytes laugh unfeignedly in going between the altar and the choir.

The musical part of the "function" which followed was delicious. Las Palmas is justly proud of its organist. At the elevation of the Host, the tender tremolo of the instrument was ecstatic. And, later, at the conclusion of the ceremony, the organ sent forth a broad joyous peal of thanksgiving that cheered heart and soul, like the bestowal of some solid and surpassing boon.

A curious scene ensued upon the concession of the episcopal blessing. The wickets connecting the aisle with the avenue between the altar and the *coro* (in the middle of the building) were thrown open; and a mob of boys and girls and tiny barelegged children scampered up the altar steps, and fell upon their hands and knees among the rose-leaves. These were scraped into heaps, packed into handkerchiefs and wrappings, and carried off with glee and chattering.

Then a new tumult arose. Priests, acolytes and some of the laity surrounded the fat paschal candle, sheathed in tin, which had stood in honour to the left of the altar since Easter week, but was now to be removed. A ladder was reared against it, to enable a nimble boy to draw from it the five symbolical nails. Afterwards, six or seven men joined their strength, and lifted the great candle from its heavy leaden stand. The boys did not scruple to clap their hands with a will when they saw the thing prone upon the marble pavement, like the dead body of a white cylindrical giant; and the infants among the rose-leaves paused to gape at it.

Finally, ropes were brought, and planks for a causeway down the altar steps. The men threw off their coats, two or three of the clergy, with beaming faces, tucked up their sleeves, and the portly candlestick was taken in tow. At first, all the tugging of all the men and boys could not stir the monster. But the encouraging shouts of the contractor, and the united efforts at length shuffled it an inch or two. And so, in due time, it was pulled down the incline, and, with a riot that sounded singular in such a place, urged all along the aisle, and out by the northern porch, into a large chamber already full to overflowing with wooden figures, machinery, and the other paraphernalia of the Church's properties.

The cathedral of Las Palmas contains few antiquities of general interest. But the bones of Viera, that model historian, and of the local poet, Cairasco de Figueroa, of whose abilities Cervantes thought very highly, redeem it from the charge of sterility. Indeed, there are plenty of bones in the well-kept vaults under the altar. I was there shown a neat row of pigeon-holes, each filled by a bishop, a dean, or a canon; and at the end of the white-washed chamber was a sunken recess where a number of prelates and other church dignitaries lay intermingled. It seems that fit accommodation is limited. Hence, the deceased vacate their niches according to seniority. When a new comer pleads for a place, his predecessor is relegated pellmell to the corner. It was noticeable that the skulls of these ecclesiastics were furnished with sets of teeth worthy of the Guanches themselves. And yet it is improbable that they, like the Guanches, systematically abstained from drinking during a hot dinner; nor were they likely to confine their post-prandial libations to cold water.

Here, as in Santa Cruz of Palma, is a wealth of copes, and other richly-embroidered vestments. And here again it is said that certain of the vestments came originally from London, in the time of the Reformation. A gold chalice, the gift of Philip IV., in 1696, is worth admiration; and so is a crimson flag of the *conquistador* of Grand Canary, be he whom he may. Sundry trivial relics (knuckle-bones and the like) of St. Placidus, in a lozenge-shaped reliquary, have a special signification. For it is to this saint that the Canarians have learnt to pray when a plague of locusts comes upon them. A certain modern chalice of gold, weighing 7 lbs. avoirdupois, is much appreciated by the sacristan of the cathedral; and so is the massive silver chandelier that hangs in the nave. This, the gift of the Bishop Ximenez, in the 17th century, weighs about $2\frac{1}{4}$ cwt., and cost more than £700.

The cathedral paintings are few, and of no great merit. An Annunciation, by I know not whom, is the most pleasing. But a series of large new canvasses of the crucifixion, by Losada, hung in the northern chapels, are much appreciated locally. Their realism is evidently a new feature here : and greatly it impresses the simple peasants who come and gape and groan beneath them. The face of Christ is uniformly rather weak than sublime. Losada excels in the brutal : his red-capped executioner, following Christ and the cross, and carrying hammer and nails, is a bold compound of cruel indifference and the presumption of a jack-in-office. Again, in the second picture of the series, the same character is depicted holding Christ by a rope round the waist, and threatening Him with a rod in the right hand. Here the brutality of his expression is worsened by a diabolical grin that must have come to the artist from a face with African blood in it. In short, Losada's pictures are remarkable for the mild inanity of the Christ, and the repulsiveness of the executioner. The latter indeed gives them a Zolaesque character almost too pronounced for their surroundings.

One other work of art must be mentioned. This is a huge rough fresco on the south part of the western wall. It represents S. Cristóbal carrying the Holy Child through the water, which reaches to his knees. But the gigantic proportions of the painting (the figure being about twenty feet high), the club in the saint's hand, and his ferocious expression, in spite of the accessories, are all acutely suggestive of an illustration from an old nursery tale of giants and bloodshed.

After the cathedral, the hospital of Las Palmas

deserves a visit. It is a comfortable public institution, gay with flowers, brightened by cheerful sisters of mercy, and covered as to its walls with the portraits of ancient Spaniards. Hundreds of so-called foundlings here spend the first years of their life. Formerly, they were hung to door knockers, or slipped into the *patios* of great houses. The hospital for *expositos* has done away with the excuse for such reckless desertion. And now, day and night, a good sister keeps watch at the revolving cupboard whereby the babes are passed from the street into the establishment without ceremony or scandal. The infants are at once bathed, examined, named after the saint of the day, and enrolled with their predecessors. The sister in charge of the department tells me, with a smile of sorrow, that the number of new inmates is so many per week. Of course it is. With such a system in vogue in England, who can doubt that the population nightmare would be even more terrifying to conscientious Malthusians than it is at present? These hospitals for foundlings were instituted in all the larger towns of the Canaries two centuries ago. Stalwart soldiers and sailors were then much in request for the various wars of the kings of Spain. Public morality was secondary to the satisfaction of State requirements. Now, however, it is vastly different. The islands are even over-populated. Yet, the foundling hospitals are kept open; immorality is encouraged: and the innocent have to bear the burdens of the guilty.

I found an English sailor in the hospital. He had

been put ashore by a passing coaler, and, after some weeks of severe illness, was now convalescing. In the meantime, he had never opened his mouth for conversational purposes. His faculty of speech had got diverted into his faculty of observation; and he smartly criticised the management of the hospital. He complained that the sisters of mercy spent too much time in praying in the bedrooms. "Three weeks in bed, and never once a wash!" And, having thus relieved himself, the simple fellow assumed that the Spaniard forbears to wash because his skin is by nature swarthy, and therefore less likely to betray him in his uncleanliness. But, whether he would or no, this British tar had gained a friend. We were sitting in the hospital garden, when a lean sickly Spaniard came by, and his cadaverous face lit up with a smile at the sight of us. He sat down by the sailor, who allowed him to fondle his big brown fingers and tatooed wrist as if he were a girl. "We gets on nicely sir, him and me," said my countryman, with an affectionate glance down his red nose at his companion. "He don't talk English any more than the others, poor fellow, but he tries to look as if he did, and he's one of the cleanest of them all. I don't know what's up with him, but he twists about awful, sometimes, though he tries to keep it to himself." When I told the sailor that his friend was dying of a cancer, it was affecting to see his change of manner towards the Spaniard, to mark his rough responsive caresses and sympathetic murmurs. "Fancy me being with him all this time, and not to know that!" he exclaimed, huskily, as if he had a lump in his throat.

Among other buildings of credit to Las Palmas, the theatre, the courts of justice, and the market halls must not be forgotten. The theatre is an imposing pile that would take high rank in Paris : erected at a cost of £26,000, and adapted for about fifteen hundred spectators. It has evidently been designed not only to do honour to present Las Palmas, but to meet the needs of the city when its importance has swelled according to the aspirations of its more enterprising citizens. The market halls adjoin the theatre, close to the sandy shore, and the spray of the big rollers at times wets both buildings alike. The fish market is a perfect institution : cool, light, airy, and graceful. Between it and the regular produce market may be seen groups of nondescript merchants, squatting on the pavements under an awning. Pedlars here offer for sale crude and home-made crucifixes, the figure of Christ rendered ghastly with bloodstains. The large red bowls and jars which are also abundant, come from Atalaya, an inland village long famed for its workers in clay. The savage-looking little girls, with large impudent eyes, who stand by the pots, have brought them to town on their heads. If they may sell to the value of sixpence, it is enough to compensate for the labour and their fifteen-mile walk. In the produce market, one notices the fine oranges. In all the islands, none can compare with these of Grand Canary. For threepence one may buy ten of them, large and juicy and sweet. But here, as in Santa Cruz, the octroi seems hard upon the people. The old woman who brings her goat into the town to sell its milk pays rather more than a half-penny a day for the privilege; and it costs her not less than two shillings to offer a pig in public market.

The courts of justice of Las Palmas occupy an old conventual building, with a church tower attached, in a back street. Here is the supreme court of the archipelago (*real audiencia*); with a pretentious appanage of officials in cocked hats. The attire of the judges is elegant, and tolerably fitted to the climate; black silk-velvet gowns, with white lace at the neck and wrists, are its characteristics. As for the executive of these courts, it is the same as in Spain. The litigator has no pleasant time of it. This very day, for example, there was a bankruptcy case which fairly showed the looseness of procedure in commercial law. Before failing, the bankrupt had transferred all his property to his sons. As many distinct lawsuits were now in progress for the recovery of this property, as there were creditors against the bankrupt's estate. In England, of course, a general representative would sue for the entire body of creditors. Imagine, therefore, the loss of time, and the expense of this Spanish method, which is so delightfully Spanish that it is likely long to continue.

The weather during the few days I spent in Las Palmas was curious. The same gloom which the clouds of the Peak cast over the valley of Orotava came daily upon us in Grand Canary, though here it was not due to the mountains. The "trade winds," now blowing lustily, brought thick banks of vapour with them, which darkened the sea horizon east and south. The combined effect of this gloom and the tremendous surf upon the coast was as suggestive of storm as the wildest north-easter of September in the Hebrides or the Shetlands.

It is to combat these high seas that Las Palmas is so busily pushing forward its harbour works. These, begun in 1885, will, when finished, extraordinarily improve the commercial standing of the town. A breakwater of nearly a mile in length is designed to run from the Isleta towards the capital. The enclosed area of water will be of depth and extent enough for the safe anchorage of a fleet. But the loose sand-hills of the land boundary of this harbour of refuge will probably be troublesome. These works are in the hands of an English contractor, so there is no doubt of their speedy achievement. More than twenty thousand blocks of concrete, averaging about thirty tons bulk each, will be used in the composition of the breakwater; and the artizans employed are numerous enough to form a village under the black volcanic cliffs of the Isleta, where they live. When the harbour de la Luz is completed, it is believed that European vessels bound for South Africa, South America, &c., will use this as their coaling station, in preference to Santa Cruz of Tenerife, or St. Vincent of the De Verde Islands. "And yet," say the Las Palmas merchants, "Santa Cruz presumes to think she is superior to us!"

But if the heat in the town during the day, notwithstanding the gale from the sea, is considerable, the cool sweet evening that follows the day is only the more enjoyable therefore. Then the beauty and fashion of Las Palmas are drawn to the promenade by the first sound of the regimental band which serenades them. Here, again, it is impossible not to notice the superb carriage of these southern dames. To be sure, it is outrageously theatrical. The ladies pace up and down the flags in the lamp-light, with elevated heads, arm in arm, keeping excellent time, talking of trifles light as air in loud consequential tones, bowing with emphasis to the gentlemen whom they recognize, and turning their pretty painted faces to the right and left, that all the world may see them. Commonly, a Spanish lady is, it must be confessed, a little dull. It is the defect of her education, and national customs. She and her husband are two, not one; or perhaps, speaking accurately, he might say but one and a quarter, if he have but the ordinary amount of respect for his spouse. Thus, circumstances have kept the Spanish lady a stranger to that mundane spirituality which, when genuine, is certainly engaging in a high degree. Nevertheless, she aspires to be witty and *spirituelle*, when she is before the public gaze. And hence the jarring spectacle of winsome faces, powdered profusely, distorted in the vain effort to be what they are not, and casting glances which would be the leers of a wanton if they were not those of a Spaniard.

Las Palmas elects to bury its dead at the time when the promenade is at its gayest. The distant chanting of priests and boys, and the periodical tolling of the cathedral bell sounds over the blare of the trumpets, and the shrill chattering of the women. Then, slowly, the head of a funeral procession appears from the street by the Bishop's palace, and passes between the promenade and the cathedral façade. Four laughing acolytes in scarlet, with crucifixes and gilded lamps on staves, come first. The priest with his book follows, attended on each side by a boy with a lamp to illumine his pages. He sings the sombre service as he stumbles over the uneven stones of the street. The body, under a pall, carried by four men, attended by a knot of others to relieve them, comes after the priest. And then, in long parallel lines, the friends and relations of the deceased, with lamps interspersed among them, close the procession.

A funeral is not by its nature entertaining. But custom and the church have so arranged it that in Las Palmas the burial of a citizen is even romantic—at least, in its initial stage. The priestly dirge, as we slowly pace through the streets of the city, the bobbing of the gilded lamps, held all awry by the acolytes, the low exclamations of interest or pity from the groups of women standing at their open doors to see the files of mourners, and the cheerful chirp of crickets when we get beyond the borough, and are passing between clumps of aloes and fields of tall maize, guided by the funereal lamps and the stars alone—all this is calculated to affect a stranger whose heart is not hardened to emotional influences of every kind.

The heavy lava-stone portal of the cemetery bears the inscription: "Do not be deaf to the voice that tells you all is illusion except death." Here all the lamps save two are puffed out by the boys, and most of the mourners return to the city, with fresh cigars between their lips. If you would see the end, however, join the ten or twelve others who accompany the chief mourner within the gates. A man with a sack of lime on his shoulders, and a pipe in his mouth, walking with the arrogance of one proud without cause, precedes the coffin, as it is lifted from iron staircase to staircase until the particular niche in the high columbarium destined to receive it is attained. It is then set on the ground; the lid is removed; and the man empties the lime over the deceased, methodically spreading and pressing it until nothing of the body is visible save the tips of the small well-shod feet. The sexton keeps his pipe in his mouth while he does his work. The chief mourner, while minutely watching the process attendant upon the burial of his mother, lights a cigarette, and chats with his friends. And the two remaining acolytes grin and play tricks by holding their lamps so that grotesque shadows flutter across the lime man, and the dead woman hid under lime. At length, the latter stands up with an interrogative grunt. "Are you satisfied, Señor?" "Perfectly," replies the chief mourner. The lid is now replaced, the coffin pushed energetically into its destined groove, and all is over. Twenty-four hours ago, the deceased was alive and well. Twenty-four hours hence, she will be half cremated. If the Spaniards are expeditious about nothing else, they lose no time in the disposal and dispersal of what remains of their dead.

CHAPTER XX.

Characteristics of Grand Canary The noisy sleeper—A sudden idea—Pancho and the Andalusian—The Caldera de Vandama—Tafira—Atalaya—Probable pedigree of the dwellers in Atalaya—Santa Brigida San Mateo—Pancho's relations—The priest and his assistants—Across country—Ginamar A pretty prospect—Telde—Troglodytes and aristocrats—A brisk ride in the dark—S.S. *Opobo*—The last of the Peak.

GRAND CANARY can boast of no living volcano like the Peak of Tenerife; nor has it an extinct crater to compare with the prodigious Caldera of Palma. But it relies for its individuality on the very beautiful mountain recesses or sheltered plateaux which cluster at the bases of the high peaks in the centre of the island. There is more water here than in Tenerife: hence the brilliant verdure of these Elysian nooks; their incredible fruitfulness; and their freshness even under a blazing June sun. The circular coastline of the island is reft systematically by *barrancos*, which ought to have streams in their deep dry beds. But the Canarians know better than to permit any of the supply of their precious springs to flow to waste into the salt sea. Tanks and conduits intervene between the springs and the *barran-*

cos, and the water, for the conveyance of which nature has arranged with so much foresight, is all turned to useful account.

It is rather by accident than design that I am able to say anything about the interior of this island. Spring was merging into summer, and the ophthalmic glare of the white houses of Las Palmas daily made me long for a homeward-bound ship. One morning, however, I found myself afoot for the day at the ridiculous hour of half-past four. It was in this wise. I had incautiously permitted the hotel manager to let the second bed in my double-bedded room to a gentleman, who was not expected to appear until late in the night. My companion proved to be the chief engineer of a Spanish steamer *en route* from Buenos Ayres to Cadiz, a rosy, great-girthed Scotchman, who lurched into the bedroom, very drunk, at one o'clock in the morning. His eccentricities of course awoke me, and when he lay in bed (in his clothes) he snored so that a continuance of sleep was, for me, impossible. I shouted to him to moderate his spirits; but of what use was it trying to arouse a man accustomed to the shrieks and groans of machinery? He was as deaf to everything as a dead man. And so, at four o'clock, I left him to snore alone, and prowled forth into Las Palmas' streets, bent on hiring a horse and a guide, and going straightway as far in a day as was possible.

By good luck, both horse and guide were found before six o'clock; and thus we started on a long tour in the prime of the morning. The horse was an odd Andalusian: so tall that his legs

seemed to have outgrown his body, and with a
movement like the jerk of a camel. He was also
hideously bony, and had a sore under the saddle
which would have kept both of us at home, if I had
known of it ere the journey began. In spite of these
apparent demerits, however, the brave fellow took me
forty miles with unflagging pluck, in the fourteen
hours between 6 a.m. and 8 p.m. My guide, too,
was not of common mould. An ordinary Canarian
would have shrugged his shoulders at the prospect
of the exertion implied in the programme submitted
to him. But Pancho, as he was called, was brought
forward to me as a lad of spirit, whose energies were
rather heightened than depressed by an exceptional
undertaking. He had lived through a stormy youth
in Havana, been criminally associated with bloodshed, could show five knife marks about his body:
and was still untamed. They told me I could have
no better guide, if I would take him with his pecca-
dilloes. Never was there such a babbler as this
Pancho. Gossip and tales of adventure raced one
after the other from his tongue; and withal he was
my very obedient servant.

The Caldera de Vandama was our first aim in the
day. This extinct crater lies in the hills about six
miles south-west of Las Palmas. It is approached
by the high road to Tafira, a pretty upland village
embosomed in palm trees, and connected with the
capital by the San Mateo daily coach. In Tafira,
Pancho had a scare. We were clambering to its
church (of which the exterior belies the trivial interior), when a man in black, holding a watch in one

hand, and a rosary in the other, stopped us authoritatively. "London is dead!" said he, solemnly, with a roll of the eyes. I was about to ask for particulars, when he broke forth into a torrent of filthy abuse—some of his expressions being too gross for Pancho subsequently to reiterate; and then stepped aside with a murmur about *otro reloj* ("another watch"). The man was a local priest who had gone mad. So affected was the superstitious Pancho by this encounter that he forgot to point out to me the Palm of Tafira, a notable tree about sixty feet high, and not without a legend attached to its melodious title.

At Tafira we diverged from the thoroughfare, and struck upon a series of basins of fertile vineland of singular appearance. The soil was a black volcanic sand, still tinctured with sulphur. But how the vines revelled in it! Their greenery was delightful; and the gorgeous hedges of geraniums and aloes (some with flowering masts twenty feet high soaring from their midst), with here and there a broad stunted umbrella pine, and the bold outline of the olive hills on all sides combined to form a landscape of rare charm. Nor must I forget the scarlet poppies among the vines, and the bushes of yellow retama which sweetened the air.

We climbed through these vineyards and by rugged red lanes to a dimple in the outline of one of the hills. Here was a large farmhouse; and a few yards from its walls the Caldera of Vandama was disclosed. This is the most perfect crater in the Canaries. It is as smooth a bowl of earth and rocks as nature well could contrive. Only at one point do the environing hills rise into pre-eminence. Thence, from the summit, to the little red farm at the bottom of the Caldera, the distance may be 1,000 feet. In upper diameter, the bowl is perhaps half a mile. I cannot conjecture as to the age of this extinct volcano. It is certainly as dead as Palma's Caldera: though the jet-black reaches of charred earth upon its sides look as if they had but yesterday been released from the flames. Euphorbia, wild vines, nopals, fig trees and brambles grow sparsely upon the slopes; and from the midst of them two brown, wide-nostrilled boys climbed up like cats at the sight of us, and besought Pancho to take me into the farm to taste their mother's wine. For threepence, a full decanter was offered us: the wine was heady, and yet I had trouble to deter my guide from drinking every drop of it.

By a short cut over the hills, Pancho now took me in less than half an hour to the village of Atalaya,[1] where the clay pots of the Las Palmas market are made. Village, however, is a name too complimentary for it. "Warren" were more apt; for it is but a number of caves in a precipitous, isolated, gritstone rock, falling boldly to a glen with a river bed in it. Atalaya is the Burslem of Grand Canary. Every cave contains the rude appliances for the manufacture of the pottery of the country; and men, women, and children, clad but lightly, were squatting in the sun at the mouths of their abodes, handling the clay with speed and dexterity.

[1] *I.e.*, The Giants' Burrow.

Pancho confirmed the prevalent opinion about the populace of Atalaya. They have no morality. They live like the beasts. The Church does not interfere with them. From the steep brow of their cliff-home, they look down at the pretty townlet of Santa Brigida, a mile away, surrounded by fruit trees, palms, and water tanks; but the priest of Santa Brigida is nothing to them. Naked urchins were rolling about within sight of their mothers; and the grown girls who left their work to follow, stare, and laugh at us, had as little clothing as they well could have had. Even the matrons of the community, broad dark dames, wore skirts to their naked legs that the Lord Chamberlain might have shuddered at. Nor were they all in the strong health of open-air life. Deformities and sores seemed to taint them. "Turn round, child, and show your hump," said a mother to one of her luckless offspring, about whose malformation she was peculiarly proud; and the little sufferer held out her hand for *quartitos* when she had duly exhibited herself.

This strange settlement is of so old a standing that it is probable its men and women, alone in the island, perpetuate the blood of the aboriginal Grand Canarians. Sosa, writing in 1678, says of the natives that they had a knack of making clay vessels without a mould, wheel, or any machinery whatever, and that such vessels were in common use in the villages. Well, Atalaya maintains this reputation. And when I had sat for a few minutes by the cave of one deft old woman, watching while she took the soft clay in her hands, briskly separated and

SANTA BRIGIDA.

fashioned it, finally in two or three minutes offering me a rude but well-shaped jar, scored with intricate decorative lines—all the unaided work of her fingers; and after an interested consideration of the features of the crowd around us, their broad cheekbones, large eyes of a lighter hazel than that derived from Spain, and wild free manners—I assured myself that here was aboriginal blood without doubt. Indeed, it is like enough. For the civilized citizens of the adjacent town would as soon marry a negress as an Atalaya woman. The people of Atalaya have cohabited among themselves from time immemorial.

The descent from this inhabited rock to the town of S^a. Brigida was tiresome, though short. The hard matrix was wrought into the most defiant of surfaces; so that the Andalusian perspired and fretted until we again reached the high road. Thence, by a charming avenue of tall palms, we soon cantered into the town, which is more remarkable for the beauty of its valley than for anything archæological or historical. In the neighbourhood, is the largest tank I have seen in the three islands. It is, in fact, a pond, and the profuse vegetation around it shows what water will do here.

We left behind us the white tobacco factories and the church, boldly situated on the edge of a rock, to push on to San Mateo for our breakfast and a rest. The distance between the two places is barely a league; but the rise is nearly a thousand feet. San Mateo is at the foot of the Saucillo mountain (6,639 feet), which contests with the Pico del Pozo de las Nieves, about two miles farther south, the supremacy of elevation in Grand Canary. Thus, as we advanced up the valley towards San Mateo, its head, these glorious mountain tops were before us, now unveiled, and now again hidden by a drift of cloud. The Saucillo is a conspicuously abrupt rock, with an imposing foreground of broken hills and green dome-shaped hillocks. One mountain immediately behind San Mateo is noteworthy, and would repay investigation. It is precisely semi-circular, with a regular depression on the summit. As we saw it, with its smooth sides dappled with light and shade, and domineered by the dark cloud-wrapt peaks beyond it, this calderetta (for such it must be) was very picturesque.

Pancho possessed an aunt and a cousin in San Mateo, and as the town has no inn, we went to his relations. These ladies received us with a half timorous reserve, that was no doubt due to his reputation for escapades. Pancho, on the other hand, was all enthusiasm, and would have kissed his cousin more than once, had she not coldly set him aside. With me, however, these good people were most hospitable. The hotel lunch on the Andalusian was supplemented with what they had in the house; and both the ladies sat with bright eyes to see me eat. Pancho forgot himself so far as to wish to join me, but the indignant protest of both his relations reminded him of the proprieties.

San Mateo is but a mean village, about 2,400 feet above the sea. Its houses are built for a temperate clime, though the aloes and geraniums in the open air testify to the warmth even here. Besides the church, it contains no building of interest. We found the church, however, in gala dress. The aisle was cumbered with boughs and heaps of fresh flowers, among which five pretty girls were kneeling or sitting, making wreaths and bouquets. The *cura* also was there, alone with the girls and a life-size wooden Virgin, in a blue dress, covered with a white gauze veil, which he lifted reverently, that I might see her features. "May is dedicated to the flowers," he remarked, alluding to the Whit Sunday decorations then being prepared. Thanks to Pancho, the priest and his fair assistants welcomed me as they would not otherwise have welcomed a Protestant. In a low voice, he explained to the delighted man that as I always enquired for the church when we passed through a village, and as I had looked sorry when told that Atalaya had no church, therefore I was *Catolico*. Neither the priest nor the pretty girls rejected this argument, and so they were all very courteous. And the priest, without a thought of the consequences, asked the prettiest of the girls (whom he unwisely addressed as such, before her companions to give me a sweet flower, that I might keep her in mind. The girl, who was really beautiful, blushed and smiled, and obeyed her spiritual master—though as she and I could not agree as to the sweetest of the flowers at her disposal, the business was a protracted one. And then, with a devout wish for a prosperous journey, they gave me "Good-bye." I again mounted the horse, and as we moved briskly out of San Mateo, Pancho told me what he thought of priests in general, and the priest of San Mateo in particular. Unless he exaggerated, I fear the prettiest of the girls in the church has, ere this, been in jeopardy.

It was two o'clock when we left San Mateo for Telde, near the east coast. I had included Telde in the programme, without much knowledge of the difficulties of the way. But Pancho said we could not go due east from San Mateo, as I desired : the mountains were too rough. We had therefore to return to S^n. Brigida, and take cross lanes for three or four hours through the richest vineyards and most enchanting country I have seen in the Canaries. We passed villas of all kinds built upon green knolls, and commanding wide views of valleys and hill tops near and distant. Some were painted as gaily as the vegetation and flowers surrounding them. Others again spoke of solid wealth : palatial stone mansions that could dispense with external decorations.

We were all weary when at length the village of Ginamar appeared below us as the forerunner of Telde. Ginamar is a trivial collection of white houses, built upon lava of no very old date. Indeed, about a mile past the village, we crossed a lava flow that had burst from a small volcano hardly more than a stone's throw from the road. The hills here were arid and forbidding ; and the grey stream of once-molten matter trending down towards the sea, and sufficiently disintegrated to support clumps of euphorbia here and there, was positively cheerful compared to its surroundings.

This dull landscape, the duller for some rain-clouds and the waning light, was, however, a fit prelude to the delicious spectacle of the plain and town of Telde, which appeared from a sharp bend in the road. We stepped from gloom into a clear soft twilight; and before us were white houses with steeples, and the semblance of minarets rising, among tall palms, from their midst. The white, compact town was set in a plain of intense greenness, bisected by a wide river bed of blue stones, and bounded beyond by some conical hills, which, though dim and parched in reality, were now etherialised by the pale golden light of evening. " Is it not fine ! " observed Pancho, when we had involuntarily paused for a moment. " Ah ! there is no place in the world like Telde—for its oranges ! "

Telde is the second city in Grand Canary, and contains about 7,000 inhabitants. Here the careful genealogist may find blood as blue as the best in Spain. For the settlement was founded, and the district peopled, by a number of noble adventurers, who joined Pedro de Vera in the completion of the conquest which Rejon actually began. The villas round the city, and the larger houses in the city, still bear imposing heraldic devices, some of which have survived the stock to which they belonged, though others have not. And truly during our short ride across the stout lava bridge which spans the river, and past the rich suburban orange groves, cochineal plantations, and gardens fringed with white lilies and scarlet geraniums, it was impossible not to admire the taste of these early colonists. But others, besides aristocrats, now people Telde. From their holes in the rocks, a number of troglodytic girls were chirping as lustily as the sparrows in the palm trees on the other side of the road, and rough-looking women with cigars between their lips met us, squatted on little asses laden with new-cut beans and flowers. Some of the men here wear a garment, too, which the blue-blooded are not supposed to love—a hempen blouse, quaintly edged with black ornamentation.

A short half-hour was all the time we could spare for Telde in the course of our madcap excursion. But the town is less attractive than its neighbourhood. The church of S. Juan has a stone portal of dainty filigree work. More of its features I could not examine, because a couple of priests were busy confessing young girls in both its aisles. The women of Telde are said to be beautiful—but where are they not? I was introduced to one young lady, who was reputed to be *muy simpático*; but she sat on the edge of her chair, with her hands folded tight in her lap, and with down-cast eyes, which she only lifted when she said, " Si, señor " to my observations; so that I could judge neither of her head nor her heart.

Of the three leagues which separate Telde from Las Palmas, I rode two in the dark. The thoroughfare is of the first class, but of course it is not lighted by lamps. In places it skirts the sea-shore, and here I had the glow of the white surf for an illumination. In one part, it is carried through the sea-cliffs by a tunnel about one hundred yards long, with a lamp in the middle of the tunnel. Elsewhere the shadow of overhanging rocks made the darkness yet more dark. Finally, the lights of the capital appeared, and our long day came to an end.

On the following morning the ss. *Opobo* came into harbour, and dashed my hopes of another scamper into the interior. Pancho early reported himself at the hotel, both ready and desirous. However, the master of the Andalusian thought the poor animal had had enough work for two or three days, and he wisely kept it in the stable.

We steamed from Grand Canary in the night, and, on the ensuing day, from Santa Cruz of Tenerife. Our farewell to the Peak was a long one: hour after hour we watched it from the deck; and it was full evening, and eight hours after leaving the island, ere its rosy cone faded completely out of sight.

APPENDIX.

THE reader of the foregoing pages may, now that he has come to the last of them, like to know a few details about "ways and means" of reaching the Canary Islands, and the manner and cost of life in the archipelago. The following particulars claim, therefore, to be exclusively practical.

Communication.—The boats of at least three Steamship Companies call regularly at Santa Cruz of Tenerife, or Las Palmas of Grand Canary. Of these, the New Zealand mail steamers (Shaw, Savill, and Co.) make the voyage from Plymouth in less than five days. They go monthly, and offer a ticket for Canary for £14, or a return ticket for £25, available for six months. The African Steamship Company's boats ply weekly between Liverpool and the West Coast, calling at the Canaries. These vessels are slow, demanding about seven days for the course; but the return tickets for £15, available for twelve months, which this Company offer, are so extraordinarily cheap that something may be forgiven them in the matter of speed and accommodation. From London, also, there is a monthly service in the boats of Forwood Bros. and Co., who give a single ticket for £12, or a return ticket for £18. In addition to these English lines, there is direct communication between Hamburg, Havre, and Cadiz, by first-class steamers of Germany, France, and Spain.

As for intercommunication between the seven islands of the Canaries, that is not so easy. A *correo*, or mail smack, goes six times monthly between Tenerife and Grand Canary; weekly between Tenerife and Palma; between Tenerife and Gomera and Hierro; and between Grand Canary, Fuerteventura, and Lanzarote. Besides this, there is occasional steam connection between the three chief islands, though that between Santa Cruz of Tenerife and Las Palmas of Grand Canary can alone be relied upon. Contrary winds may at any time lengthen the voyage by the *correo* most inordinately, and as victualling is not provided on board, the passenger's appetite may become as rabid as his impatience.

Accommodation.—Already there are English hotels in Santa Cruz, Orotava, Laguna, and Las Palmas, where a man may hear no Spanish, and dine as he dines at home, only, maybe, more luxuriously. At these hotels the charges are European, ranging from about 8s. to 14s. a day. The Grand Hotel at Orotava is incomparably the best of them. Here, in early spring, I found about seventy-five English people—a colony quite enough to Anglicize the small town of Puerto. Elsewhere, however, the hotels and *ventas* of the country are Spanish to the backbone. In Palma, English is unknown, and so is English cuisine. But a dollar (4s.) or even only four pesetas (3s. 4d.) per diem is, in these native inns, the tariff, instead of the 8s. of the English hotels. The Fonda Europa, in Las Palmas, is a good Spanish hotel. Fleas, however, are too distinctive an attribute of the native inns. In outlying villages, where there is no *venta*, or wine shop, with a truckle bed for a stranger, the traveller must be dependent upon letters or his guide's *savoir faire*.[1]

Roads.—Except in the vicinity of the capitals, the roads of the islands are very bad. Bicycles would serve between Santa Cruz of Tenerife and Orotava, between Santa Cruz and Guimar and, in Grand Canary, for a few leagues, in two or three directions from Las Palmas; but elsewhere not at all. When the authorities finish the Canarian scheme of roads, the islands will be admirably provided. But the work will be a tedious one.

Horses, &c.—Every one rides in the Canaries. At Orotava, it is possible to get excellent steeds for about a dollar a day, or £1 weekly. Two or three Spaniards make a good living by letting their beasts to visitors. The horses are strong and gentle, and unused to luxurious feeding. In Las Palmas and Santa Cruz, horses are rarer than in Orotava. In Palma, mules serve instead of horses. In the eastern islands of Fuerteventura and Lanzarote, the traveller may hire a camel.

Guides.—For tours round the islands, a guide is necessary, as much for the roads, as for his help

[1] In the neighbourhood of Orotava and Las Palmas, and probably in Palma, with a little trouble, villas and apartments may be obtained at moderate rental.

towards a bed in the evening. It is usual to pay two dollars a day for each man and each horse used in an ascent of the Peak of Tenerife, and the same estimate, or a little less, may hold for other protracted tours. A boy to look after the horse may, however, take the place of a man for a *toston*, or a shilling a day instead of two dollars.

Language.—It is difficult to say how a man would control or associate with his guide, or hold satisfactory communion with the native Spaniards, without a certain knowledge of Spanish. In Palma, such knowledge is essential. I believe there are but two people in that island who could say " How do you do ? " It is equally essential in the country parts of Tenerife and Grand Canary.

Climate. — On this subject, the Canaries compel superlative praise. Our winter and spring are the best seasons for visiting the islands. In summer, though the heat is not on the whole excessive (except on the south and south-eastern sides of the islands), the mosquitoes are troublesome. Equability and dryness are the characteristics of the climate. The average temperature of Puerto in January is 62·2, and in August 77·2—a difference of but 15°. On a like comparison, Pau varies no less than 35·8, and Nice 29·9. Again, the mean temperature for the winter months at Puerto is 63·8, compared with London 41·7, Pau 44·6, Nice 49·6, Rome 51·6, Algiers 58·3, and Madiera 61·7. Even Florida, with its winter mean of 58·7, is thus inferior to Tenerife. But the extraordinary dryness of the Canaries gives them a vast advantage over most health resorts. The day and night temperature differs but three or four degrees. Paper left exposed to the night air retains its crispness as if it were in a heated room; and it is the custom to sleep with open windows.

The *Necessaries* for a tour in the Canaries are but few. Patience, civility, a knowledge of Spanish, a certain amount of money, and a broad-brimmed straw hat are indispensable. I do not think " Keating " is much use, unless it be taken in bushels: the Canarian fleas (whom, by the by, Peter Pindar memorialized for their agility) are so active. The Canarians are a peaceful folk. A revolver is therefore useless, except as a work of art, to exhibit for the stupefaction of the peasants.

Sport.—In this particular, the islands are sadly deficient. Their nature and limited extent, of course, accounts for it. A country that begins and ends its catalogue of mammiferous animals with " the horse, the ass, or the donkey, and elegant mules as a crossbreed between the two," must be considered rather tame. In fact, the only food for powder that I know of are the different kinds of birds (many of which do but hibernate in the Canaries, and return to England and the north in the summer), rabbits, and partridges. Locally, as in the time of the aborigines, ferrets are used for the rabbits. On the south, that is, the hot side of Tenerife, there are many partridges. Rats abound in the islands, and, though they cannot be said to offer much sport to the sportsman, they are peculiar in that in times of drought and scarcity they hunt each other, and eat those of their comrades they succeed in killing.

The Gresham Press,
UNWIN BROTHERS,
CHILWORTH AND LONDON.

www.ingramcontent.com/pod-product-compliance
Lightning Source LLC
Chambersburg PA
CBHW022334230426
43664CB00040B/726